Talking to Strangers

Talking to Strangers

Anxieties of Citizenship since *Brown v. Board of Education*

DANIELLE S. ALLEN

THE UNIVERSITY OF CHICAGO PRESS
CHICAGO AND LONDON

Danielle Allen is professor in the Department of Classical Languages and Literatures, the Department of Political Science, and the Committee on Social Thought at the University of Chicago. Author of *The World of Prometheus: The Politics of Punishing in Democratic Athens,* Allen received a MacArthur Fellowship in 2001 and directs the Civic Knowledge Project.

The University of Chicago Press, Chicago 60637
The University of Chicago Press, Ltd., London
© 2004 by The University of Chicago
All rights reserved. Published 2004
Printed in the United States of America

13 12 11 10 09 08 07 06 05 04   1 2 3 4 5

ISBN: 0-226-01466-5 (cloth)

Library of Congress Cataloging-in-Publication Data

Allen, Danielle S., 1971–
     Talking to strangers : citizenship after Brown v. Board of Education /
Danielle S. Allen.
         p. cm.
     Includes bibliographical references and index.
     ISBN: 0-226-01466-5 (cloth : alk. paper)
     1. Political participation—United States. 2. Pluralism (Social
sciences)—United States. 3. Civil society—United States. 4. Trust—
United States. 5. Intergroup relations—United States. 6. United States—
Race relations. I. Title: Citizenship after Brown v. Board of Education.
II. Title.
JK1764.A44 2004
305.896'073—dc22

                                                        2004001836

♾ The paper used in this publication meets the minimum requirements of
the American National Standard for Information Sciences—Permanence
of Paper for Printed Library Materials, ANSI Z39.48-1992.

I wrote this book in memory of Ralph Waldo Ellison—
may his spirit endure—
and dedicate it now to my husband, Robert von Hallberg.

THIS SOCIETY *is not likely to become free of racism,*
thus it is necessary for Negroes to free themselves by becoming their idea
of what a free people should be.

RALPH ELLISON, Working notes to *Juneteenth*

Contents

Key to Brief Citations

Citations with single numbers refer to page numbers in the cited text. For instance (*LSLR* 3) would refer to page three of *The Long Shadow of Little Rock*. In order to decode numbers that include decimal points, please refer to the citations below to determine whether the numbers refer to volumes, books, chapters, paragraphs, or pages.

CE   Ralph Ellison, *Collected Essays,* ed. J. Callahan (New York, 1995).

DC   Thomas Hobbes, *De cive,* trans. T. Hobbes (Indianapolis, 1991). First Latin edition 1642, 2nd Latin edition 1647, English translation 1651. Citations refer to chapter and paragraph.

EL   Thomas Hobbes, *Elements of Law,* ed. F. Tönnies (Cambridge, 1928). Citations refer to part, chapter, and paragraph.

HC   Hannah Arendt, *The Human Condition* (1958; repr., Chicago, 1989).

IM   Ralph Ellison, *Invisible Man* (1952; repr., New York, 1995).

L   Thomas Hobbes, *Leviathan* [1651], ed. E. Curley (Indianapolis, 1994). Citations refer to chapter and paragraph.

LSLR   Daisy Bates, *The Long Shadow of Little Rock* (New York, 1962).

MDT   Hannah Arendt, *Men in Dark Times* (New York, 1968).

NE   Aristotle, *Nicomachean Ethics,* trans. H. Rackham (1926; repr. Cambridge, Mass., 1975). Citations refer to book, chapter, and paragraph of the Loeb edition. I have not included Stephanus numbers in order to simplify citations for those who are not specialists in ancient literature.

NPUC   J. Levi, *The Neighborhood Program of the University of Chicago* (Washington, D.C., 1961).

P   Aristotle, *Politics,* trans. H. Rackham (1932; repr. Cambridge,
        Mass., 1990). Citations refer to book, chapter, and paragraph of
        the Loeb edition. I have not included Stephanus numbers.

PUR   P. H. Rossi and R. A. Dentler, *The Politics of Urban Renewal*
        (1961; repr. Glencoe, 1963).

R   Aristotle, *The Art of Rhetoric,* trans. J. H. Freese (1939; repr.
        Cambridge, Mass., 1975). Citations refer to book, chapter, and
        paragraph of the Loeb edition. I have not included Stephanus
        numbers.

RLR   Hannah Arendt, "Reflections on Little Rock," *Dissent* (1959) 6:
        45–56.

SECC   South East Chicago Commission, *South East Chicago Renewal
        Project,* no. 1 (Chicago, 1954).

TCA   Jürgen Habermas, *Theory of Communicative Action,* vol. 1., trans.
        T. McCarthy (Boston, 1984).

TWW   J. L. Austin, *How to Do Things with Words,* 2nd ed. (1962; repr.,
        Cambridge, Mass., 1975).

WNJ   Ralph Ellison, Working notes for *Juneteenth,* appendix in *June-
        teenth,* ed. J. Callahan (New York, 1999).

WS   Interview with Ralph Ellison by Robert Penn Warren, in R. P.
        Warren, *Who Speaks for the Negro* (New York, 1965), 343–44.

Prologue

A GREAT DEAL of interracial distrust now is a product more of retrospection than of immediate personal experience and prevails along fossilized boundaries of difference. We still have economic policies and social patterns to frustrate yellow, green, blue, black, pink, brown, and red. Yet continually this frustration—with unemployment, crime, and public education—is understood in racial terms. "White" blames "black" and "black" blames "white" and who knows what others blame one another and then slip also into the black-white muck. It takes time to build up a record of experiences and narrative to justify distrust, and our repeated fallback upon race as an explanation exposes history's gravity. Within democracies, such congealed distrust indicates political failure. At its best, democracy is full of contention and fluid disagreement but free of settled patterns of mutual disdain. Democracy depends on trustful talk among strangers and, properly conducted, should dissolve any divisions that block it.[1]

When citizenly relations are shot through with distrust, efforts to solve collective problems inevitably founder. Here is a trivial example: my sweet, shy thirteen-year-old friend, Malik Burnett, who was growing up in Chicago's housing projects until his family was shifted recently to a run-down West Side house (so the high-rise projects can be demolished), loves his teachers and is proud to be third in his class in a school he doesn't know is terrible. How often have my husband and I said to him, "You know all those famous universities all over Chicago? They want you to come and they have great financial aid packages to make sure you'll have the money to go. You just keep concentrating on your reading and your math." One of his responses is simply to register disbelief in terms I remember as: "The white people who won't come live in my neighborhood, or even visit it, will welcome me in theirs? Why should they feel any differently about my coming to live with them than they do about coming to live with me?" Even all the policies for recruiting minorities to universities and for funding poor students, even the best-intentioned and least controversial of policies, suffer from the distorting effects of distrust.

One more example. In the 1950s and 1960s the University of Chicago (my employer) cooperated with the City of Chicago and the U.S. government in a project of urban renewal of the South Side neighborhoods around the university. Just as the city had once reversed the flow of the Chicago River to run away from Lake Michigan, so now the effort was to reverse the effects of an influx of poor African Americans to the neighborhood and to stanch the rush of whites to the suburbs. The goal was also to reduce crime and improve the housing stock in the area by demolishing homes that had been converted into rooming houses with despicable living conditions. As another part of urban renewal, in remarkably far-reaching applications of eminent domain, the city and university, with federal help, cleared out businesses that served a poorer clientele, in some cases leveling business districts of several blocks. Fifty years later new economic growth in that area is only just now again sprouting up. Why has it been so slow? No doubt the reasons are multiple but among them is this: what entrepreneur will undertake the risk of a new business in an area where she can't trust the region's powerful institutions to leave her property and client base alone? Empowerment zone policies, too, will succeed at disparate rates, as they encounter distrust's paralyzing effects. This is no secret to social scientists. Political scientist Robert Putnam's marvelous book, *Making Democracy Work*, describes precisely the ways in which strongly contrastive patterns of trust and distrust differentiate life in Northern and Southern Italy. An honest look at the political situation in the United States leads to a related recognition that among our core political problems is not racism, but interracial distrust. It flows all ways, but especially "both ways," across the black/white divide. Despite demographic change, the question "Whom can you trust?" keeps reconstituting the color line.[2]

But is interracial distrust in fact a political problem, as opposed to, say, simply an embarrassment? The answer is clearly yes. When Putnam turned his attention to the United States, he found a decline in "social capital," by which he meant networks and habits of cooperation that provide a cultural basis for collaborative democratic decision making. Initially, he traced the decline by focusing mostly on the decrease in participation in homogeneous groups, like Elks Clubs, Boy Scout troops, and bowling leagues. His catchphrase is common now: Americans who used to bowl in leagues now too often bowl alone. But then he found that some U.S. towns that rate high in social capital, because of the number and vigor of local social organizations, also unfortunately rank low in interracial trust. In a study of forty regions, Charlotte, North Carolina (and counties surrounding it), ranked second in giving and volunteering and fourth in the level of church activity (which is to say high in social capital) but thirty-ninth (out of forty) in cultivating trust across racial divisions. Social organizations for those who are like each other turn out (no surprise) not to cultivate social capital across historic boundaries of difference. Quite the contrary, in fact. But why should we worry that Charlotte, North Carolina, still has deep divisions, if the city has managed to sustain robust habits of cooperation among a significant number of citizens?[3]

Interracial distrust is a problem not only for its own sake—that is, raising the question of whether ethnic minorities and majorities can overcome their pasts. It also has farther reaching effects on our political culture. One study after another has reported declines in U.S. citizens' trust of their government and other institutions of authority since the 1960s. Most recently the University of Chicago's National Opinion Research Center announced that whereas 53 percent of U.S. citizens in 1964 thought "most people can be trusted," by 2002 only 35 percent of them thought so. Buried in all these statistics is the telling fact that African Americans are even less trusting than other citizens.[4] African Americans have been cultural leaders and anticipators in respect to distrust's increase. Unsurprisingly, this group's distrust comes back again and again to interracial questions. Could that be true for other citizens also? After all, interracial distrust powerfully distorts the implementation of all policies aimed at issues coded as "race" problems (welfare, employment, crime, drugs, gangs) and also any that require implementation across race lines (health care, abortion, housing and real estate, city planning, public education). These distortions result in racially disparate effects for the policies, which then feed narratives of distrust and so extend its reach and power. Is it possible that the expansion of the active citizenry in the 1950s and 1960s to include African Americans brought inside the citizenry the patterns of trust and distrust that had previously defined the boundary of the citizenry? Is it possible that, once included in the official public sphere, interracial distrust has been a catalyst of more general distrust?

But perhaps I have not yet convinced you of the basic level at which distrust pure and simple, leaving aside interracial distrust for a moment, is a problem for a democracy. Perhaps you agree with John Hart Ely, who wrote in *Democracy and Distrust* that the continuance of democracy depends on the meticulous cultivation among citizens of distrust in government.[5] We should all, he argues, be so many jumpy watchdogs, a whole citizenry of Ralph Naders. On one level he's right. We citizens should cast a skeptical eye on all claims made by governing officials on our behalf, and we should vet their behavior seriously at election time, holding them accountable for choices good and ill. But intellectual skepticism about policy is perfectly compatible with efforts to encourage citizens' trust of one another and, more important, their trustworthiness in the eyes of others. Trust in one's fellow citizens consists in the belief, simply, that one is safe with them. This trust can be registered cognitively, as when one believes that a particular fellow citizen is unlikely to take advantage of one's vulnerability (and any number of reasons might legitimately support such a belief); or it can be registered emotionally, as when one feels confidence, or a lack of fear, during a moment of vulnerability before other citizens.[6] When an election rolls round, citizens will cast a doubting eye on prospective representatives, but they can vote—that is, they can think it reasonable to participate in public institutions—only if they trust that the effects of the votes of other citizens, combined with their own, will not produce their political oppression. The conviction that one's fellow citizens are vigilant against governmental abuses of power ought only to support a citizen's belief in the efficacy of the vote. As for distrust of one's fellow citizens, however, when this pervades democratic relations, it paralyzes democracy; it means that citizens no longer think it sensible, or feel secure enough, to place their fates in the hands of democratic strangers. Citizens' distrust not of government but of each other leads the way to democratic disintegration.

How corrosive is such distrust over time? Won't the fossilized distrust in Charlotte, North Carolina, simply dissolve on its own eventually? In fact, the civil rights movement has already answered these questions, provided that we can see it for what it was: an interconnected set of low-grade civil wars in the states of the former Confederacy that arose out of long-term distrust.[7] In the standard story of the movement, grassroots organizations in the South challenged local segregation; when local segregationists resisted, the federal government eventually disarmed Jim Crow. Because of the civil rights movement, the late 1950s and early 1960s are conventionally identified as the period when U.S. politics completed a shift (begun in the FDR New Deal era) from a protection of states' rights and local governance to dramatically increased centralization. In many accounts, even in some sympathetic to desegregation, the federal government is portrayed as a bully who took one side in a fair fight that ought to have been left to resolve itself. But what would have happened if the Southern states had in fact been independent countries, and there had been no federal government? In fact, the civil wars in the Southern states, which in combination added up to the civil rights movement, were won by the transfer of African American citizens' loyalties from their state governments to federal institutions.

Members of a political unit will not remain within it if they cease to trust its ability eventually to serve their interests, unless they are compelled by force or terror to remain. Emigrants flee impossible economic circumstances at home to join, even if unofficially, a political unit that they expect will better serve their interests. Theorists of this "exit" phenomenon too often speak of it as something that individuals do.[8] Congealed boundaries of distrust, however, convert dissatisfied individuals who might leave their polities into groups that, unless restrained by force, eventually secede or start a civil war. Of course, these can amount to the same thing, as when in the nineteenth century the South ceased to trust that continued collaboration with the North was compatible with its interests. In the early twentieth century African American citizens of Southern states gave up on their local governments and economies in great numbers and migrated to northern cities; thus arose "The Great Migration." But with the civil rights movement, African Americans who had remained in the South after others had gone North rose up instead of departing and, with acts of rebellion like sit-ins and protests, began a series of civil wars within the former Confederate states. The tense standoffs surrounding school desegregation acquired nicknames like "The Battle of Little Rock": citizens on both sides of the Southern racial divide prudently armed themselves against fellow citizens. Even Martin Luther King, Jr., knew the activities were rebellion: "There will be neither rest nor tranquility in America until the Negro is granted his citizenship rights. The whirlwinds of revolt will continue to shake the foundations of our nation until the bright day of justice emerges."[9]

To call that period of struggle a civil war will probably seem like an exaggeration, given how the history of the civil rights movement is typically told. The outcome of events allows us to peddle a softer version of the tale than the origin of those events points to. At the very least, in the period of the civil rights movement, large groups of citizens had decided no longer to obey a fair portion of the laws of their states.[10] And citizens on each side of the ethnopolitical divide had difficulty imagining a future together. These two phenomena—the break from law and the failure of citizens to imagine a shared future—have historically been first steps toward civil war.[11] In this case, African Americans in Southern states had no reason to trust the Southern whites in control of the state governments; Southern African Americans in the early 1960s therefore increasingly committed their allegiance to another political body (the federal government) in the belief that it was still reasonable to trust the national majority, if not local power blocs.[12] Victory lay in this switch of allegiance.

When theorists argue that democracies are based on consent, they mean that the entirety of a democracy's legitimate strength and stability derives from the allegiance of citizens. That allegiance endures only so long as citizens trust that their polity does generally further their interests; minorities must actually be able to trust the majorities on whose opinions democratic policies are based. When distrust among electoral minorities endures over time and congeals, such that citizens recognize themselves as constituting a disaffected group, only four outcomes are possible: (a) distrust of the electoral majority will be dissolved and converted into trust; (b) the group will leave the polity; (c) the group will rebel against the polity; or (d) the group will be retained by repressive acts of state force.[13] (When distrust flows in the other direction, and the majority distrusts the minority, there is the possibility that the minority will be expelled or eradicated.) The first eventuality—the conversion of distrust into trust—alone suits democratic practice.

Distrust can be overcome only when citizens manage to find methods of generating mutual benefit despite differences of position, experience, and perspective. The discovery of such methods is the central project of democracy. Majority rule is nonsensical as a principle of fairness unless it is conducted in ways that provide minorities with reasons to remain attached to the polity. The central feature of democratic politics is therefore not its broad definition of citizenship or its ultimate dependence on majority rule, but rather its commitment to preserving the allegiance of all citizens, including electoral minorities, *despite* majority rule. Would we join a club if we knew that all its policies would go against our own interests? No. Would we join if we knew that every vote would find us in the minority? We might, provided that we trusted that the majority decisions, despite our dissent, would still generally advance our own interests. The central challenge for democracy is to develop methods for making majority decisions that, despite their partiality, also somehow incorporate the reasonable interests of those who have voted against those decisions, for otherwise minorities would have no reason to remain members of a democratic polity. Without such methods, popular government cannot become a stable form of political organization.[14]

Fossilized distrust indicates failure at this key democratic task of holding majorities and minorities together. The Southern "civil wars" of the 1950s and 1960s were contained because rebellious citizens turned their allegiance to the national majority. But the experience of the local power holders should be a lesson to all democratic citizens. Not all cases of fossilized division will erupt in civil war, but all will generate significant economic and psychological costs. People talk about "climates" of trust and distrust because high levels of distrust make life uncomfortable, even difficult, and require extra measures for basic survival, just as climates of excessive heat or cold do. Citizens who try to do business or conduct politics against a backdrop of distrust inevitably expend financial and psychic resources in maintaining protections against those in whom they have no faith. Worse still, as we shall see, in democracies that are marked by settled patterns of distrust, citizens develop modes of political behavior designed to maintain boundaries; such citizenly habits corrode democratic citizenship from within.

None of this is to say that, given current levels of distrust, the end of the world is at hand. The United States is nowhere near an internal apocalypse. Rather, we are at a historical point where we have the time and the confidence of our successes to reorient our political practices in order to strengthen and prolong the democratic experiment. Our stability and confidence arise from the history of liberalism, meaning the ideas behind political protections of rights and liberties against state power. Liberalism originated in efforts to solve the problem of radical distrust in political life, but in the seventeenth century the dangerous distrust arose from religious contention. Theorists like Thomas Hobbes and John Locke proposed institutional solutions for the problem, among them representative government; later, the framers of the U.S. Constitution devised institutions that went a long way toward solving the problem of radical distrust within a democratic citizenry. That those institutions could not solve the problem once and for all is proved not only by the U.S. Civil War of 1861 but also by the small U.S. civil wars of the 1960s. Like citizens in Israel and Palestine, in Rwanda, in Ireland and Northern Ireland, the early theorists of liberalism faced dissension so extreme that they could not both invent democratic institutions of social control and identify those ongoing practices that might dissolve distrust within a citizenry. This second part of the task has been reserved for us. Liberal democratic institutions give us the opportunity now to think patiently and directly about citizenship.

This book is a modest contribution to liberal political theory. I argue not for institutions that can dissolve distrust but for forms of citizenship that, when coupled with liberal institutions, can do so. The forms of citizenship I advocate here tend to support some forms of liberalism more than others (I identify these in chapter 9 and the epilogue), but in general these forms straightforwardly complement institutional politics based on equal human dignity and the protection of the liberty of citizens. I bring up Northern Ireland, Palestine, Israel, and Rwanda to emphasize the peculiar advantage we in the United States have. Even our most long-lived distrust is less severe than that suffered by citizens of these other polities. Precisely for this reason, we should learn how to deal with our own. If we cannot resolve our own distrust, how can we offer guidance to those who face more radical versions of it? Interracial distrust in the United States serves as a case study for thinking about the modes of citizenship that are generally needed to deal with congealed distrust.

In part I, I recast the problem of interracial distrust in the United States as a symptom of a more general problem of citizenship. This democracy has repeatedly failed to develop forms of citizenship that help break down distrust and generate trust, a failing closely linked to a second failure to develop citizenly habits that can contend with the unequal distribution of benefits and burdens inevitably produced by political decisions. In part II, I explore why the U.S. democracy has been so bad at developing the forms of citizenship needed and also discuss the ideals that are proper to this trust-generating citizenship. A word of warning for the philosophically faint at heart: chapter 5 is the hardest going. Finally, in part III, I outline the substance of a citizenship of trust-building by exploring how the ordinary practice of friendship provides all citizens with knowledge that can be carried into the political realm to good effect. In the epilogue, I return to the intersection of these arguments about citizenship with efforts to reform political institutions. I ask all citizens to see themselves as founders of institutions, to whatever degree they interact regularly within institutions (churches, schools, universities, businesses, and bureaucracies) that have reach enough to affect the shape of life in their surrounding communities. If a citizen sees the institutions of which he or she is already a part as a medium in which to exemplify the citizenship of trust-building, institutional reform will already be underway.

This is not an argument that we should all just be friends—in the spirit, say, of Hollywood's popular interracial buddy movies.[15] Nor is it an argument that each of us should seek some human commonality that binds us even to strangers, and base our relationships to them on that. In my youth, to quote Lewis Carroll, I tried that line and found it failed. In the present argument, friendship is not an emotion, but a practice, a set of hard-won, complicated habits that are used to bridge trouble, difficulty, and differences of personality, experience, and aspiration. Friendship is not easy, nor is democracy. Friendship begins in the recognition that friends have a *shared* life—not a "common" nor an identical life—only one with common events, climates, built-environments, fixations of the imagination, and social structures. Each friend will view all these phenomena differently, but they are not the less shared for that. The same is true of democracy. The inhabitants of a polity have a shared life in which each citizen and noncitizen has an individual perspective on a set of phenomena relevant to all. Some live behind one veil, and others behind another, but the air that we all breathe carries the same gases and pollens through those veils. More important, our shared elements (events, climates, environments, imaginative fixations, economic conditions, and social structures), when considered at the political rather than the private level, are made out of the combination of all our interactions with each other. We are all always awash in each other's lives, and for most of us that shared life, recorded as history, will be the only artifact we leave behind.[16]

Political friendship begins from this recognition about what we share with the people who live around us and in the same polity. It moves from this recognition of a shared horizon of experience not to a blind trust in one's fellow citizens but rather to a second recognition that a core citizenly responsibility is to prove oneself trustworthy to fellow citizens so that we are better able to ensure that we all breathe healthy air. But in order to prove oneself trustworthy, one has to know why one is distrusted. The politics of friendship requires of citizens a capacity to attend to the dark side of the democratic soul. My ideal reader is simply the democratic citizen, any citizen, but my argument is neither Pollyanna's nor Hollywood's.

Let us begin, then, with the photograph that has served as a national icon of our interracial distrust for nearly fifty years now. It is an icon too of the basic problems involved in democratic citizenship generally.

PART ONE: LOSS

I

⁓

Little Rock, a New Beginning

ON SEPTEMBER 4, 1957, when Elizabeth Eckford set off for her first day at Central High School in Little Rock, Arkansas, as was her legal right, and when she was kept from entering the school by a mob of her fellow citizens who called out for her lynching and when, on top of this, photographs of her exclusion were blazoned across the nation (and the world) by the major news organs, the U.S. democracy was reconstituted. In the photo (fig. 1), we see her after she has been turned away from the school's entrance by the Arkansas National Guard and is on her way back to the bus stop to get away. But her real escape occurred elsewhere. Her bowed shoulders and quiet presence slipped past the psychic defenses—and into the hearts and minds—of citizens (in the North especially) and fired public opinion in favor of the civil rights struggle. Earlier that year Congress had passed its first civil rights legislation since 1875. But only her suffering—intense, contained, and quiet, under Hazel Bryan's curses in the public square during September's still warm early school days—forced a psychic transformation of the citizenry.

Why did U.S. citizens respond so powerfully to this image? What did their engaged imaginations discover in the photo, about their own democracy, about democratic citizenship, and about democracies in general? And what can we learn now about all this by scrutinizing the picture? Here begins an investigation into democratic practice and its difficulties, and also into the relationship between citizenship and trust. How U.S. citizens think about their citizenship has changed dramatically since 1957; tolerance, for instance, is an ethical

FIGURE 1. Elizabeth Eckford being cursed by Hazel Bryan in front of Central High School, Little Rock, Arkansas, September 4, 1957. Photo by Will Counts.

norm of ever-increasing authority. But if we are to understand the nature of citizenship since 1957, and its requirements, we need to analyze the moment of desegregation, when the polity was coming unstitched and being rewoven. Much as a violent wound reveals bone, sinew, blood, and muscle, the picture stripped away idealized conceptions of democratic life and directed the eyes of the citizenry to the ordinary habits that in 1957 constituted citizenship despite the standing law. As we shall see, habits of citizenship begin with how citizens imagine their political world. And what changed with the photographs? Exactly that: how citizens of the United States imagine their political world.

For decades, white Southern citizens had been accustomed to maintaining key public spaces as their exclusive possession; for the sake of preserving life and stability black Southern citizens had been accustomed to acquiescing to such norms and to the acts of violence that enforced them. Each set of customs, exclusionary on the one hand and on the other acquiescent, constituted the practical rules of democratic citizenship for a set of citizens; together the two sets of rules guided citizens into the diverse forms of behavior that secured stable (though undemocratic) public spaces. In that one moment on September 4 caught in the photo, neither Hazel nor Elizabeth was acting unusually. Hazel was insisting on her habitual prerogatives (with power behind her to back up her demand), and Elizabeth was (realistically) acquiescing. But the photo had a new frame, thanks to the 1954 Supreme Court decision in *Brown v. Board of Education* outlawing legally enforced segregation in schools. The irony of the photo, what gives it its immediate aesthetic charge, is that the two etiquettes of citizenship—the one of dominance, the other of acquiescence—that were meant to police the boundaries of the public sphere as a "whites-only" space have instead become the highly scrutinized subject of the public sphere. At the same time, the new legal framework meant that old habits could no longer stabilize the public sphere; the photo therefore also promised that more was to come.

Here the function of the photograph becomes clear. It rendered visible democracy's "public sphere," as it existed in 1957. The mob encircles Elizabeth in the street; she and they meet to contest the value of a political decision (*Brown v. Board of Education*) before the public eye. In one quick instant, looking at photos of Elizabeth and Hazel, viewers saw, as we still do too, the skeletal structure of the public sphere, and also its disintegration. Once the citizenship of dominance and acquiescence was made public, citizens in the rest of the country had no choice but to reject or affirm it. The photo forced a choice on its U.S. viewers, and its power to engage the imagination lay in this. The picture simultaneously recorded a nightmarish version of a town meeting and, by presenting to a broad public the visible structure of segregation, elicited throughout the citizenry an epiphanic awareness of the inner workings of public life and made those mechanics the subject of debate. Even today, the photo provokes anxiety in its audience not merely about laws and institutions but more about how ordinary habits relate to citizenship. Like the German poet Rilke's archaic torso of Apollo, the image of Hazel cursing Elizabeth raises the challenge of transformation not of laws but of ourselves: *Du mußt dein leben ändern,* wrote Rilke. Or, you must alter your way of life.

Nineteen fifty-seven forced citizens to confront the nature of their citizenship—that is, the basic habits of interaction in public spaces—and many were shamed into desiring a new order. The time had come for new conceptions of democratic life. With their epiphanic power, the photos achieved psychic pressure significant enough to make the demand for such new conceptions inescapable. The year therefore inaugurated a new constitution.

An overstatement? I don't think so.

A constitution is more than paper; it is a plan for constituting political rights and organizing citizenship, for determining who has access to the powers of collective decision making that are used to negotiate a community's economic and social relations. Indeed, a constitution need not even be written out. It may, as in Britain, rest on laws and customs that accrete over time to establish a particular distribution of political power through institutions. Or it may, as in ancient Athens, consist of laws and customs that determine who has access to the instruments of political power. As it happens, in the United States the Constitution of 1788–89 by no means even then contained the whole plan for determining political rights and powers. It left the regulation of voting rights to the states. One can't claim to understand the Constitution of the United States without looking beyond the document, which bears that title, to the state laws and the customary habits of citizenship—unspoken norms for interaction that constrain who can speak where in public and how—that helped route the basic circuitry of political power.[1]

If one takes "constitution" in this broad sense, the United States has had several foundings. What we're used to calling the Constitution took years to settle into place as states decided how much property white men needed in order to vote. Some Eastern states retained property requirements even as late as 1860.[2] But the plan of 1789 was eventually superseded, thanks to the Civil War, after which constitutional amendments began to federalize control over voting rights. That refounding, the Reconstruction, incorporated much of the plan devised in 1789 but finally established universal white male suffrage, prohibited slavery and, in designating newly freed African Americans as citizens with full voting rights, connected citizenship for native inhabitants to place of birth rather than to blood. This plan was itself made moot in 1876 when the Hayes-Tilden Agreement led to the withdrawal of federal troops from the South and gave white Southerners free rein to employ extralegal violence to redraw the basic parameters of political and civil rights. Also, in this period literacy requirements in both North and South restricted the voting rights not only of African Americans but also of poor whites and immigrants. This step away from universal suffrage was confirmed at the end of the nineteenth century when the United States acquired Puerto Rico in the Spanish American war and determined that the U.S. Constitution would not be binding there. Now there was federal sanction for maintaining different types of citizenship in different parts of the polity. Puerto Ricans still may not vote in national elections, and citizenship has since then had an imperial cast.

Nineteen twenty reconstituted U.S. citizenship again—with a turn back toward universal suffrage; women acquired the right to vote through a constitutional amendment. Then in the 1950s the fight over race, and its political significance, was joined once more. Over the course of a single decade, between 1954, when the Supreme Court invalidated legally enforced segregation in schools, and 1965, when the Voting Rights Act was passed to supplement the 1964 Civil Rights Act, the citizens of the United States once again reorganized their basic plan for assigning and protecting political rights and powers, this time to protect the rights of minorities. Now it was not state but federal laws that supplemented the text of the Constitution to organize the circuitry of political power.

Let me take note of one last major refounding. In 1971 a constitutional amendment lowered the voting age from 21 to 18, in response to arguments that men old enough to die for the country were also old enough to vote in it. The amendment recast the generational struggle of the late 1960s, and no doubt contributed to sapping the vigor of the protest movements following 1968, by redirecting (at least to a degree) the political energy of the young into official channels. With each set of constitutive legal changes, whether at the level of federal or state law, basic habits for the interaction among citizens also changed. But the amendment of 1971 came about only after young men were dying apace in Vietnam and their age cohort had taken to the street, abandoning parental norms. Shifts in basic habits for interaction can themselves rise to the level of constitutional change, preceding and necessitating changes in the law.

Of all the refoundings, that from 1954 to 1965 is my concern here. It is not the only epochal shift in the country's history, but it does remain still undigested. When in December 2002 Senator Trent Lott, newly elected Republican majority leader, praised Strom Thurmond's

1948 presidential campaign on a segregationist platform at a birthday party for the old senator, it was unclear what political consequences would follow from his nostalgia for the pre–civil rights era. Several weeks of widespread conversation in the media and on the street preceded Lott's decision to resign the leadership post. Until the last few days of the furor it was unclear whether he would have to. Citizens in the United States have not yet fully come to grips with what has changed for them since the 1950s, at the basic level of how they interact with strangers, despite the fact that the political restructuring of the civil rights movement drew so much of its initial energy precisely from challenges posed to ordinary habits, as with the photo of Elizabeth Eckford. We have not yet hammered out all the provisions of the new constitution that, in 1957, "took," or "quickened" in the womb of the old. Yet the epiphanies the photo of Elizabeth provoked then (and still provokes now) destabilized old understandings of citizenship thus making room for and requiring something new. After that moment there could be no turning back. The road from 1957 to the present in the United States has been a rocky one of, among other things, trying to articulate new accounts of democratic citizenship. The photographs of Elizabeth Eckford have made this project inescapable. In this regard 1957 inaugurated a new constitution.

2

⤸

Old Myths and New Epiphanies

I WANT TO SAY MORE about the epiphanies provoked by the photos. Plenty of letters to the editor appeared in newspapers across the country in response to them in September 1957. Most writers expressed only a general recognition of the effects of segregation on U.S. public life. The photos of Elizabeth did more, however, than merely draw back the veils that had previously hidden the inner workings of this country's public sphere. They also provoked, and do so even today, specific epiphanies about the nature of democratic citizenship. Audiences at the time, hurried readers of newspapers, perhaps registered these epiphanies only half-consciously. We, in contrast, have the luxury to study the photos at length as if they were texts. Although they no doubt inspired diverse epiphanies for their many viewers, they still produce three that directly reveal the difficulties of democratic practice and citizenship. Two of these epiphanies also gut old myths.

Here let us add a few more photos to our iconographic archive (figs. 2 and 3).

Old myth 1: Citizenship consists primarily of duties (like voting, paying taxes, and serving on juries or in the military) to institutions that protect citizens' rights. Students are regularly taught that the political structure of democratic countries depends on written documents called constitutions and on the institutions, rights, and duties for which those documents are the blueprint.[1] This account seems to many an adequate answer to the question, What is citizenship?

Epiphany 1: In a quick instant, looking at Elizabeth and Hazel (fig. 1), we see how long-enduring habits of interaction give form to

FIGURE 2. Journalist Alex Wilson, under attack by a mob near Central High School, Little Rock, Arkansas, September 4,1957. Photo by Will Counts.

public space and so to our political life.[2] We see two different political etiquettes directed together toward the restoration of order. Habits stabilize and shape the public sphere. For instance, we notice a measured spatial distance between black and white citizens and also a strong distinction not only between the demeanor of the girls and of the boys, but also between the political tasks assigned to each gender. Girls attack the girl with curses and taunts; men turn to physical violence and also stand guard at the boundary of the public space (the bus stop). Political order is secured not only by institutions, but also by "deep rules" that prescribe specific interactions among citizens in public spaces; citizens enact what they are to each other not only in assemblies, where they make decisions about their mutually intertwined fates, but also when, as strangers, they speak to one another, or don't, or otherwise respond to each other's presence.

These photos remind me of the single story we have from ancient democratic Athens of the political activity of the citizen women; it too concerns a crisis in which the distinct roles of different members of society stand out with unnerving clarity. Once during the stress of war, a member of the Council (the agenda-setting body for the As-

FIGURE 3. Elizabeth Eckford at the bus stop after having been refused entry to Central High. Photo by Will Counts.

sembly) was thought by his colleagues to have spoken out of treasonous motives; they rose up to stone him on the spot, and men outside the chambers joined in.[3] When a hue and cry about the events spread throughout the city, the women "of their own accord" went and stoned the man's wife and children. In the Athenian story, men secure the political realm, and women do act politically but only in order to do what they, as nonpolitical actors, would normally do: secure the sanctity of the Athenian household. In the moment when the Athenian order was coming undone to the extent that women were acting politically and in public, its customary structure was made most dramatically apparent. Citizens know the deep rules of their society by intuition and habit and become expressly conscious of those rules only when the order they secure is disintegrating. As we saw in the last chapter, the photos provoke anxiety in their audience not merely about laws and institutions but more about how ordinary habits relate to citizenship. That ordinary habits *are* the stuff of citizenship is the first epiphany.

Now to the second.

Old myth 2: Out of many, a democratic people should become one. The metaphor of "oneness" has for centuries been central to descriptions of the proper aspirations of a democratic people. *E pluribus unum* is only the most common statement of this ideal, which is a staple in our political vocabulary.

I quote Arthur Schlesinger, Jr.'s *The Disuniting of America* as a highly influential recent example of important commentary on American politics that uses the metaphor of "oneness" to describe the democratic people the author hopes we can become.[4] In 1991, Schlesinger argued that the turn toward ethnicity of the 1970s and 1980s was gutting the old American ideal of the melting pot, wherein all citizens believed themselves a part of "one people." He tells a simple fable of historical decline: before World War II, we were one people; now no longer one, we are in danger of losing our remaining unity to balkanization. To fix this, he argues, we must restore our commitment to being one people, and to "assimilation." But he is hopeful: "[T]he vigorous sense of national identity accounts for our relative success in converting Crèvecoeur's 'promiscuous breed' into one people and thereby making a multiethnic society work. . . . [T]he historic forces driving toward 'one people' have not lost their power."[5]

Schlesinger is not alone in imagining the democratic populace through the metaphor of "oneness." In the 2000 presidential campaign, nearly every major politician drew on it. When former vice president Albert Gore conceded the election, he argued that the "very closeness [of the election] can serve to remind us that we are *one people* with a shared history and a shared destiny" (Dec. 14, 2000; emphasis added). Gore was, unsurprisingly, heir to the rhetoric of the previous president, William Clinton, who, in his valedictory address to the Democratic National Convention just a few months earlier (Aug. 14, 2000), had celebrated his administration for success at leading the United States closer "to the one America of our dreams" and urged voters to persist in their commitment "to one America." But the Republican victor, George W. Bush, was no less Clinton's heir. In his acceptance speech, he pledged to move "the country forward, as one nation indivisible," insisting that he was "not elected to serve one party, but to serve one nation" (Dec. 14, 2000). For all of these citizens, the metaphor of oneness is crucial to holding a democratic people together.

Epiphany 2: The metaphor of "oneness" could not in 1957 and cannot now capture Elizabeth and Hazel's experiences of citizenship, for they lived radically different versions of democratic life. Though they were members of the same democracy, each was expert, as we have seen already, in a different etiquette of citizenship: dominance on the one hand and acquiescence on the other. The picture recorded the two-ness of citizenship as it existed in 1957.

Indeed, the metaphor of oneness is generally inadequate to describe the proper aspirations of a democratic people to solidarity and community, and not merely in relation to the events of 1957. To explain this point, I must set a bit of my own historical work against Schlesinger's. When President-elect Bush in his acceptance speech invoked the ideal of "one nation indivisible," he quoted the Pledge of Allegiance—not as we know it today, but as it read prior to 1954. In that year, the year of the Supreme Court decision in *Brown v. Board of Education,* in fact, just a month after the decision, Congress voted to insert the phrase "under God" after "one nation."[6] World War II and the onset of the Cold War in the early 1950s had brought a wave of literature on citizenship and the question of how to cultivate appropriate allegiances within the citizenry. Congress added the phrase "under God" in order to distinguish the United States from its new enemy, the atheistic Soviet Union, thus legislating a decidedly religious turn for citizenship in the United States. Many states also passed laws requiring public schools to lead students in reciting the pledge on a daily basis and so drafted schoolchildren into the armies of the Cold War.[7] But more important for our purposes is the congressional debate surrounding the emendation of the pledge. This concerned not *whether* to emend but only *where* to insert the new phrase "under God." When Congress decided to place it after "one nation" and before "indivisible," "one nation under God" became the most famous phrase in the pledge and revitalized the language of "oneness" that had been so important when it was first written in the 1890s as a response to staggeringly high rates of immigration.[8]

The new phrase also at last made explicit that the language of the pledge had originated in Civil War–era efforts to unify Northern and Southern whites. During the congressional debate on emendation, advocates justified the phrase "one nation under God" by reference to Lincoln's Gettysburg Address, which uses it; and the author of the original pledge, Francis Bellamy, had drawn much of its language from Daniel Webster's famous January 26, 1830, speech against the prospect of Southern secession. Webster's speech ended in the following ringing peroration:

> I hope that I may not see the flag of my Country, with its stars separated or obliterated, torn by commotion, smoking with the blood of civil war. . . . I hope I shall not see written, as its motto, *first* Liberty, and *then* Union. I hope I shall see no such delusion and deluded motto on the flag of that Country. I hope to see spread all over it, blazoned in letters of light, and proudly floating over Land and Sea that other sentiment, dear to my heart, "Liberty *and* Union, now and forever, one and inseparable!"

The Pledge of Allegiance, as we know it today, is simply the junior sequel to this remarkable piece of Civil War–era rhetoric.[9] In an effort to draw rebellious Southern whites into accord with their white brethren up north, Webster had celebrated "Union, now and forever, one and inseparable." Under Bellamy's pen, the national ideal became "one nation indivisible."[10]

It was no accident that "oneness" should be emphasized once again in 1954 just a month after the high court had momentously decided to invalidate school segregation. When Congress legislated schoolchildren into the minor armies of the day, they gave them a ritual that was intended to respond not only to Communism but also to rising tensions that threatened to divide the country's white citizenry once again on questions of race and "equality."[11]

Now, Bellamy had deliberately left that last word, "equality," out of the Pledge in order to avoid this country's most divisive issue.[12] What, then, was the significance of the turn in national rhetoric in the 1950s back to the trope of "oneness," in a political context where

FIGURE 4. "Stop the Race Mixing March of the Anti-Christ."
Photo by Will Counts.

the issue of equality could no longer be postponed? Was the rhetoric supposed to unify, once again, Southern and Northern whites, or was it at last to unify white and black?

When Elizabeth and her antagonists met in the streets in 1957, all of them had, for the three previous years, been daily pledging their devotion to "one nation under God," the one in her black school, the others in their white schools. Had Elizabeth made it to school on that September day, she would have recited the same phrase in a room full of black and white students, for the first time in the lives of all those students. What a mockery, then, the photo of the battle in the Little Rock streets made of those students' morning ritual, their daily devotion of themselves to the cause of "one people." Division, not unity, had marked their lives; they knew that "oneness" could capture their experience only by idealization. In our second epiphanic moment, we see clearly in the photo that the democracy of the United States in 1957 was made up of not one but at least two, and maybe three, four, or more, peoples, all living in the same polity but under different laws, with differential rights and powers, and with different habitual practices of citizenship. The photo, in one flash, makes explicit

FIGURE 5. "Race Mixing is Communism." Photo by Will Counts.

the mythological status of the country's ideal of "oneness," but it also forces us to wonder whether that myth could ever accurately guide diverse and disagreeing citizens in their attempts to establish relationships within the democratic whole.

Happily, the photo also suggests an alternate metaphor that might be more useful for discussing the solidarity of the citizenry in circumstances of diversity. Schlesinger's desire to restore "oneness" despite its transparent flaws as a metaphor derives from his awareness that democratic peoples *need* metaphors to make "the people," the body of which they are a part, conceivable to themselves. Citizens who hold the conviction that politics is by, for, and of the people can assume a place in politics only by imagining "the people" and a place for themselves in, or in relationship to, that body. But where, what, and who is this "the people"? And how does it act? The term produces a quandary for the imagination. If modern democratic citizenship seems mostly to be about voting, this derives from the belief that "the people" exists only when a "will" has been expressed and that this occurs only through a mass compilation of votes. Voting does not merely legitimate democratic politics but also provides a practical solution to that imaginative dilemma. Metaphors, no less than institutions, are vehicles for the imagination and, indeed, are central to securing "the people" for democratic life. In short, citizens can explain their role in democracy only by expending significant conceptual and imaginative labor to make themselves part of an invisible whole.[13]

Now, with that phrase "invisible whole," we have hit upon the central term. Citizens must imagine themselves part of a "whole" they cannot see. "The people" is the name for that "whole," and, in fact, wholeness, not oneness, is the master term in the history of the production of democratic peoples. Indeed, the effort to make the people "one" should be seen as but a single version of the more general endeavor, necessitated by the more fundamental democratic project, to make the people "whole." The word derives from Old English and Germanic forms meaning "uninjured, sound, healthy, and complete." Now it means rather "full," "total," "complete," and "all." Neither the *Oxford English Dictionary* (2nd ed.) nor *Merriam Webster's Collegiate Dictionary* (10th ed.) treats "one" as its synonym. The reason for this is simple. A speaker cannot use the word "one" to mean multiplicity, but the word "whole" entails just that. The effort to make the people "one" cultivates in the citizenry a desire for homogeneity, for that is the aspiration taught to citizens by the meaning of the word "one," itself. In contrast, an effort to make the people "whole" might cultivate an aspiration to the coherence and integrity of a consolidated but complex, intricate, and differentiated body.

Why does it matter how democratic citizens imagine "the people" of which they are a part? As a democracy develops an explanation of how its citizenry is a coherent body, "the people," and makes this body imaginable, it also invents customs and practices of citizenly interaction that accord with that explanation. The democracy's self-explanation must necessarily focus in some way or another on securing the wholeness of "the people" in the minds of democratic citizens, for only if it does can the imaginary body that is the foundation of any democracy come into existence. But different metaphors, for instance the metaphor of "oneness," may be laid on top of the aspiration to "wholeness," redirecting the aspiration to integrity and communion toward, in this case, homogeneity. And with the particular metaphors that give force to the pursuit of wholeness come also particular *practices* that help give those metaphors recognizable and living form.

The aim of Hazel's curses is precisely to restore oneness to the public sphere. The moment that Elizabeth reaches the bus stop Hazel succeeds. The two modes of citizenship that I discussed in the last chapter—dominance on the one hand and acquiescence on the other—secured not only the pre-1957 public sphere but also the myth of "oneness." The commitment to unity for which Schlesinger grieves was intimately bound together with *practices* of citizenship that involved making citizens who were not part of "the one people" politically invisible. Those practices stand revealed in the photographs of Elizabeth Eckford. Most important, the citizenship of oneness consisted not so much, as we like to think, of exclusion as of domination and acquiescence.[14] Thus a movement beyond 1957 requires not merely the inclusion of the excluded within political institutions but also, more fundamentally, a transformation of the citizenship of dominance and acquiescence into a single more truly democratic citizenship shared by all citizens, through which we would aspire to make the citizenry not one but whole, mutually trusting and therefore healthy.

To see how the metaphor of oneness has been tied to particular habits of citizenship gives us access to a different view of the history of this country. It is not the case that the United States has experienced a decline and fall from a period of prewar unity to a later stage of division. Rather, the United States has moved through several different stages of the citizenry's effort to make the people "whole." In the period from the Civil War to World War II, the effort to make the people "whole" was defined by the attempt to make it "one." But in that same period, within the citizenry of the United States, several peoples were subject to different laws, and even those who were subject to the same laws often had radically different experiences of legality in America. The decisive thing was that those who were unassimilated had no mainstream public voice. The divisions within the citizenry were not given public articulation, and the dominant practice of citizenship among those who *had* melted together was to uphold the idea of being one people by ignoring or even undermining the citizen status of those who had not been assimilated. Citizenship taught habits of domination and acquiescence that, in conjunction, produced invisibility and a seeming oneness.

During the period of World War II and the civil rights movement

that followed, minorities gained mainstream public voices and vocal-
ized the perspectives of citizens who had for decades lived "beyond
the pale" (to quote Schlesinger) of the "one people." Thus Elizabeth
ended up in the middle of the public square and in so doing did not
create but only revealed the division that had always constituted it.
The civil rights movement not only advocated legal and institutional
changes but also insisted that U.S. citizens acknowledge the deep divisions that had long existed within the citizenry. The movement
condemned practices of citizenship that entailed ignoring the second
and third peoples within the polity and thus implicitly challenged the
populace to cultivate new habits of citizenship. During the postwar
period, there was no transition from unity to division, only from
whitewashing those divisions to their explicit acknowledgment. In
the new project of citizenship initiated by this move to acknowledge
difference, exclusion, and domination, citizens' habits for interacting
with one another still needed to foster the integrity of the citizen
body as a whole, but now the question was how practices of citizenship might evolve so as to accommodate frankness about difference.

We are still in this second period. We long ago abandoned modes
of citizenship that laid claim to unity by means of domination, acquiescence, hypocrisy, and the production of invisibility. The second
epiphany provoked by the photograph leads us finally to the discovery that wholeness, not oneness, is the appropriate metaphor with
which to discuss the aspirations of a democratic populace to integrity
and solidarity. But since the 1950s and 1960s we have met the challenge to develop new forms of citizenship with only limited success.
The seesawing back and forth of African American political ideology
between assimilation and separatism is itself a product of our failure
to address directly the question: what modes of citizenship can make
a citizenry whole without covering up difference? Both the assimila-
tionist and the separatist positions arise from the "one people" mode
of citizenship—the one as its product, the other as a reaction against
it. Similarly, the antagonisms within the white citizenry between
those who argue for assimilation and English-only policies and those
who argue for multiculturalism, group rights, and bilingual education
for non-native English speakers equally arise from the one people
ideology as product and reaction. Indeed, exhortations, like that of
Schlesinger, to return to an ideology of one people, which neces-

sarily ignores how diversely the laws of the land can affect different members of the citizenry, persist because citizens and theorists of democracy have not closely examined the practices involved in the citizenship of "the one people"; nor have they yet adequately articulated positive alternative visions of the citizenly practices that might foster wholeness though acknowledging difference.

A focus on the wholeness of the citizenry, rather than on its oneness, might allow for the development of forms of citizenship that focus on integration, not assimilation, and on the mutual exchanges and appropriations that have already occurred among different groups and that will always keep occurring. Such a citizenship might focus on multilingualism, where citizens all expect to learn each other's languages, rather than on multiculturalism, which seems to set up permanently distinct cultural blocs.[15] In short, the metaphor of wholeness can guide us into a conversation about how to develop habits of citizenship that can help a democracy bring trustful coherence out of division without erasing or suppressing difference. This second epiphany prompts us to reimagine the very idea of "the people," work that I will take up again in chapter 6. Now it is time for the final epiphany.

The third epiphany does not upend any particular old myth but turns our attention to the neglected topic of the psychology of democratic citizenship.

Epiphany 3: A small detail in the Little Rock photos sparks a sharp awareness of the psychologically complex ways the human imagination factors into democratic citizenship. Look closely at the photographs of Elizabeth Eckford and notice that the bottom portion of her skirt is made up of black-and-white checks.

As far as Elizabeth was concerned, this was the salient feature of her back-to-school dress. In a memoir of the Battle of Little Rock, written in 1966, the dress is simply, "my black and white dress—I had made it to wear on the first day of school" (*LSLR* 73). One might wish to disregard as bathetic the intuition that Elizabeth had made herself a dress in which she would embody the new world of integration she hoped to enter, were it not for remarks she made again about the dress as late as 1997. On that morning of the first day of school, she had heard television reports about white supremacists gathering outside Central but says of them in 1997, "I was more con-

FIGURE 6. Elizabeth with guards. Photo by Will Counts.

cerned about what I would wear, whether we could finish my dress in time . . . what I was wearing, was that okay, would it look good?"[16] What should we make of the dress? Why does it matter?

Strangely, the dress itself has become a museum piece, one item among many in exhibits on the history of desegregation. It is best understood as something like a souvenir T-shirt that reads, "I tried to go to an integrated school, and all I got was this lousy dress." The dress reports on the gap between ideals and actualities, and also on the importance of symbols to the efforts of democratic citizens to deal with that gap. Although her fellow citizens across the country did not, Elizabeth knew that the integration of the public school system would require a made-from-scratch reweaving of the relationships among citizens. When she made the dress, she expressed the autonomy of the democratic citizen who desires to be sovereign and to effect new political orders but must also confess her own disempowerment.[17] She had at her disposal the means to reconstitute not the "fabric" of society but only her daily uniform, and hers alone. Insofar as democracy is touted as a project of self-rule for citizens, it is, for all citizens, an effort of trying to subdue matter to form, so that the world matches our desires. But, as Elizabeth discovered, it is much

FIGURE 7. The dress as displayed at the Chicago Historical Society.
Published with permission of Facing History and Ourselves.

easier to bend a piece of cloth to one's will than one's fellow citizens; it is much easier to fashion material symbols of the state we desire than that state itself. If democratic citizens rule themselves, they do so fully, in reality, only in their symbol worlds. The manipulation of ideal symbols, however, gives a democratic citizen psychological access to political power.

Is it possible that democratic citizens have a special need for symbols and the world of fantasy precisely because their real political world does not and cannot give them the autonomy, freedom, and sovereignty it promises? The ancient Athenian historian Thucydides suggested this about democratic Athens, which he recognized as a city that, in contrast to its oligarchic enemy Sparta, was devoted to the production of symbols.[18] Athens was building so many monuments that long after both cities were gone, he argued, people would see the impressive ruins of Athens, find nothing at Sparta, and believe that the democracy had been the greater of the two when, in fact, Sparta had won the war between them. The Athenians' high regard for their own power and autonomy would live on, despite being a misrepresentation of reality. Could this Thucydidean observation be an insight into democracy more generally? After all, democracies inspire in citizens an aspiration to rule and yet require citizens constantly to live with the fact that they do not. Democracies must find methods to help citizens deal with the conflict between their politically inspired desires for total agency and the frustrating reality of their experience. Elizabeth's dress reveals one such method, and served as a symbolic outlet to the desire for political power. The important thing, though, is that the symbolic required real power, real fashioning, on Elizabeth's part. Her ability to subdue matter to form with the skirt no doubt helped secure her belief in the possibility of doing the same with her fellow citizens, and her conviction that eventually she and they would together reweave their social fabric. The dress may well have reassured her of her ability to help reform the future.

Captured flying in the photo, then, is Elizabeth's flag for a project of reconstitution. She knew the habits of citizens would have to be unknit and rewoven. She had an aspiration for the form that weave would take: her skirt is a model of wholeness, not oneness, and her desire to wear it reveals her intuitive knowledge that citizens embody their political forms. If they wish to change their politics, they must clothe themselves in new forms of citizenly action. As Ralph Ellison put it, "This society is not likely to become free of racism, thus it is necessary for Negroes to free themselves by becoming their idea of what a free people should be." This is an exhortation not merely to African Americans but to all who would truly be democratic citizens. Elizabeth needed neither an epiphany nor an exhortation to learn that democratic citizens embody their political norms in their interactions with one another in public spaces or to learn that democratic citizenship is as much a matter of how strangers interact in public spaces as of institutions. Nor did she need an epiphany to learn that wholeness, rather than oneness, is the appropriate metaphor with which to guide efforts at the production of democratic solidarity. Without having to see some photograph of a nightmarish public square, she recognized that the constitution of democratic practice in the United States was under strain in 1957, and near the point of change. With her dress, she named the political moment as one of reconstitution and told her fellow citizens it was so. By wearing her flag modestly and quietly before a mob, she helped initiate the transition from symbolic invention to real transformation. The final epiphany for those who look at her photo is that Elizabeth intended, even if only intuitively, to provoke political epiphanies with her dress so that real, and not merely symbolic, reconstitution might occur.[19] It was her way, the only one available to her, of talking to strangers. Quiet at the center of all that yelling, she could not be heard, nor would those immediately around her listen. Yet walking silently she was also, all the while, talking to strangers, and so provides an example of the powerful inventiveness that belongs to the true democratic citizen. Happily, a photographer was there to amplify what Elizabeth had to say.

If we take Elizabeth's lead, and identify September 4, 1957, as a moment of reconstitution, as an opportunity for weaving a new social fabric in which to clothe ourselves, we should, if we scrutinize the situation, see a democracy coming apart and trying to put itself together again. And to see a democracy in a moment of unknitting and reweaving is to have the chance to learn things about the inner workings of democracy that we do not normally see. Two political theorists were among the newspaper audience of the events in Little Rock and, like Elizabeth, identified the day as both a moment of reconstitution and a time for talking passionately and frankly to strangers. Philosopher Hannah Arendt and novelist and democratic theorist Ralph Ellison both took the trouble to ascertain what could be learned about democracy by considering the events at Little Rock. I turn to them now for the sake of refining our understanding of what democracy is and how it works. This will also require that we turn to the full story of the Battle of Little Rock.

3

⁓

Sacrifice, a Democratic Fact

PHILOSOPHER HANNAH ARENDT wrote a controversial article against school desegregation in the wake of the September 1957 struggles in Little Rock, Arkansas, and published it two years later in *Dissent* magazine. The city had exploded over whether nine African American students who had been admitted to the previously whites-only Central High would in fact attend. Arendt's article, "Reflections on Little Rock," criticized the National Association for the Advancement of Colored People (NAACP) and the parents of the Little Rock Nine for using political institutions like the courts and the public sphere generally to effect what she considered not a political program but self-interested social advancement. Much affected by the news photographs of Elizabeth being menaced by a nasty mob as she, unaccompanied, tried to enter the school, Arendt argued further that the parents, in pursuing social advancement, were exploiting their children. "The girl obviously was asked to be a hero," Arendt wrote, "[which] is, something neither her absent father nor the equally absent representatives of the NAACP felt called upon to be" (RLR 50).[1]

Arendt objected to any strategy that drew children, white or black, into a political fray, but when she accused the African American parents of a lack of heroism, she also more specifically charged the desegregation movement with a failure to rise to the level of political action. Her position depends heavily on the argument she published almost simultaneously in the *Human Condition* of 1958 that politics, properly understood, is a heroic activity; Achilles, the Greek hero of the Trojan War, is her paradigmatic political actor. In her analysis, the parents mistook a "social issue" for a legitimate political battleground. This contention that school desegregation was not an appropriate object of political action rested on her strong distinctions among private, social, and political spheres. To the private realm she assigned intimacy and activities like marriage, love, and parenting; in the social world we secure our economic livelihood and also, importantly, discriminate against others by choosing friends who are like ourselves for ourselves and our children. Finally, in the political realm, in her account, we secure political rights, like the rights to vote and hold office, and also private rights, like the right to marry whom we please. The public sphere is also the arena for conversations with strangers and for epic action that brings glory to the actors.

Arendt's central concern in *The Human Condition* was to translate an epic approach to politics into a democratic context. Democratic political agents must construct a common world out of difference and speak to one another qua men and not qua members of society (*HC* 219). In a democracy, the ability to "fight a full-fledged political battle" (*HC* 219) consists of articulating "one's own ideas about the possibilities of democratic government under modern conditions," and of "propos[ing] a transformation of political institutions" (*HC* 216). Most important, political action in a democracy is the opposite of what we do as members of society, which is merely to "defend economic interests," ask for "due consideration of vital interests" (*MDT* 11), and function as "interest parties" (*HC* 218). In Arendt's view, only nonheroic economic and "vital" interests were at stake in Little Rock.

In short, Arendt criticizes the actions of the African Americans involved in Little Rock as failures of citizenship. Their "nonpolitical" actions in Little Rock caused a crisis that could be solved, she argued, only by converting the public to new citizenly practices of tact and restraint. If the U.S. democracy were to succeed at its new post-1957 constitution, developing enough trust and stability to preserve democracy, its citizens would heroically have to surrender their concern with social issues. Only this genteel mode of citizenship, she believed, could convert long-standing divisions into the stuff of public debate and also preserve the public sphere.

Ellison disagreed with Arendt's account of Little Rock and democratic citizenship and twice responded publicly to her article, presenting a different take on problems like distrust, and on their solution.

In an interview with Robert Penn Warren he remarked, "I believe that one of the important clues to the meaning of [American Negro] experience lies in the idea, the *ideal* of sacrifice. Hannah Arendt's failure to grasp the importance of this ideal among Southern Negroes caused her to fly way off into left field in her 'Reflections on Little Rock.'" He continues:

> [S]he has absolutely no conception of what goes on in the minds of Negro parents when they send their kids through those lines of hostile people. Yet they are aware of the overtones of a rite of initiation which such events actually constitute for the child, a confrontation of the terrors of social life with all the mysteries stripped away. And in the outlook of many of these parents (who wish the problem didn't exist), the child is expected to face the terror and contain his fear and anger *precisely* because he is a Negro American. Thus he's required to master the inner tensions created by his racial situation, and if he gets hurt—then his is one more sacrifice. (WS 343–44)[2]

Ellison had developed the concepts of ritual and sacrifice at length in his 1952 novel *Invisible Man,* and amplified his accounts of both terms in his many essays; these concepts were the foundation for a provocative account of democracy.[3] But just how are ritual and sacrifice relevant to an analysis of Little Rock, or of democratic citizenship?

Democracy puts its citizens under a strange form of psychological pressure by building them up as sovereigns and then regularly undermining each citizen's experience of sovereignty. Ellison explicated what it is like to be an individual in a democratic world of strangers, where large-scale events are supposed to arise out of one's own consent and yet never really do.[4] He recognized that every human life is full of rituals that initiate people into the symbol world, ideals, and political structure of their community. These are the link between any particular life and the larger political structure. The rituals may be as overt as the requirement that students say the Pledge of Allegiance in school every day or as little noticed as the adult habit of asking a child upon a first meeting, "What's your name and how old are you?" (*CE* 195).[5] For Ellison, that particular ritual at least partially explains the modern concern with identity. Similarly, a ritual may be as obviously political as one's first trip to the polls, or may (wrongly) seem to be merely social, like getting drunk legally at the age of twenty-one. But since the purpose of rituals is to create, justify, and maintain particular social arrangements, they are the foundation also of political structures, and an individual comes to know intimately central aspects of the overall form of his community by living through them. Significantly, since every ritual is for Ellison also a form of initiation, or reinitiation, children are not exempt.[6]

In the moment that Hazel and Elizabeth, two teenagers, met in the public square, neither was inventing her form of behavior. Each had already been initiated into the requirements of adult life in the South. In the Battle of Little Rock, they were simply tested once more to see how well they had learned their lessons. Elizabeth knew the drill and was lucky that she did. This is the force of Ellison's argument to Warren that the parents of the Little Rock Nine understood how integral to childhood are rituals initiating the child into the symbol world and ideals of adults, and so also into adult politics. Whereas Arendt developed a political theory that might protect children from politics, by transforming politics into an epic arena for full-grown warriors only, Ellison has a more tragic vision: rituals to solidify social order inevitably involve children in politics, however much one might wish the case otherwise.

Of all the rituals relevant to democracy, sacrifice is preeminent. No democratic citizen, adult or child, escapes the necessity of losing out at some point in a public decision. "It is our fate as human beings," Ellison writes, "always to give up some good things for other good things, to throw off certain bad circumstances only to create others" (CE 208).[7] But sacrifice is a special sort of problem in a democracy. Democracies are supposed to rest on consent and open access to happiness for their citizens. In the dreamscape of democracy, for instance à la Rousseau, every citizen consents to every policy with glad enthusiasm. No one ever leaves the public arena at odds with the communal choice; no one must accept political loss or suffer the imposition of laws to which she has not consented. But that is a dream. An honest account of collective democratic action must begin by acknowledging that communal decisions inevitably benefit some citizens at the expense of others, even when the whole community generally benefits. Since democracy claims to secure the good of all citizens, those people who benefit less than others from particular

political decisions, but nonetheless accede to those decisions, preserve the stability of political institutions. Their sacrifice makes collective democratic action possible. Democracy is not a static end state
that achieves the common good by assuring the same benefits or the
same level of benefits to everyone, but rather a political practice by
which the diverse negative effects of collective political action, and
even of just decisions, can be distributed equally, and constantly re-
distributed over time, on the basis of consensual interactions.[8] The
hard truth of democracy is that some citizens are always giving things
up for others. Only vigorous forms of citizenship can give a polity the
resources to deal with the inevitable problem of sacrifice.

As we shall see, one of the achievements of the protagonist of Ellison's novel, *Invisible Man,* is to develop criteria for distinguishing legitimate from illegitimate forms of sacrifice, and also to outline a form
of citizenship that helps citizens generate trust enough among themselves to manage sacrifice. Here it is necessary rather to outline the
conceptual bases of such a citizenship. Most important, recognition
of the necessary fact of loss and disappointment in democratic politics vitiates any effort, such as Arendt's, to hold the social firmly separate from the political. As citizens struggle over political questions,
they will necessarily come to understand how political choices affect
social experience. The site of sacrifice is between the social world—
of custom and of mental, physical, and economic harm from other
citizens—and the political world of institutions and practices for
the sake of which one wants to master that harm. Thus Ellison says to
Warren of the African American parents behind the events at Little
Rock, "We learned about forbearance and forgiveness in that same
school, and about hope too. So today we sacrifice, as we sacrificed
yesterday, *the pleasure of personal retaliation in the interest of the common
good*" (WS 342; emphasis added). The initiation of citizens into public
life entails pains and disappointments that, though generated in the
public sphere, are experienced in the social and personal realms. No
wonder, then, that Ellison, in powerful contrast to Arendt, so frequently uses the term "socio-political."

In Ellison's view, African Americans had, within the confines of a
citizenship of acquiescence, developed powerful insights about democracy based on this recognition of the inevitable blending of social and
political. Because African American parents had long recognized the

centrality of sacrifice to their experience of life in America, they found it necessary to cultivate in their children habits for dealing with the sacrifices that would come their way. They felt obliged, according to Ellison, to teach their children that the political and legal worlds are imbricated in a social context (sometimes of terror) that constrains the possibilities for action supposedly protected by law. These parents also taught their children both that they would have to pay a social price for exercising the democratic political instrument provided them by legal institutions, and that the use of the democratic political instrument and its preservation were worth that price. The ability to make such a sacrifice constituted, for Ellison, "the basic, implicit *heroism* of people who must live within a society without recognition, real status, *but who are involved in the ideals of that society* and who are trying to make their way, trying to determine their true position and their rightful position within it" (WS 342; emphasis added). The sacrifices of African Americans living in a segregated polity were sufficiently extreme to constitute scapegoating in Ellison's terms rather than legitimate sacrifice, and yet, he argued, they nonetheless revealed a truth that applies to all democratic citizens: the political world cannot be entirely separated from the social world, and learning how to negotiate the losses one experiences at the hands of the public is fundamental to becoming a political actor, not only for minorities suffering political abuses, but for all citizens. For Ellison, as not for Arendt, the Little Rock parents were heroes. They were acting politically, even in Arendt's own terms, for, as Ellison describes them, they were illustrating ideas about how a democratic community might organize itself. They were providing rich lessons in citizenship by revealing the sacrifices citizens make for each other and the necessary connections between the social and the political.

On Ellison's reading of the events of September 1957, the figure of Elizabeth Eckford brought before the public eye not only the truth about then existing modes of citizenship but also the glimmerings of a new account of democratic agency. Her parents and those of the other children were enduring social abuse—the taunts and threats addressed to their children—and asking their children, many of whom had wanted to attend Central High over their objections, to endure too, in order to render functional a legal system that had recently banned the legal imposition of segregation on schools. They suffered the abuse of their children, a challenge "they wish[ed] didn't exist," to help assure that the law worked. Elizabeth's solitary walk was one more sacrifice. In the face of disagreement she sought forms of political action that might generate enough political friendship to secure a democratic legal system and convert the distrust arising from political disappointment into trust.

Which account of democracy and citizenship, Arendt's or Ellison's, is the more accurate analysis of the events at Central High and their political significance?

The story of Little Rock, briefly, is this.[9] In the spring of 1957 the Little Rock school board formulated, and was required by courts to abide by, a plan for integrating Central High School the following September. Over the summer many African American students applied for admission to Central, very often against their parents' wishes, and nine students were finally selected by school authorities.[10] As the NAACP was readying the students, with extra academic training, to enter Central, Governor Orval Faubus worked to pass new legislation reinstating segregation in the state's schools, and citizen groups organized against the projected opening of an integrated Central High. (Strangely, several other schools in Arkansas had been integrated in preceding years without incident.) On September 2, the day before school was to start, 250 National Guardsmen, under the supervision of the State of Arkansas, surrounded Central on Faubus's orders. He announced on television that this was his response to warnings that carloads of white supremacists were headed to Little Rock; he also announced that on the next day Central High School would be off-limits to black students, and Horace Mann, the black school, would be off-limits to white students.

Central High sat empty on September 3, but the Little Rock school superintendent reasserted his local authority and, rescheduling the opening for the fourth, authorized proceeding with the integration plan. When the morning of the fourth arrived, so did large crowds, watching and waiting as the guardsmen began to let a few white students through their ranks to the school. Then Elizabeth Eckford, the first black student, arrived. As the crowd surged around her with curses and cries that she be lynched—radios reported, "A Negro girl is being mobbed at Central High"—she walked the length of the mob to reach the school entrance (*LSLR* 66). She had seen the white stu-

dents enter between the ranks of guardsmen but, when she also tried
to pass through, the soldiers thrust their bayonets at her chest. She
tried twice before turning and returning, passing again along the
whole length of the crowd, to the bus stop, where she sat. There Benjamin Fine, a white reporter for the *New York Times,* sat down with
her, putting his arm around her. With a white woman he tried to help
Elizabeth escape, first by cab (the mob prevented this) and then at last
by bus. This was the first event in what has come to be called "The
Battle of Little Rock," where victory was determined, though the
fighting not ended, by the arrival of federal troops (as distinct from
the guardsmen) on September 24. "Sure we're in Central. But how
did we get in?" one of the students said, on the twenty-fifth. "We got
in, finally, because we were protected by paratroops. Some victory!"
(*LSLR* 106). This student regretted that the law could not prevail
simply through the ordinary interaction of citizens.

Daisy Bates, president of the Arkansas State Conference of
NAACP branches, gives an account of the events at Little Rock, and
some of the negotiations of legal authority involved in them, that
confirms Ellison's analysis of both the centrality of sacrifice to democratic politics and the close relationship between sacrifice and democratic legal authority. On the afternoon of the third, the school superintendent Virgil Blossom called a meeting of leading African
American citizens in Little Rock along with the children's parents
and "instructed the parents *not* to accompany their children the next
morning when they were scheduled to enter Central. 'If violence
breaks out,' the Superintendent told them, 'it will be easier to protect
the children if the adults aren't there'" (*LSLR* 63). The parents were
extremely troubled by this—Superintendent Blossom had not explained *how* the children would be protected—but they agreed. Bates
was also worried by the instructions and, doing what she could to
provide protection for the children while also following the superintendent's orders, she spent the night making phone calls: first, to a
white minister to ask if he could round up colleagues to accompany
the children in place of the parents; second, to the police to ask that
they accompany the children as close to the school as Faubus's National Guardsmen would permit; third to the parents to tell them not
to send their children straight to school but rather to the ministers and

police. The Eckfords had no phone, so Daisy missed them, but planned to go by their house early enough in the morning to fill them in. Then, after a late night, she overslept. In the morning, not knowing of the new arrangements, the Eckfords simply followed the superintendent's instructions and sent Elizabeth to school alone.

After being mobbed, Elizabeth slipped inside herself, remaining there wordless during all of the news reports in the following days, screaming at night in her dreams (*LSLR* 72). When she began to talk again, she described the morning of September 4. Her focus is on her parents:

> While I was pressing my black and white dress—I had made it to wear on the first day of school—my little brother turned on the TV set. They started telling about a large crowd gathered at the school. The man on TV said he wondered if we were going to show up that morning. Mother called from the kitchen, where she was fixing breakfast, "Turn that TV off!" She was so upset and worried. I wanted to comfort her, so I said, "Mother, don't worry."
>
> Dad was walking back and forth, from room to room, with a sad expression. He was chewing on his pipe and he had a cigar in his hand, but he didn't light either one. It would have been funny, only he was so nervous.
>
> Before I left home Mother called us into the living room. She said we should have a word of prayer. . . . Then I caught the bus and got off a block from the school. . . .
>
> Someone shouted, "Here she comes, get ready." I moved away from the crowd on the sidewalk and into the street. If the mob came at me, I could then cross back over so the guards could protect me. The crowd moved in closer and then began to follow me. . . . They moved closer and closer. Somebody started yelling, "Lynch her! Lynch her!" . . . Someone hollered, "Drag her over to this tree! Let's take care of the nigger."
>
> [Then Elizabeth walked to the school, could not get in, and returned to the bus stop, where she was helped onto a bus.]
>
> I can't remember much about the bus ride, but the next thing I remember I was standing in front of the School for the Blind where Mother works. . . . Mother was standing at the window with her

head bowed, but she must have sensed I was there because she turned around. She looked as if she had been crying, and I wanted to tell her I was all right. But I couldn't speak. She put her arms around me and I cried. (*LSLR* 76)

Elizabeth's parents obeyed Superintendent Blossom's instructions not to accompany their daughter in order to support the rule of law and the institutions that were purportedly available to help all citizens obtain their democratic rights, and which claimed to offer all citizens equal protection. The result was psychological terror for them and for their daughter, which was endured in hope of future benefit. This constitutes sacrifice. Ellison was right to identify this as a central feature of these political events.

Those involved in events on the ground knew that they were negotiating sacrifices demanded by the rule of law, as their own words reveal. One exchange, between Daisy Bates and the father of one of the students, even indicates the degree to which the superintendent's orders were equated with the law of the land. On September 24, the night before the students were to reenter the school with the protection of the 101st Airborne Division, Daisy Bates went to visit one of the families. She found an angry father, unwilling to let his daughter face the mobs again. When Bates, "in [her] most pleasant, friendliest voice, and trying to look at him instead of the gun, . . . said that the children were to be at [her] house by eight-thirty the next morning, and that those were the instructions of Superintendent Blossom," the father answered, "I don't care if the President of the United States gave you those instructions! . . . I won't let Gloria go. She's faced two mobs and that's enough" (*LSLR* 102–3). Here was a father who explicitly viewed the sacrifices demanded of him and his daughter as originating from the demands of legal authority.

These are the sacrifices Arendt did not see—one father pacing with pipe in mouth and cigar in hand; another ready to throw the legal system to the winds—when she chastised Elizabeth Eckford's parents and the "absent representatives of the NAACP" for allowing Elizabeth to go to Central High alone, and when she insisted that they were not acting politically. The invisibility of their sacrifice made the NAACP representatives seem "absent" when they were not. Their invisibility in turn ensured the invisibility of those whom they repre-

sented. Rushing around at midnight to find white ministers to accompany the children to school instead of their parents, they were unable to shed public light on their situation or on that of the children
and parents. Indeed, in *Invisible Man,* invisibility regularly surrounds
the experience of sacrifice without recognition or honor. Ellison,
by invoking the idea of sacrifice in a discussion of Little Rock in his
Robert Penn Warren interview, suggests that the source of this invisibility was not merely the failure of one theorist to see individual
sacrifice but, more broadly, the general absence from democratic
practice of a language to comprehend sacrifice, or the losses and disappointments people accept for the sake of maintaining the communal agreements that constitute legality.

A language of sacrifice did, however, exist on the ground; citizens
of Little Rock could remark, "We've had the Constitution since
1789 . . . Last night they came into our neighborhood and rocked
our homes, breaking windows and all that. *We've taken a lot because we
didn't want to hurt the chances of Negro kids, but I doubt whether the Negroes
are going to take much more without fighting back.* I think I'll take the rest
of the day off and check my shotgun and make sure it's in working
condition" (*LSLR* 99; emphasis added). But the public language of
political theory, which can directly interact with policy, did not reflect
a precise awareness of the practical sacrifices involved in the production of democratic agreement and laws. As a result, political theory
was not in a position to offer a full account of democratic citizenship
or of the full range of potential citizenly action. Ellison's accuracy in
analyzing the events in Little Rock points to theoretical work that still
needs to be done.

Both Arendt and Ellison, then, treat the Battle of Little Rock as an
occasion to inquire how to develop habits of democratic citizenship
for a passage beyond exclusion, domination, acquiescence, and a
hypocritical "oneness." But each theorist of democracy offers different suggestions for how to develop new habits for interacting with
strangers. For Arendt, citizens should focus on reforming political institutions, ensuring their inclusiveness, and maintaining public peace
by defining some questions as outside of politics. For Ellison, in contrast, the evolution of a newly inclusive citizenship required addressing those aspects of democratic decision making that the dream of
unity had previously hidden: loss and disappointment. This new cit-

izenship would also have to address those phenomena that follow from loss and disappointment, namely resentment and distrust. Could diverse citizens, he asks throughout his writing, find ways to talk and act that could convert loss into a freely given gift to be reciprocated, and that could transform distrust into trust? First, we must directly address the question of what is at stake in acknowledging sacrifice to be a central feature of democratic citizenship.

4

⌒∂⌒

Sacrifice and Citizenship

NINETEEN FIFTY-SEVEN PRESENTED the citizens of the United States with the prospect of reconstitution. New citizenly habits would be necessary to produce a public sphere in which "wholeness," not "oneness," would be the objective. Ellison showed that those new habits needed, above all else, to include methods for dealing with political loss and for developing forms of interaction among citizens that would allow for the constant redistribution of patterns of sacrifice. But how important, in fact, is this dynamic to the democratic tradition?

Ellison's intuition that sacrifice is fundamental to democratic citizenship was absolutely accurate.[1] He zeroed in on a central and neglected term in the social contract tradition. The enlightenment philosophers Thomas Hobbes, John Locke, and Jean-Jacques Rousseau all draw on the same Old Testament story in grounding their accounts of consent and political obligation. And it is the story not of Isaac, in which Abraham's mere willingness to sacrifice his son satisfied the Lord, but of Jepthah (Judges 11).

Jepthah, offspring of an illegitimate union, is cast out of the Israelite tribe, but in exile develops into the greatest warrior in the region. When Israel faces an overwhelming military adversary, the Israelites ask Jepthah to fight for them, promising that, in return, they will give him rule over the tribe. He returns and turns the tide of the battle, but in the middle of fighting vows to God that, if given the victory, he will sacrifice the first thing he sees when he gets home. Is there any need to say what happens next? First out to greet him is his daughter.

We might have expected this. Jepthah is torn about what to do—whether he should carry out the sacrifice he has sworn to Yahweh and kill her—when his daughter saves him: "My father, if you have opened your mouth to the Lord, do to me according to what has gone out of your mouth" (11:36).[2] Importantly, she insists that she have the chance to honor her own death before it comes. She will allow herself to be sacrificed provided that she can first go with her friends to the hills for two months to lament her virgin death. How painful, then, that the text never names her.

Jepthah thus gains his citizenship among the Israelites through military heroism, but cements a system of promise and consent only on the basis of his daughter's self-sacrifice. For Hobbes, Jepthah's promise to God is paradigmatic of the promises that underlie consent-based politics, but the daughter's self-sacrifice is the basic model for the relationship between citizen and sovereign (L 21.7). Locke, too, treats Jepthah's story as a model for a political order founded on contract (First Treatise, sec. 163; Second Treatise, sec. 109).[3] Beneath the promise and consent that found the social contract is the most extreme loss. Ellison's analysis thus unearths, through astute observation of practice, the principle buried beneath the operations of a consent-based politics.[4] James Madison understood what was at stake: "In absolute Monarchies, the prince is sufficiently neutral towards his subjects, but frequently sacrifices their happiness to his ambition or his avarice. In small Republics, the sovereign will is sufficiently controuled from such a sacrifice of the entire Society, but it is not sufficiently neutral towards the parts composing it."[5] In large republics, too, some citizens are always giving things up for others. The question Madison hoped to answer was how to make this manageable.

Recent political analysts have noticed the importance of military sacrifice, in particular, to modern forms of democratic citizenship. Judith Shklar was one of many recent commentators to note that the military service of African American men in the Civil War and World War II was the most effective fillip to dramatic changes in civil rights in the United States.[6] Ellison's point, in contrast, is that military sacrifice is only the most dramatic and honored form of an activity that in fact occurs less conspicuously throughout democratic life. In Ellison's analysis of Little Rock and of the photo of Elizabeth Eckford, he attends to the sacrifices not only of sons but also of daughters in order to expand our ability to see quotidian sacrifices and ordinary benefactions.

In chapter 3 I described an encounter between Daisy Bates of the NAACP in Little Rock and an angry, armed father who did not want his daughter to face the mobs again. In response to Bates's request that the daughter be dropped off at her house the following morning, the father refused. But he changed his mind: "[The next morning,] Mr. Ray, shy and smiling, led Gloria into the house. He looked down at his daughter with pride. 'Here, Daisy, she's yours. She's determined to go'" (*LSLR* 102–3). Like Jepthah's daughter, Gloria chose to sacrifice herself to fortify for others the legal order her father was willing to thwart. Ellison's recognition of the centrality of sacrifice to democratic politics leads directly to an explanation of the power of the photos of Elizabeth Eckford with which we began. "Here, Daisy, she's yours." This might have been said of Elizabeth. The famous photos show us yet another sacrifice of a daughter to solidify new promises and democratic contracts. One might learn yet more from the story of Jepthah's daughter's self-sacrifice about the experience of women in democratic polities, but for the time being the point is to look beyond the battlefield to other moments of sacrifice.[7] Discourses identifying and recognizing sacrifice are common for soldiers, firemen, and policemen; for all of these, Jepthah's military sacrifice is the model. Like him, generals, fire chiefs, and police heads often win leadership roles in their communities. The daughter's self-sacrifice, however, is the model for a whole other range of anonymous loss in democratic politics, which, as it happens, democratic citizens generally do not see clearly; nor do they honor it. And just as the political theory of the 1950s was not equipped to acknowledge the sacrifices of Little Rock, neither do our present terms of political analysis come to grips with this kind of sacrifice.

Consider a more recent example from two *New York Times* articles written in a period of recent prosperity. One is about loss, the other about gain, but both stories arose from a single event. On June 3, 2000, citizens of the United States woke to news of the first large rise in unemployment in eight years. This growth in joblessness had a history. Between January and April 2000 the Federal Reserve had, for the good of the country, raised interest rates several times in hope of slowing the economy. Joblessness was increased by design and justified by the idea of the common good, which shows that political decisions can impose loss not by accident, but by intention. Indeed, the intentions behind the Fed's decisions in the spring of 2000 had developed as early as 1968 (at least) when economist Milton Friedman, as president of the American Economics Association (but not yet a Nobel laureate), addressed that group ex cathedra and argued for the existence of a natural rate of unemployment, or a "non-accelerating inflation rate of unemployment"(NAIRU).[8] This phrase designates the precise level of unemployment that is thought by many economists to ensure stable, nonexcessive levels of inflation. Friedman argued, in macroeconomic terms, that attempts to reduce unemployment below a "natural rate equilibrium" would "appear successful in the short run, but would soon generate accelerating inflation, whose intolerability would force a retreat [in unemployment figures] to the natural rate."[9] He added the microeconomic argument that, when unemployment falls beneath a certain level, labor shortages generate wage increases, which in turn spark inflation. In other words, some amount of unemployment above that produced by people's movements from job to job is good for the economy as a whole. In the early 1980s the natural rate of unemployment was thought to be 7 percent. Anyone who advocated a policy to lower the rate any further had to argue against nature itself.

For nearly thirty years, political leaders and Federal Reserve bankers have feared to let unemployment fall below its designated "natural" level. But events have regularly foiled economists' predictions; levels of unemployment have repeatedly sunk below the assigned natural rate without being followed by dramatic inflation. As a result economists have constantly revised their estimates of the natural rate of unemployment: in 1990, the natural rate of unemployment was generally assessed at 6 percent but by 1996 economists George Akerlof, William Dickens, and George Perry estimated it in the range of 4.6 to 5.3 percent. Indeed, their estimates were timely: by September 1996 unemployment fell to 5.1 percent, again without inflation. This brings us back to the Fed's decision in the spring of 2000. In January 2000 most estimates put the natural rate of unemployment at 4.5–5 percent; the drop to 3.9 percent set off an alarm.[10] When the Federal Reserve raised interest rates to cut back on jobs, it acted in accord with nearly thirty years of policy.

Let's presume for the moment that the natural rate of unemployment is a valid ideal. At 5 percent, this would mean that the best interests of the country as a whole dictate that seven million citizens look for work without success, another four million work part-time involuntarily, and another 700,000 be counted as discouraged workers.[11] Optimistic public policy does indeed construct notions of the common good on the basis of differential distributions of loss and gain. The phrase "for the good of the country" says everything fundamental about democratic decision making. Collaborative action requires sacrifice from one or another citizen at particular times, and the preposition "for" betrays the phrase as plea, exhortation, and finally justification. But however much increased unemployment might benefit the polity as a whole, the effects of unemployment on those who lose jobs cannot be easily undone. How are citizens to think about the fact that a regime constructed for the good of all (liberal democracy) must make day-to-day decisions that are better for some or that are directly hurtful for others?

Since sacrifice is ubiquitous in democratic life, and the polity often makes decisions with which one disagrees, all citizens must confront the paradox that they have been promised sovereignty and rarely feel it. Herein lies the single most difficult feature of life in a democracy. Democratic citizens are by definition empowered only to be disempowered. As a result, democratic citizenship requires rituals to manage the psychological tension that arises from being a nearly powerless sovereign. For a long time, in this country, the solution to this paradoxical fact that most democratic citizens are, at the end of the day, relatively powerless sovereigns was the two-pronged citizenship of domination and acquiescence. These old bad habits dealt with the inevitable fact of loss in political life by assigning to one group all the work of being sovereign, and to another group most of the work of accepting the significant losses that kept the polity stable. This approach to the place of loss in politics is a breeding ground for distrust. The challenge set to us by 1957, then, is to develop healthier habits for handling the problem of loss in politics, and other roads to empowerment.

The front page of the *New York Times* business section, which reported the June 2000 rise in unemployment, separated the stories of loss and gain. The left-hand, or less significant column, reported,

"The nation's private sector employers shed 116,000 jobs in May. It was the largest drop in more than eight years and the first decline since the economy began to soar in the mid-1990's. The unemployment rate edged up to 4.1 percent from 3.9 percent, with blacks and Hispanics *absorbing most of the loss*" (June 3, 2000; emphasis added). On the right-hand side of the same page, the lead article spun the story thus: "The Nasdaq composite index soared 6.44 percent yesterday, ending its best week ever, as investors cheered data suggesting that the nation's economy is slowing and the Federal Reserve may be almost done raising interest rates." This headlined article was illustrated with a photograph of frantic traders on the market floor. How differently these two groups of citizens—marginally employed laborers on the one hand and investors on the other—experienced the "common good" as served up by the Federal Reserve!

Significantly, the stories of loss and gain were not merely separated but also prioritized. The front page of the paper had also made the stories visually separate from one another, but had introduced them as if to give the story of increased unemployment greater weight: it is the right-hand-column story, and the information about the increase in the stock market is a small inset box, marked off with a black outline. If one looks closely, however, both stories are continued not in the front section of the paper, but in the business section. The story on unemployment, which looks like the lead story on the front page, is demoted to the twenty-third page of the business section while the story about Nasdaq is continued on page 1 of the business section. The business section tells the truth about editorial priorities. There the lead story was the positive outcome, the soaring stock market. But the story about the laborers absorbing losses has the deeper significance. At the end of *Invisible Man,* the protagonist realizes that all the people he had idolized had been sacrificing him to achieve goods for themselves or others; he falls into a troubled sleep and has a bizarre dream of castration. Toward the end of the dream, he addresses all the figures who had abused him about the blood dripping from his wound: "But if you'll look, you'll see . . . It's not invisible . . . there hang not only my generations wasting upon the water . . . But your sun . . . And your moon . . . Your world . . . There's your universe, and that drip-drop upon the water you hear is all the history you've made, all you're going to make. Now laugh, you scientists. Let's hear

Business Day

The New York Times

SATURDAY, JUNE 3, 2000

Stocks Post Big Gain on Report That Shows Slowing Economy

By ALEX BERENSON

The Nasdaq composite index soared 6.44 percent yesterday, ending its best week ever, as investors cheered data suggesting that the nation's economy is slowing and the Federal Reserve may be almost done raising interest rates.

The gains in many technology stocks echoed the wild trading seen in January and February, with many big technology companies rising 10 percent or more on heavy volume. Over all, the Nasdaq rose 230.88 points, to 3,813.38, up 19 percent. Other indexes also gained. The Dow Jones industrial average rose 142.56 points, or 1.34 percent, to 10,794.76, and the Standard & Poor's 500-stock index jumped 38.45 points, or 1.36 percent, to 1,477.26.

With unemployment in May rising unexpectedly and wages nearly flat, Wall Street strategists believe that the Federal Reserve is no longer likely to raise short-term interest rates later this month and may not have to push rates much higher this year. To slow the economy and keep inflation down, the Fed had already raised short-term rates six times since June 1999, and until this week many economists thought at least two more increases were likely.

Higher different rates are usually considered bad for

Continued on Page 4

The Only Sure Thing Has Been Volatility

By FLOYD NORRIS

Is this move real, or is volatility just going wild?

That is the most difficult question for stock market watchers, particularly with regard to the Nasdaq composite index, which is dominated by technology stocks that regularly rise and fall.

This week was the best ever for the Nasdaq composite, which rose 19 percent. That was nearly twice the size of the previous best week for the index, a 9.71

percent rise recorded only six weeks ago.

Yet, even with the two best weeks ever for the Nasdaq market, the index is down 6.3 percent since the end of 1999. Four of the five worst weeks came between the two great weeks over this year.

Moreover, this year has also had the worst week ever for the Nasdaq market, a 25.3 percent plunge in the week ended April 14. That decline set off warnings of severe economic effects if the stock market continued to fall, which it did not.

You can also see the extraordinary volatility more colorfully in the history of the Nasdaq stock market, dating back to 1971.

There have been 36 days in which the average closed with a gain or loss of at least 5 percent. Exactly half of them have occurred in 2000, three of them this week. When there were only four trading days in the week, as there was this week.

Volatility is not as great in the broader market, as it is in the Nasdaq market, largely because other stocks do not swing as violently as do many technology stocks. But it is unusual: So far this year, the Standard & Poor's 500 has risen or fallen by 1 percent or more on 49 percent of the

Continued on Page 4

As stocks rallied in response to a government economic report yesterday, traders checked prices at the New York Stock Exchange.

BUSINESS Digest

Unemployment Rate Rose To 4.1 Percent Last Month

In the strongest signal yet that the booming economy is finally slowing, the Labor Department reported that the private-sector employers shed 116,000 jobs in May. It was the largest drop in more than eight years and the first decline since the economy began to soar in the mid-1990's.

The unemployment rate edged up to 4.1 percent from 3.9 percent, with blacks and Hispanics shouldering most of the loss. Wage increases remained muted.

More H.M.O.'s Are Exiting Medicare

How Do You Spell Volatility? Nasdaq.

Yesterday's 6.44 percentage rise in the Nasdaq composite index capped off its best week ever that the index had risen nearly 19 percent of itself, making this its most volatile year in its history.

FIGURE 9. Front page of *New York Times* from June 3, 2000

you laugh!" (*IM* 570).[12] The blood that drains from him constitutes the world of his tormentors and their only legacy. So too the sacrifices of some citizens are the bedrock of other citizens' lives. Citizens of democracies are often implored to realize that they are all in the same boat. Ellison instead asks us to recognize that our fellow citizens *are* the boat, and we in turn the planks for them.[13]

Side-by-side but not touching, what are these citizens—laborers and investors—to each other? Inevitably, they are one another's supports, though in diverse ways and at different moments. When citizens find themselves newly jobless as a result of collective decisions and accept their losses without violence or rebellion, they grant their fellow citizens stability, a gift of no small account. Are they owed something in return? If so, what? And by whom? Citizens who benefit from the stable polity find themselves, on this view, in debt to the newly jobless. Now, clearly, not all instances of law-abidingness constitute the same level of gift. When a citizen gives up driving 90 miles per hour, for the sake of sustaining community norms about safety and fuel efficiency, the loss is not substantial. A democratic polity must develop criteria for assessing different levels of loss and for distinguishing between reasonable and unreasonable claims on this front. What distinguishes obedience to policies whose aim is to produce unemployment from acquiescence to laws that slow down speedy drivers? As Shklar points out, being able to work and having work are defining elements of citizenship in the United States. Marginally employed citizens who peaceably accept the Federal Reserve's policies to nudge up unemployment suffer a loss that touches not merely idiosyncratic pleasures but also a primary good, their standing as citizens within the polity.[14]

Ellison challenges us not only to see our comforts as constructed out of the sacrifices of others, but also to develop terms for assessing how significant these sacrifices are. On the same page or in the same city, alongside each other without touching, citizens of different classes, backgrounds, and experiences are inevitably related to each other in networks of mutual benefaction, despite customary barriers between them, and despite our nearly complete lack of awareness, or even disavowal, of these networks. This relationship *is* citizenship, and a democratic polity, for its own long-term health, requires practices for weighing the relative force of benefactions and for responding to them. Ellison was right, then: democratic citizenship should properly involve a discourse about loss and mutual benefaction. But such a discourse confronts significant philosophical and practical difficulties. It requires developing terms not only for assessing relative levels of sacrifice but also for analyzing the intersection of social experiences and politics, and this leads us onto the terrain of political emotion.

Social or economic loss becomes political when citizens believe themselves disadvantaged by a collective decision. Regardless of whether their beliefs are reasonable, they will be registered in negative emotions like anger, resentment, disappointment, and despair. These bring with them psychological stress for the individuals and, worse still for the polity, they sow the seeds of distrust. One can imagine three different ways in which political loss might manifest itself in negative emotions within the citizenry: (1) citizens may reasonably believe they have suffered losses from collective decisions and feel anger about those losses, even though the loss has been reasonably enough demanded of them; (2) citizens may reasonably believe they have suffered losses and feel anger about those losses in cases where the losses have not been reasonably imposed; and (3) citizens may unreasonably believe they suffer losses and may feel anger over what appears to them as a loss, even if it cannot reasonably be described as such. Criteria for differentiating reasonable from unreasonable feelings of loss are crucial to the effort of converting negative emotions like anger, resentment, and disappointment into less painful states, but they are not in themselves enough to convert distrust into trust. Again, let's take the policies of the Federal Reserve as an example. The policy of raising interest rates in face of an unemployment rate of 3.9 percent is justifiable enough; one might explain it to the marginally employed as a reasonable policy for the common good and no doubt gain the assent of many to it. Yet such marginally employed citizens could perfectly well assent rationally to a policy for the common good, and nonetheless feel anger at having to be the people who bear the costs of preserving the polity as a whole. Their judgment of the common good would simply have come into irreconcilable conflict with their opinion about their personal good. The divergence between the two goods may well jeopardize their own sense of security within the state.

Even in cases where a citizen believes that the loss she suffers is reasonably imposed, her increased sense of vulnerability will be a breeding ground for distrust. The emotions of anger, resentment, and disappointment that attend political loss arise not merely on the basis of opinions about particular policy decisions but also as judgments about a citizen's hope for future security. Democratic citizenship must involve practices not only for assessing whether a given experience is reasonably identified as a loss and whether that sacrifice is reasonably requested but also for responding even to those emotions that remain after the criteria of reasonableness have done their work. Such practices would address citizens' fears about their own security within the polity.

Why do such fears require a response?

Here let me take up the connection between political loss and trust. Democracy depends on the ability of citizens to submit their fates willingly to the hands of others, not only to their own representatives, but also to the politicians with whom their representatives debate in the assembly house. Is it reasonable for a citizen to accept the uncertainty of representative democracy? Only if he trusts his fellow citizens. When can a citizen trust his fellow citizens? Only when he is not burned by collaborative action. If citizens are to maintain their trust in the institutions of democratic life, they need to see a positive connection between their political membership and their general well-being. They can trust political institutions only if those are worth something to them and do not generally work their harm. Disappointment and resentment, the aftereffects of loss, deplete the reservoirs of trust needed to sustain democratic life. Since democratic decision making necessarily brings about losses for some people, decision makers act responsibly only when they also develop techniques for working through that loss and its emotional surround. A democracy needs forms for responding to loss that make it nonetheless worthwhile or reasonable for citizens who have lost in one particular moment to trust the polity—the government and their fellow citizens—for the future.[15]

Do policy makers who engineer loss say anything useful about accommodating the lived experience of loss within democratic politics? The phrase "the common good" manages the problem of loss in politics simply by asking citizens to bear up in moments of disappoint-

ment, as does a strict Arendtian distinction between social and political realms. So it goes too in utilitarianism, or cost-benefit analysis. In
a utilitarian calculus, costs and benefits cancel each other out until
policy makers can see options that produce either net gains or net
losses; their job, then, is only to choose the net gain. The idea of "net
gain" erases the problem of loss by insisting that analysts proceed to
"the bottom line." Democratic theory has, unfortunately, learned too
well how to protect itself from direct consideration of the nonacci-
dental losses that follow from political decisions. It ignores the complicated relationships among citizens, and this is a real problem. We now
see that citizenship, in contrast, is the practice of attending to the losses
that produce the bottom line, and of negotiating both our status as
one another's mainstays and the need for taking turns at losses as well
as gains. Not only decision makers, but also citizens themselves have
to cope with the losses of others suffered for the good of the whole.
Since the entire citizenry is implicated in networks of gain and loss,
its members all share responsibility for resisting the corrosion of trust.

Here the central question emerges: What approach to loss in politics is compatible with working to sustain networks of democratic
trust over the long term? Trust is not something that politicians alone
can create. It grows only among citizens as they rub shoulders in daily
life—in supermarkets, at movie theaters, on buses, at amusement
parks, and in airports—and wherever they participate in maintaining
an institution, whether a school, a church, or a business. How can we
successfully generate trust in all these contexts?

It's hard to imagine a moment in this democracy when politicians
and citizens are not lamenting the absence of a civic education in citizenly interaction. But this lament misdiagnoses the situation. In fact,
the United States does provide a forceful civic education. One political lesson is inscribed as deeply as possible into the hearts and minds
of all children. "Don't talk to strangers." Yet another childhood ritual,
this admonishment is the central tenet of our current education in
citizenship.

Again, the two stories in the business section illustrate the problem. They depict diverse groups affected by a single communal event
who share an experience and a memory. But the stories, running
along side-by-side without touching, seem related to each other like
the citizens. Saying comprehensively how they are involved with each

other is difficult, and citizens have also developed methods of ignoring each other and their mutual implication in one another's experiences. The newspaper reports, like the citizens, don't talk to each other; they generate no language or conceptual space for relating the winners and losers of communal decisions.[16]

The *New York Times'* own analysts eventually became aware of this blind spot. When the scenario—of increased unemployment leading to joy on the trading floors—repeated itself several times in the spring of 2001, analysts began to notice the ethical awkwardness. A May 5 article entitled, "More Bad News, and the Stock Markets Are Happy to Hear It," quoted the president of a money management firm as saying, "We're at this seemingly anomalous situation where stocks rise on bad news."[17] Awareness of the interrelatedness of different citizens here, as too often, elicits only curiosity and confusion and not concentrated ethical and political thought. We have no nuanced language for understanding the coincidence of good and bad news in democratic life. When it comes to seeing how strangers are related to each other, we are aphasic.

The ancient Greeks encouraged one another to be hospitable to strangers on the ground that any of them might turn out to be a god in costume. We teach our children, "Don't talk to strangers!" in order to protect them from dangers. But democracy requires vulnerability before one's fellow citizens. How can we teach children, as they begin to near adulthood, to develop countervailing habits that allow them to talk to strangers? And what should these habits be like anyway? These are important questions in a democracy where our fellow citizens are strangers to us.

PART TWO: WHY WE HAVE BAD HABITS

5

಄಄ಿ

Imperfect Democracy

IN PART I, I argued that the United States was reconstituted between 1954 and 1965 during the civil rights movement. We have fresh aspirations and reformed institutions but, I contended, not yet new forms of citizenship. We cultivate habits neither for dealing with political loss nor for generating trust among strangers. This leads to two questions. Where do our old bad habits come from? And what would a new trust-generating citizenship look like? I save the latter question for part III, and turn now to a project of collective autobiography for an answer to the question about our habits' origins.

What is a collective autobiography? It's not as if all those currently in the United States have exactly the same experiences, or the same heritage or cultural horizons. Yet, as I argued in the prologue, although some of us live behind one veil, and others behind another, we all breathe the same air. We all share, and take in as unselfconsciously as we do air, our political institutions and a network of words, names, metaphors, and tropes for describing them and their work. These terms establish the contours of our collective political imagination. Some features in the landscape of that imagination stand out more sharply for one person than for another, or for one group more than for others, and the landscape is extensive, but by and large citizens of the United States analyze political problems on roughly the same conceptual turf. A collective autobiography ought to explain how the landscape of our political imagination has come to have its own particular topography.

What, then, are the prominent features of this landscape as it currently exists? The tale must begin from those. In chapter 2, I pointed out the idealization of oneness in our political ideology and argued for its close ties to practices of racial domination and so to the etiquettes of dominance and acquiescence that constituted proper citizenship until 1957. That ideology and those habits provide only a partial explanation of why U.S. citizens are bad at seeing ordinary sacrifices and dealing with distrust. Lying beneath the ideology of "oneness" is a philosophical tradition that idealizes unanimity. The social contract tradition, out of which our political institutions arise, dreams of an ur-moment of total consent as the legitimating foundation of liberal institutions. In some state of nature, all men will unite and consent unanimously to establish a shared government. A close look at this tradition reveals, however, that this idealization of unanimity brings with it a severely impoverished understanding of language as the medium of politics. And without a rich understanding of language's political capacities and effects, how can we deal with distrust?

In what follows, I examine in some detail the work of the philosopher who has made the most impassioned case in recent years for orienting political practice on the aspiration to unanimity. The German philosopher Jürgen Habermas focuses, as I do, on how citizens should talk to each other in order to sustain legitimate political practice. I take his remarkably widespread influence on political theorists working in the United States to reveal the compatibility of his arguments with the political imagination of this country's citizens, and so I introduce him now not really in his own right but rather as a representative of modern democratic theory. The specific questions now before us are these: What are the conceptual side effects of Habermas's (and liberalism's) insistent focus on unanimity as our orienting ideal? How do these side effects shape modern forms of citizenship?

Habermas's arguments are by now quite familiar. He advocates a "deliberative" form of democracy where the aim is to make policy decisions by coming to consensus through speech rather than relying on majority vote. He proposes modes of speech that should, if used properly and in ideal conditions, generate perfect agreement. The aim is to achieve unanimity where "*all* participants harmonize their individual plans of action with one another and thus pursue their illocutionary [or nonstrategic] aims *without reservation*" (*TCA* 294, emphasis in original). Not only will citizens consent to the outcome of deliberations carried out in accord with Habermasian speech techniques, but they'll be happy about it.[1] Disappointment, resentment, and even half-hearted agreement would not exist.

What speech techniques can pull this off? Habermas first recommends that speakers cast their arguments in the form of universalizable principles, and not in terms of their own interests. In fact, they should ban interest from the political forum altogether and agree not to take an interest in one another's interests.[2] Second, speakers should steer clear of what Habermas, ostensibly following philosopher J. L. Austin, calls the perlocutionary elements of speech. These are all those maneuvers by which a speaker engages with the emotions and subjective states of her listener. In conventional parlance, this means avoiding rhetoric, which has a bad name precisely because it engages not only with reason but also with the emotions. The third recommendation is that deliberators must be mutually well-intentioned toward each other and offer one another "reciprocal recognition." Speakers who heel to these rules (this list is not exhaustive) successfully employ "communicative action," which aims for consensus, instead of "strategic action," which is the mode of speakers who instrumentalize their listeners. Only speakers who employ communicative action, eschewing strategic action, establish the basis for politically legitimate agreement, argues Habermas.

Now these techniques of speech, and the claim that under ideal conditions they would result in unanimity, have come under regular critique along two familiar lines. First, there is the double-pronged criticism that interest cannot be ruled out of the deliberative arena, and that its play in politics ensures that agreements will never seem fully acceptable to everyone. Take desegregation and Little Rock as an example. Hannah Arendt argued that all parents have the right to send their children to a school of their choice.[3] In the abstract, this principle is universalizable, but in the context of debates over desegregation in the United States in the 1950s, it was not. Allowing white parents their free choice of public schools meant the abrogation of the same right for black parents, and vice versa. Insofar as public policy engages abstract and universalizable principles, it generally concerns their application to concrete contexts, but, in their application, few abstract principles are in fact universalizable. The particularity of individuals' interests ensures that general rules will affect citizens differently, and the diversity of experience resulting from universal principles is a fundamental cause of distrust. No effort to advocate universalizable rules, no matter how noble, could have on its own solved the political problems of desegregation. Public discussion that wishes to address problems of distrust, and generate reciprocity, must not banish the problem of interest, but tackle it directly.

The second line of criticism challenges Habermas's repudiation of rhetoric. Critics argue that it is just as impossible to exclude emotion from politics as to ban interest, and equally so for a speaker to avoid affecting the emotions of his listeners. Or they argue that to rule out rhetoric is to exclude practices like greetings and acknowledgments that can set a stage for friendly interchange, and that such practices may be more necessary as a prelude to conversation in some cultural contexts than others. And some make the especially trenchant criticism that Habermas's theory of discursive practice cannot explain how reason, stripped of all affect, can motivate people to action or secure social integration.[4]

Few critics have recognized, however, that these problems with interest and emotion originate entirely in Habermas's decision to ignore the question of how to create trust. The weak link in his proposed speech techniques is the third rule, that speakers should enter the deliberative forum already mutually well-minded toward one another. If they do so enter, the battle to achieve a reasonable policy outcome is already 75 percent won. The hard part is getting citizens to that point of being mutually well-intentioned. Although Habermas thinks reciprocity is critical for agreement, he has very little to say about how to generate it. He addresses its production simply by assuming that "the relevant attitudes and modes of orientation that enable participation in moral argumentation are seen as the result of a historical learning process. They are thus now socially available to a high degree."[5] Experience can, however, undo the basis of trust as easily as it establishes it. How should we respond when that happens?

As soon as one begins to take trust and distrust seriously, and to ask how trust can be generated, one realizes that reason, interest, and emotion cannot be entirely disentangled. The criticisms of Habermas for encouraging his speakers to ignore interest and emotion reflect more significantly that he leaves his citizens without a basic political resource, namely, techniques for cultivating trust. What can explain this counterintuitive alliance between a commitment to perfect agreement and a neglect of trust production? After all, trust enables agreement. To answer this, we have to turn to Habermas's theory of language, including some of its technicalities. The goal is to ascertain what happens to trust production under the pressure of a focus on unanimity.

As we have seen, the central rule of Habermasian speech is that speakers pursue communicative, and not strategic, action. Although the terms "communicative action" and "strategic action" are Habermas's own, his definitions of them rely heavily on J. L. Austin's philosophy of language. Austin distinguishes between three facets of speech: locution, illocution, and perlocution. "Locution" designates the fact that, when someone speaks, certain sounds are produced. "Illocution" designates the fact that when someone speaks, the world is affected. That is, "illocution" refers to the effectiveness, as opposed to the expressiveness or referentiality, of statements. In the standard example, a bridal pair's "I do's" may indeed express their willingness to be with one another, but their utterances also and more importantly actualize the marriage deal. The words themselves change the relationship between the bride and groom as they stand before a presiding official; by speaking them, they transform their world and their subject positions in it. Words, therefore, not only "tell" but also "do." Finally, "perlocution" designates the effects of a statement not on the world itself but on those who hear the statement. For all the importance of an utterance's illocutionary effect on the setting in which actors find themselves, its transformations of context tell us nothing about how particular auditors will react to it. When we hear the bride and groom exchange vows, we know that they have changed the world and become husband and wife in the eyes of the law, but we do not know how the utterances have made either of them *feel*. Thus Austin writes, "[S]aying something will often, even normally produce certain consequential effects upon the feelings, thoughts, or actions of the audience, or of the speaker, or of other persons. . . . We shall call the performance of an act of this kind the performance of a 'perlocutionary' act" (101).

Austin's terms feature prominently in Habermas's distinctions between communicative and strategic action. Habermas defines the former as "those linguistically mediated interactions in which all participants pursue illocutionary aims and *only* illocutionary aims, with their mediating acts of communication" (*TCA* 295), and defines strategic action as "those interactions in which at least one of the participants wants with his speech acts to produce perlocutionary effects on his opposite number." Speakers who seek to "come to agreement" must think only about illocution, and this requirement transforms agreement itself into a wholly illocutionary event. Habermas writes, "What we mean by reaching understanding has to be clarified *solely* in connection with illocutionary acts" (*TCA* 293, emphasis in the original). This definition of agreement as an illocutionary event has extremely important consequences, as we shall see.[6]

To sustain the idea that agreement is wholly illocutionary, Habermas has to redefine perlocution. Austin's most regular examples of the perlocutionary function of language were "persuading" and "convincing," and for Austin, "being persuaded" was simply one among many possible ordinary reactions of an auditor to a world made new by the illocutionary force of language (*TWW* 102; cf. 109, 118). For Habermas, perlocutions are less innocent. He redefines perlocution by adopting, via Peter Strawson, a proviso that is nowhere to be found in Austin's *How to Do Things with Words*:

> I would like to suggest that we conceive perlocutions as a special class of strategic interactions in which illocutions are employed as means in teleological contexts of action. . . . A teleologically acting speaker has to achieve his illocutionary aim . . . without betraying [*verrät*] his perlocutionary aim. This proviso lends to perlocutions the peculiarly asymmetrical character of concealed [*verdeckt*] strategic actions. . . . A speaker can pursue perlocutionary aims only when he deceives [*täuscht*] his partner concerning the fact that he is acting strategically. (*TCA* 293–94)

Perlocution here entails interest or strategy, and successful perlocution, or successful strategic action, even requires deceit. This revision of Austin constructs a rigid boundary between interest-free and interested speech, and asserts that interest necessarily entails deceitfulness. In drawing this stark distinction, Habermas also defines that aspect of language that Austin meant to capture with the term "perlocution"—the fact that speakers interact with one another's subjective states of mind—as necessarily abusive.[7]

And yet this redefinition of perlocution is importantly arbitrary.[8] The idea that a speaker can achieve strategic aims only if she conceals them is without justification. Although some speakers may indeed convince their audiences through trickery, others will openly admit that their goal is persuasion and will succeed nonetheless. Consider Gandhi and Martin Luther King, Jr. Also, whereas Habermas argues that communicative action must proceed by illocutionary, not perlocutionary, means, and that it is possible to separate these two features of speech from one another, Austin had described all speech acts as always simultaneously involving locutionary, illocutionary, *and* perlocutionary features. In his account, there is no illocutionary speech act without perlocutionary effects; every speech act will impress itself upon an auditor's subjective reactions.

Why then does Habermas insist so strongly on this unstable distinction between interest-free and interested speech, and arbitrarily connect interest and deceit? Some critics have argued that his exhortation to citizens to exclude perlocutionary speech from the deliberative forum is not an attempt to make empirical distinctions between different types of speech act, but rather a method of encouraging speakers to assume nonstrategic ethical orientations, or at least to prioritize their nonstrategic above their strategic aims.[9] On this account, he is concerned not with whether illocutionary and perlocutionary aspects of speech are separable, but only with whether speakers are restricting their own attention and, more important, intentions to the illocutionary force of their words. This is the best way to understand Habermas's injunction against perlocutionary speech. But it does not get at the implications of his condemnation of all perlocution as deceitful or of his claim that agreement is a wholly illocutionary event. Both these moves are necessitated by his prior commitment to perfect agreement. That commitment produces significant errors in his account of language.

Let us return to Austin's original distinction between illocution and perlocution, and its conceptual stakes. Austin often explained what the terms meant by comparing two communicative experiences: warning people and alarming them. He calls the former an illocutionary act and the latter a perlocutionary effect of that speech act. If in the library in the middle of the day, a fire alarm goes off, or if somebody runs through the building yelling "Fire!" both the symbolic gesture of the alarm and the utterance "Fire!" effect a warning. Auditors who recognize the conventions that constitute an alarm (and the shout of "Fire!" as an alarm) and who, in recognizing these conventions, provide "uptake," will now consider their setting possibly to involve danger. But will these auditors take the warning seriously enough to be alarmed by it? Or will they rather be annoyed? To borrow from Austin, we "may entirely clear up whether someone was [warning] or not without touching on the question of whether he was [alarming] anyone or not" (*TWW* 104). The illocutionary aspect of language captures the effect language has on the situation that auditors confront (now they *are* warned of a danger). The perlocutionary aspect of language designates the effect language has on auditors' reactions to the situation they confront (now they *may be* alarmed).

Austin makes another important distinction. The illocutionary, but not the perlocutionary, aspect of language is conventional (*TWW* 119–32).[10] Any language is a conventional symbol system that helps structure its users' reality. The fire alarm and the shout "Fire!" are effective warnings because convention has already constituted them as warnings, provided that they are used in appropriate contexts and with the right gestures. Utterances arise from the symbol system and reorient the attention of auditors to their realities in ways consistent with the conventions constituting the symbols employed. We can assess the illocutionary effect that an utterance is expected to have on the world of things simply by determining its role within a language's symbol system.

But whether a fire alarm in fact alarms people as well as warning them is wholly underdetermined by convention. One person may be alarmed and another not. Among those who are alarmed, each may have his own reason: one person may never have heard such a loud buzzer before; another may recently have been in a fire. An individual's particular relations to conventional symbols are nonconventional and idiosyncratic. No one, Austin therefore argues, can predict an utterance's perlocutionary effects, though anyone can predict its illocutionary effects, provided that the utterance conforms to appropriate conventions in front of an audience sensitive to them (*TWW* 110–

22). Austin makes the same point about retrospective judgment when he argues, "[A] judge should be able to decide, by hearing what was said, what locutionary and illocutionary acts were performed, but not what perlocutionary acts were achieved" (*TWW* 122).

As we have seen, persuading and convincing are the two acts most frequently designated as perlocutionary by Austin. Each involves the subjective reaction of an auditor to a locution and its illocutionary effects. As with all other perlocutions, those who are persuaded understand themselves as reacting to a change in their situation (brought about by illocution) that can be attributed to particular agent-speakers. The subjective reactions of the persuaded to the illocution necessarily incorporate a sense of relationality to that speaker. Whereas for Austin the techniques for felicitous illocution can be taught, perlocution cannot be. One can teach people how to warn but not how to alarm, to speak but not how to persuade. The subjective reactions of auditors to an illocution and to its speaker are simply too numerous and various to be the subject of a teacher's lesson.

With this claim, Austin invites himself into a very old argument. Plato and Aristotle disagreed about whether there could be an art or *technê* of persuasion. Were there such an art, persuasion itself would have to be, to some degree, conventional (i.e., predictable). Since a speaker's impact on a listener depends partly on extralinguistic causes, an art of persuasion would have to reduce to conventional form not merely language but also much more of the subjective interactions of speaker and actor. Plato doubted that there is anything either essential or conventional about the intersubjectivity involved in persuasion, and therefore also that there is anything teachable or philosophical to be said about it. After Plato, Aristotle would argue the opposite position, namely that the elements of intersubjectivity involved in persuasion could indeed be conventionalized and subject to art. Aristotle squarely tackles the relations between speaker and audience in his book *The Art of Rhetoric*. But Austin's argument lines up with Plato's. His insistence on the nonconventional status of perlocution is equivalent to Plato's argument that there can be no art of rhetoric.[11]

Where does agreement fit in? Did Austin think that agreement, like persuasion, is a perlocutionary phenomenon? Is it nonconventional and so unteachable? Or is it illocutionary and therefore teachable? As far as Austin was concerned, "being convinced" is a matter of perlocution, and he made the case for this idea thus: "We may entirely clear up whether someone was arguing or not without touching on the question of whether he was convincing anyone or not" (*TWW* 104). Similarly, one can determine whether someone is deliberating or arguing, without saying whether anyone is agreeing. Agreement would be, for Austin, a perlocutionary effect of language. Like persuading and convincing, it depends on the subjective reactions of auditors to speech situations and to speakers, and would therefore not be teachable. Moreover, since agreement, as an effect of perlocution, cannot be conventionalized, it can also never be perfected.

This is why Habermas must recategorize agreement as the product of illocution, not perlocution. Understood as an illocutionary phenomenon, agreement can be said to arise from shifts in the status quo that are produced simply through the regularized application of linguistic conventions. His arbitrarily negative definition of perlocution walls off consideration of problems of interaction from an analysis of agreement and protects the status of agreement as illocutionary. This status justifies treating agreement as perfectible by defining it entirely as a matter of conventional signs. Illocutionary effects either happen or they do not, and for everyone or for no one. When the fire alarm goes off, everyone is warned and completely so. They are *warned,* as it were, *without reservation* or, better, *without doubt,* although they may be *alarmed* to different degrees. Just as warnings are effected on the basis of linguistic conventions about what constitutes a warning, agreement would be effected on the basis of linguistic conventions about what is agree-able (for instance, "universalizable arguments," "public reasons"); suitably constructed arguments must therefore always give rise to total agreement. In short, Habermas rejects the Aristotelian hope of reducing the perlocutionary aspects of speech to convention. He accepts Austin's argument that only the illocutionary results of speech are predictable, and therefore susceptible to being regularized and perfected. Then, for the sake of protecting the conceptual possibility of agreement's perfectibility, he defines the complexities of human interaction, captured by Austin's idea of the perlocutionary aspect of speech, as external to the basic processes of speech. Trust and distrust, likewise, become phenomena external to speech.

Speech, however, is a crucial tool of trust production. It is not the only instrument available for dissolving distrust, but it is indispensable. The production of agreement always involves the impact that people feel others have on them, and so no reasonable account of agreement, or of language, can ignore the complexity of human interaction and say much that is useful. Habermas solves the problem of generating agreement only by undoing the need to work hard for it. The relationality between speakers and auditors is what a Habermasian pragmatics of citizenship must overlook in order to see forms of language that can convince all parties "in the same way" or "without reservation." Similarly, when ordinary citizens commit themselves to the aspiration to perfect agreement, they lose sight of the complex contributions that human interaction, broadly understood, makes to communal decisions. In contrast, if they attend to the perlocutionary aspects of language, they will find that the agreement they pursue can only ever be imperfect, but they will also discover an array of citizenly practices—oriented toward issues of subjectivity—that were invisible so long as perfection was the orienting aspiration. The real project of democracy is neither to perfect agreement nor to find some proxy for it, but to *maximize agreement while also attending to its dissonant remainders:* disagreement, disappointment, resentment, and all the other byproducts of political loss. A full democratic politics should seek not only agreement but also the democratic treatment of continued disagreement.[12]

Why, then, do we idealize the public sphere as a place of full agreement and free of rhetoric? Why aren't we content to hope that it will be a place where disagreements and disappointments will be ideally treated? Habermas's mistake on this point is relevant here not because it is his but because it represents widespread errors produced by liberalism's orientation toward unanimity. The source of his commitment to total agreement is no secret; it rests on a Kantian account of reason and communication.

In the *First Critique,* Kant writes,

Persuasion is mere illusion [*Überredung ist ein bloßer Schein*]. . . . But truth depends upon agreement with the object, and in respect of it the judgments of each and every understanding must therefore be in agreement with each other. . . . The touchstone whereby we decide whether our holding a thing to be true is conviction [*Überzeugung*] or mere persuasion [*bloße Überredung*] is therefore external, namely the

possibility of communicating [*mitzutheilen*] it and finding it to be valid
for all human reason. (A820/B848, p. 645)[13]

Here, persuasion is set in opposition to truth, which only communication can access. The worry about persuasion is that it is content to
work with people's first, private, illusory impressions of what is good
for them. Communication provides an opportunity to test the rationality of arguments, so that citizens may reach a second, truer im-
pression. Reason is the same for all mankind. As a result, "What experience teaches me under certain circumstances," Kant argues, "it
must always teach me and everybody; it and its validity are not limited to the subject nor its state at a particular time. . . . Therefore objective validity and necessary universality (for everybody) are equivalent terms" (*Prolegomena*, 46–47). "Communication" requires the
rationalization of language so that our historically situated subjectivity cannot distort our identification of moral truths. Since moral rules
are "necessary for everybody," they will also, if language and reason
function properly, *seem*, on second glance, if not on the first one, necessary to everybody. The ultimate aim of Kantian communication is
perfect agreement on the content of moral rules. Reason, if it is to
discover norms of "objective validity," must also discern forms of language that can cast experiential and moral claims in universal terms
all will recognize and accept. Communication is a much-sought linguistic treasure, a mode of speaking derived from the idea that the human community can achieve total agreement. When civilization has
reached its apogee, it makes this work of universal communication
and communicability "almost its main business" (*allgemeinen Mitteil-
arbeit*); such communication is finally a support to true legislation
(*Critique of Judgment*, sec. 41).[14]

   Kant derived his own commitment to perfect agreement at least
in part from the work of the seventeenth-century English philosopher Thomas Hobbes, who analyzed politics by positing a state of nature out of which all human communities arise. In it life is war and
famously "nasty, brutish, and short." Although the inhabitants of the
state of nature live in distrust, and even fear, of one another, this situation somehow eventually inspires them to band together for mutual protection. They contract with one another to establish civil society, each agreeing to sacrifice to a sovereign his ability to harm the

others. This absolute authority, or Leviathan, will protect them all from each other, but will also have absolute right and power to harm anyone who causes trouble for the state. This idea of the social contract, an original moment of total agreement, has, of course, become the standard metaphor for political legitimacy in modern liberal democracies. But the social contract is not the only form of total agreement in Hobbes's account of politics.

The civil state of the Leviathan will also be a place of consensus, but its unanimity will arise differently than did the ur-consensus in the state of nature, and not as a product of everyone's autonomous choice. The state of nature is unstable because of fear and greed, but also because of disagreements about what belongs to whom, or about laws and principles of justice. The Leviathan-style sovereign, in order to bring peace out of war, must provide firm definitions of words, virtues, and vices (*L* 18.9–10). After he has come to be, decisions about "what is mine" and "what is thine" should be straightforward.[15] The sovereign is responsible for educating people to these opinions; he also has the power to repress as crimes the consequences of any actions stemming from wayward views. Hobbes derives his commitment to full agreement from a strong desire for stability and suggests that if the state should once fall away from homogeneity of opinion, all hell would break loose. Total agreement is the objective, but in a sinister form.

In order to preserve consensus, the civil state proscribes rhetoric. Although *Leviathan* is full of rhetorical figures, metaphors, and tropes, Hobbes excoriated rhetoric and argued, throughout his corpus, for its suppression in the ideal state.[16] Rhetoric inflamed the passions, he argued, and so stirred up sedition and civil war. His other worry about it was more profound. He had written a Latin brief of Aristotle's *Rhetoric,* from which the first English translation of that text derives, and would have been familiar with Aristotle's arguments there that metaphors are central to good rhetoric. They add an element of foreignness to language, and their central effect, Aristotle argues, is to produce fluidity in our conceptual universe. Metaphor is an "extension by means of a foreign word."[17] Although an overdose of foreign (*xenikon*) words produces riddles, strangeness of contrast, if effectively crafted, is nonetheless the foremost "virtue of rhetorical language."[18] Metaphors "must not be far-fetched, but we must give names to things that have none by deriving the metaphor from what is akin and of the same kind."[19] Naming the unnamed, metaphors change language, and with it politics. They allow a speaker to lead an audience onto new conceptual terrain.

For Hobbes, metaphor is a wicked source of absurdity. Those who "use words metaphorically" "deceive others" (L 4.4). Worse still, "metaphors are like *ignes fatui;* and reasoning upon them is wandering amongst innumerable absurdities; and their end, contention, and sedition, or contempt" (L 5.20). Like false lights, they lead not to new places but merely astray. Rhetoric does not only rouse passions. Because it produces conceptual change, it can destabilize sovereign definitions of justice and virtue. Hobbes fears the very fact that its object is to change minds he wants unchanging. Language itself is powerful enough, he thought, to unsettle social orders, and therein also lies its power to produce contention and civil war.

Hobbes left as his legacy this idealization of full and stable agreement combined with a rejection of rhetoric, and Habermas received this inheritance through Kant. Although fewer copies of Hobbes's *Leviathan* circulated than, say, of John Locke's *Two Treatises on Government,* philosophers read him.[20] Kant describes the aspirations of his critique of reason in highly Hobbesian terms:

> In the absence of this critique, reason is, as it were, in the state of nature, and can establish and secure its assertions and claims only through war. The critique, on the other hand, arriving at all of its decisions in light of fundamental principles of its own institution, the authority of which no one can question, secures the peace of a legal order. (A751–52/B779–80, pp. 601–2)

Kant seeks agreement based on an authority no one can question. Later in the *First Critique* he is even more explicit about the Hobbesian dimensions of his argument:

> The endless disputes of a merely dogmatic reason thus finally constrain us to seek relief in some critique of reason itself, and in legislation based on such criticism. As Hobbes maintains, the state of nature is a state of injustice and violence, and we have no option save to abandon it and submit ourselves to the constraint of law. (A778/B806, pp. 617–18)

Kantian reason and the law of Hobbes's Leviathan both establish a peace of total agreement without any remainders of disagreement or conflict. But there is one notable difference. Hobbes seeks peace by arguing that everyone should use the words and hold the opinions established as necessary by the sovereign; he bans rhetoric to shore up the king's power. Kant, too, seeks peace but wants everyone's identical ethical conclusions to be those established by reason as necessary; he proscribes persuasion and rhetoric in order to shore up reason's authority. Habermas, like Kant, argues that citizens should submit to the "force" of reason. The Hobbesian history of his figure should be clear by now.[21] In its origins, the idealization of full agreement was closely bound to authoritarian politics; more important, it was rendered viable precisely through a rejection of rhetoric and its engagements with subjectivity.

Yet the simple recognition that some modern political aspirations have Hobbesian antecedents does not complete the project of collective autobiography. We still need to discern the root causes of those aspirations. Hobbes developed his arguments about unanimity and rhetoric as *solutions* to a particular conceptual puzzle. What was it? He was keen to tackle the practical problems of distrust, strife, and civil war that confronted him in England in the mid-seventeenth century. What, amid all that turmoil, was the conceptual problem that he identified as critical and "solved" with the argument in favor of consensus and against rhetoric? This puzzle, if we can figure out what it was, is the real source of our modern idealization of unanimity and our rejection of the arts of persuasion. The next chapter aims to figure out what that puzzle was.

Before we go on, however, one more small digression on philosophy's rejection of rhetoric is necessary. Modern critics frequently employ a strict dichotomy between philosophy and rhetoric, where the former denotes pure reason directed at the discovery of truth and the latter, an art that engages the passions not to aid the discovery of truth but only to engender belief. The argument between philosophy and rhetoric is cast as one over the role of emotion in politics, as if philosophers argue against it and rhetoricians argue for it. This argument between reason and passion is attributed to Plato and Aristotle. In fact, neither ancient philosopher thought that philosophy could ignore the emotions, nor did their argument about rhetoric turn on the question of whether political debate should engage citizens' emotions. They recognized that political speakers simply do engage emotions and subjective interests, and do so with the very specific purpose of gaining their audience's trust. Instead, they debated two questions relevant to modern efforts to understand trust: (1) is producing trust in one's audience, instead of knowledge, by definition to deceive one's listeners? and (2) can there be an art for producing trust? To the first question, about whether trust necessarily deceives, Plato said yes, and Aristotle no. To the second one, about whether there could be an art for generating trust, Plato said no, and Aristotle yes.

The debate about rhetoric, then, was not about passion simply but, first, about whether engendering trust is a morally legitimate practice and, second, about whether anything scientific or rule-bound can be said about the effort to do so. Insofar as the modern rejection of rhetoric can be traced back to Hobbes, its origins lie with someone who understood very well that these questions about trust, and not simply the question about the role of passion in politics, were the central philosophical issues raised by defendants of the art of rhetoric. The burden of his political project was to devise a new solution, independent of the traditional reliance on the art of rhetoric, to the problem of distrust in politics. Its success still shapes the landscape of our imagination.

6

⤜⤏

Imperfect People

THE IMPORTANCE OF BOTH the idealization of unanimity and the repudiation of rhetoric to the liberal tradition is not merely coincidental. The two ideas are linked historically in the period of the English civil war and intellectually in Hobbes's thought, which no one has considered arbitrary. They are joined in Hobbes's political analysis, however, not in an argument but in a metaphor. It is an important one. Democracy's basic term is neither "liberty" nor "equality," but "the people." But where and what is this thing, the people? How on earth does it act? How can one even hold an idea of this strange body in one's head? Only with figures, metaphors, and other imaginative forms. "The people" exists finally only in the imaginations of democratic citizens who must think themselves into this body in order to believe that they act through it. Democratic politics cannot take shape until "the people" is imaginable. Politicians of Hobbes's day had brought the term to the forefront of English political life, but could not solve this quandary of the imagination. Hobbes did.[1]

He at first refused to use the term for political analysis, and in his early works (*Elements of Law* from 1640 and *De cive* from 1642) criticized its popularity among his contemporaries. In this regard, he was the last major European thinker to try to understand politics without reference to the people. But his criticisms of the term soon dissolved into revisions of its conceptual structure, and as his writings matured, a metaphor for the people coalesced in them and stabilized that idea. Finally, in *Leviathan,* he adopted "the people" as a basic term of art, crafting formulations that sound familiar to the modern ear: "[S]overeign power is conferred by the consent of the people assembled" (*L* 18.1); "[a] good law is that which is *needful* for the *good of the people*" (*L* 30.20; emphasis in the original). Hobbes generated imaginative forms for conceptualizing the people of sufficient cogency to influence philosophers who wrote after him. And he did this by defining the idea of "the people" in terms of oneness, unanimity, and a disdain for trust production. Hobbes built the idealization of perfect consent and the repudiation of rhetoric into the basic conceptual structure of the fundamental term of modern politics: "the people." The political habits of modern citizens are guided in an important way by how they imagine "the people," and Hobbes did his part to make sure that an orientation toward unanimity and a rejection of rhetorical art would be central to those habits. The final step of this collective autobiography, then, is to figure out how our basic habits for imagining "the people" came to be, and to analyze the political content of the metaphors and other imaginative forms which sustain this idea. We are off, quickly, to the ancient world and then to the period of the English civil war, in which Hobbes wrote.

In the political worlds of ancient Greece and Rome, the terms for "the people," *ho demos* in Greek and *populus* in Latin, each had two meanings, a *factionalist* one where the term refers merely to "the poor" and an *aspirational* one, where "the people" designates the whole citizenry, rich and poor. In the latter usage, the term aspired to combine into one collective agent heterogeneous and even conflicting subsets within a citizenry. Athenian politicians and Roman republicans insisted on the aspirational sense while elite philosophers like Plato and Aristotle preferred the factional meaning, trying to demote forms of politics in which the poor participated. So influential were these two philosophers that the factionalist usage dominated in Catholic Europe throughout the medieval period, even up to the beginning of the seventeenth century, when the House of Commons spoke for "the people" but not for the aristocrats.

Significantly, the factionalist and the aspirational usages of "the people" engage the imagination differently, and lay divergent foundations for citizenship. The factionalist definition of the people as "the poor" segregates citizens according to class and economic interest; it identifies a collective actor as existing only after a preceding homogeneity of opinion or experience establishes some set of individuals as a group. On this factionalist definition, it is easy to imagine how the people, or any other collective actor, acts: the constitutive principle of its identity is presumed to define its motive or interest. Since homogeneity constitutes the group, any member or subset of the group can act for all; group choices simply amplify extant individual opinions. To be a part of the people is simply, if one is poor, to be oneself. No imaginative labor is required for interpretation exactly because the part-whole relation is understood as simple and straightforward.

Ancient writers used this factionalist meaning of the people to analyze politics as always satisfying one faction more than the others. Regimes were democracies, oligarchies, or monarchies depending on whether the city was ruled by the many, the few, or the one, where the many were the poor or the people, and the few were the wealthy or aristocratic. The interests of the people might sometimes be ascendant, sometimes not. To say that a government went against the interest of the people was not necessarily a charge of illegitimacy.

The aspirational usage of "the people," by including members of different classes or interest groups within a single collective body, sets heterogeneity, not homogeneity, at the heart of politics. The account of collective action on which this definition depends is correspondingly more complex. Now "the people" designates a collective actor prior to the development of a substantive account of its members' shared interests above and beyond a basic desire to flourish. Members' interests often do not coincide but conflict, and no homology exists between an individual's and the group's interest. Instead, politics must devise methods to *find* the interest of the people, and these must also prevent any one faction from dominating policy.[2] Where the factionalist definition suggests that groups merely amplify individual preferences, the aspirational definition connects individuals to a collective body that, when all decisions are tallied up, chooses differently than would any individual member. Being a member of this sort of people poses a challenge to citizen subjectivity. Whereas membership in the factionalist people requires no more than that one be oneself, citizens of an aspirational people must develop sophisticated relationships to one another and to a collective that is constantly reconstituting itself in time, as they find their own interests and desires modified by group decision making. Each individual must have a relationship not only to her own will but also to a collective will that is distinct from her own.

In the period leading up to the English civil war, politicians from diverse quarters challenged centuries of tradition and tried to restore vitality to the aspirational meaning of "the people." In 1625, Charles I, king of England, ruled Scotland also. For three-quarters of a century, radical Scottish Puritans had been resisting monarchs who had tried to impose on them first Catholicism and, then, Anglicanism. From a tradition of using "the people" to refer to their church congregations, the Protestant agitators politicized the term. The Scottish Calvinist George Buchanan argued, for instance, that the people themselves had a right to resist sovereigns rather than delegate their resistance to magistrates: "it is lawful not only for the whole people (*universo populo*) but also for every individual in it to kill the [tyrant]."[3] When Charles I tried to force the Scots to adopt Anglicanism, the result in 1639 was war. In England this triggered the issue of taxes. Charles had shut down Parliament from 1629 to 1640, and when it came time to request money from it in the 1640s, he met resistance. Soon he found himself preparing to fight not only the Scots but also Parliamentarians, and here too political debate coalesced around the idea of "the people."[4]

Parliament had developed out of a medieval adaptation of the Roman law principle that what touches all ought to be tested by all (*Quod omnes similiter tangit ab omnibus comprobetur,* Code VI.59.5.2).[5] In practice, the principle meant "that [all] parties who have legal rights at stake in a judicial action are entitled to be present or at least consulted in its decision" and was applied especially to taxpayers.[6] In the thirteenth century, when the king needed to raise tax money, he gathered the titled lords of the realm before him to be consulted about taxation in a group that would become the House of Lords. But he designated the "knights and burgesses" of the realm as "procurators" and "attorneys" to speak to him on behalf of the far vaster number of gentry and freeholding commoners. This body of delegates eventually became the House of Commons.[7] Although in the sixteenth century this lower house included many second sons of the aristocracy, it nonetheless spoke for "the people," or those citizens without titles.[8] The phrase "the people" designated a specific faction within the citizenry, and at the end of the sixteenth century Shakespeare could still write about the two houses of Parliament that "Our People, and our Peeres, are both mis-led."[9]

Since the House of Commons was the platform for rebellion

against the king, this struggle, like the Scottish one, also pitted "the people" against its monarch. Here too politicians began to radicalize and extend the idea of "the people," claiming that the House of Commons represented not merely one faction but the whole citizenry. One political pamphlet of the 1640s argued that in the House of Commons, "the *whole community* in its underived Majesty shall convene to doe justice" (emphasis added).[10] When Parliament allied itself with Scotland in September of 1643, the king found himself fighting both parties of "the people" simultaneously.

The language of rebellion developed by Protestants trying to overthrow Catholic overlords in France and Scotland combined with the terms of resistance developed by members of the House of Commons trying at first to limit, then to overthrow, a monarch who claimed a divine right to rule. In the process, the idea of "the people" became the basis of new accounts of the rights of political rulers and of political order. It was made to do serious political work, but any number of pamphleteers, politicians, and theorists acknowledged that its prominence had produced a sizeable conceptual problem. George Buchanan's invitation to his reader to picture the whole (*universus*) people coming together to kill a tyrant, and even "everyone out of the whole multitude of mankind" gathering under the name of "the people" for the act of tyrannicide was a call to new habits of imagination. Fictions or images would be necessary to convert an abstraction into a political actor.

Indeed, Buchanan's invitation engaged his readers' imagination with the adjective *universus,* which modified *populus.* What does it mean to imagine the people as *universus?* Above I translated this as "whole," but the prefix also implies oneness. Does Buchanan mean that we should imagine the people as characterized by the singularity of the universe, or by its integrated complexity? Does oneness or wholeness better stabilize the idea? In 1680 Buchanan's translator translated *universus* as "whole," and his contemporaries probably would have done the same, for this was the adjective they tended toward. In 1583 Sir Thomas Smith argued in *De republica Anglorum,* "the Parliament of Englande . . . representeth and hath *the power of the whole realme,* both the head and the bodie. For everie Englishman is entended to be there present, either in person or by procuration and attornies. And the consent of the Parliament is taken to be everie man's consent" (emphasis added).[11] This is the earliest recorded instance of the verb "represent" in English; political representation from the out-set was charged with making present the "wholeness" of the realm.[12] Smith was just one of many thinkers invoking the idea of wholeness. As the civil war advanced, various public bodies and political groups increasingly claimed to represent the wholeness of the realm. As we saw, one pamphleteer described the House of Commons, which rep-resented the people, as convening the "whole community." The rad-ical Puritan anti-Loyalists, the Levelers, took the connection between the people and the wholeness of the realm to an extreme, arguing about their upstart army, "This Army are truly the *people of England* and have the nature and power of the *whole* in them" (emphasis added).[13]

But critics of the populist arguments frequently lampooned at-tempts to develop these novel habits of imagination. How could any collective actor legitimately claim to represent or have the power of the whole? For instance, royalist Dudley Digges argued,

> As for Power inherent in the People, how should one imagine such a thing? unlesse also he would imagine People to be *juvenes aquiline creari,* men like *Grasshoppers* and *Locusts* bred of the Winde; or like *Cadmus* his men sprung out of earth.[14]

Digges suggests that attempts to picture the people lead to absurdity. No one could imagine a credible figure for the agent that "the people" was supposed to be. Its proponents must finally turn to thoroughly embarrassing myths and metaphors.

Robert Filmer, another seventeenth-century critic of the populists, also insisted that "the people" was inconceivable without flights of fancy. His point is that this category itself involves a double track of language; the idea of "the people" entailed fresh, explicit attention to the figurative dimension of language:

> For the people, *to speak truly and properly,* is a thing or body in contin-uall alteration and change. It never continues one minute the same, being composed of a multitude of parts, whereof divers continually decay and perish, and others renew and succeed in their places . . . they which are the people this minute are not the people the next minute [emphasis added].[15]

"True and proper," or nonfigurative and nonfictitious, speech requires admitting that "the people" never exists for more than a split second. Oliver Cromwell neatly summarized the conceptual problem when he declared, "I am as much for government by consent as any man, but where shall we find that consent?"[16] One might schematize Cromwell's question as in fact consisting of three central puzzles. First, what is the will of the people and how does one find it, if the group designated by the term is composed of individuals with diverse opinions? Second, how does "the people" act, if diverse citizens can be expected to respond diversely to particular political issues? And third, what is the relationship between the individual wills of citizens and the completely unstable, always changing, impossible to pin down, collective will? Neither Calvinists nor Levellers managed to generate imaginative forms or symbols adequate to answering such questions.

Hobbes too starts off as a critic of efforts to base politics on the idea of "the people," but even with his early criticisms, he begins to develop a novel take on the problem. This story begins with Hobbes's criticism of his contemporaries in a lengthy but important passage from *Elements of Law.* He irritably notes the confusing instability that characterizes usages of "the people" in the politics of his day and proposes an initial clarification of the term:

The controversies that arise concerning the right of the people, proceed from the equivocation of the word. For the word people hath a double signification. *In one sense [people] signifieth only a number of men, distinguished by the place of their habitation; as the people of England, or the people of France; which is no more, but the multitude of those particular persons that inhabit those regions,* without consideration of any contracts or covenants amongst them, by which any one of them is obliged to the rest. *In another sense, it signifieth a person civil, that is to say, either one man, or one council, in the will whereof is included and involved the will of every one in particular; as for example: in this latter sense the lower house of parliament is all the commons, as long as they sit there with authority and right thereto; but after they be dissolved, though they remain, they be no more the people, nor the commons, but only the aggregate, or multitude of the particular men there sitting; how well soever they agree, or concur, in opinions amongst themselves;* whereupon they that do not distinguish between these two significations, do usually attribute such rights to a dissolved multitude, as belong only to the people virtually contained in the body of the commonwealth or sovereignty. (2.2.11; emphasis added)

Here Hobbes acknowledges that his contemporaries use both the factionalist and the aspirational version of the term; they desire sometimes to designate all the inhabitants of a particular nation and sometimes only "the commons," one faction among many. He criticizes the aspirational usage of the term by rejecting the claim that invocations of the authority of, say, the people of England have any meaning. The inhabitants of England are, in his view, just a disorganized multitude without status as a political actor. Similarly, the House of Commons should be called "the people" not because its members' interests coincide "how well soever they agree"—this would be the factionalist approach—but because it is "a person civil," an institution capable of binding decisions. Authoritative institutions, not shared interests, constitute "the people." Already here Hobbes proposes an institutional definition of "the people," and this will eventually prove to be the crucial move for making the people imaginable, and laying to rest the confusion surrounding the term.

Slightly earlier in *Elements of Law* he had already introduced a distinction between "the people" and "the multitude" in order to underscore the conceptual problem facing anyone who wanted to talk about the people of England as an agent: "First, for their persons they are many and (as yet) not one; nor can any action done in a multitude of people met together be attributed to the multitude, or truly called the action of the multitude, unless every man's hand, and every man's will (not so much as one excepted) have concurred thereto" (2.1.2). No group deserves the name "the people" before an explanation is available of how diverse individuals can produce one action such that it belongs to all collectively and not merely to each individually. Hobbes will grant the multitude the status of a political actor only if it achieves perfect unanimity in will and homogeneity in action. Out of many, the multitude must become one, before it can be the people. But enduring unanimity is not possible. The parenthetical remark "(not so much as one excepted)" serves as a reductio ad absurdum to reveal how pointless would be an effort to depend on actual moments of unanimity to define the people. The conceptual problem confronting those who wish to draw their authority from a group that contains all of the inhabitants of their country is severe. One might be all for government by consent, but where is one to find the consent of the people, if even a single dissenting individual undermines the idea of the people's will?

His contemporaries had failed, Hobbes suggests, to base their usage of "the people" on an account of collective action that explains how a heterogeneous group can count as a unitary political actor. His remark on the difference between the multitude and the people not only advances this criticism but also prescribes how a political thinker might be able to convert "the multitude" of the diverse inhabitants of the whole realm into a body called "the people." Since the multitude cannot become one through unanimity, institutions that contrive oneness are the only option. The passage with which we began continues (again the quotation is lengthy) and provides just this sort of prescription:

> When a great number of their own authority flock together in any nation, they usually *give them the name of the whole nation*. In which sense they say the people rebelleth, or the people demandeth, when it is no more than a dissolved multitude, of which though any one man may be said to demand or have right to something, yet the heap or multitude, cannot be said to demand or have right to any thing. For where every man hath his right distinct, there is nothing left for the multitude to have right unto; and when the particulars say: *this is mine, this is thine,* and *this is his,* and have shared all amongst them there can be nothing whereof the multitude can say: *this is mine;* nor are they one body, as behoveth them to be, that demand anything under the name of *mine* or *his;* . . . On the other side, when the *multitude is united into a body politic, and thereby are a people in the other signification, and their wills virtually in the sovereign, there the rights and demands of the particulars do cease* and he or they that have the sovereign power, doth for them all demand and vindicate under the name of his, that which before they called in the plural theirs (*EL* 2.2.11; some emphasis added)

The only way to stabilize the idea of "the people" is to shift its source of authority from the individual wills of a multitude to an institutional will. Institutions stand in for a consensus that is impossible to achieve. They do not displace the need for unanimity so much as simply assert it. Hobbes believes it is possible to stabilize the idea of "the people's will" only by severing it from any individual citizen's subjectivity. The theoretical problem of the people is solved when the individual wills and demands of the particulars exist only virtually in the sovereign.

Although Hobbes is already refashioning the conceptual structure of "the people" in the *Elements of Law,* he does not in this text adopt the term for his own political analysis. When he describes the multitude unanimously contracting to set up civil institutions, they become not the people, but "the city," and their new government is charged with instantiating the will of the city. Hobbes will not himself begin to use the term "the people" until he has completely separated the subjectivity of individual citizens from this collective will. This occurs in a long passage of *De cive:*

> In the last place it is a great hindrance to civil government, especially monarchical, that men distinguish not enough between a *people* and a *multitude*. The *people* is somewhat that is *one*, having *one will,* and to whom *one action* may be attributed; none of these can properly be said of a multitude. The *people* rules in all governments. For even in *monarchies* the *people* commands; for the *people* wills by the will of *one man;* but the multitude are citizens, that is to say, subjects. In a *democracy* and *aristocracy,* the citizens are the *multitude* but the *court* is the *people*. And in a *monarchy,* the subjects are the *multitude* and the king is the *people.* The common sort of men and others who little consider these truths, do always speak of a *great number* of men as of the *people,* that is to say, the *city.* They say that the *city* hath rebelled against the *king* which is impossible, and the *people* will and nill what murmuring and discontented subjects would have or would not have; under pretence of the *people* stirring up the *citizens* against the *city,* that is to say, the *multitude* against the *people*. (*DC* 12.8; emphasis in original)

Here Hobbes redefines a term, "the people," that seems to emphasize the opinions of individual citizens and instead requires that it be defined so as to suppress that subjectivity. It is not merely the case that citizens must act through institutions in order to be the people. Rather the institutions structuring a state simply are the people. The mass of citizens (or subjects) ruled by the state are "the multitude," not "the people." The people, understood as institutions, *rule;* the multitude, understood as the mass of individual citizens, *are ruled.* Citizens are politically active insofar as they are members of the people, but since "the people" now means institutions, their political activity consists only of acting through state institutions. Each citizen's subjectivity is irrelevant to this endeavor; only his institutional role and obligations matter. The second part of citizenship is membership of the multitude. Here one's subjectivity does matter, but only to the extent that one can oppose at the level of a murmur. Otherwise, one just obeys the laws. The repudiation of rhetoric is a rejection of political techniques that transform the subjectivity of citizens into opinion and then action. As membership in the people, Hobbesian citizenship requires only participation in institutions that aim at oneness. As membership in the multitude, it requires only political passivity.[17]

By detaching individual subjectivity from the will and policies of the people, and developing a theory of institutional agency to explain collective action, Hobbes solves the conceptual problem with which he began. First, his contemporaries had asked, What is the will of the people? He answered, It has nothing to do with the wills of individual citizens; it is the will of the one man or the court that is responsible for acting in the name of the people. Second, they had asked, How does the people act? He answered, The acts of individual citizens have little to do with the actions of the people; "the people" acts through the one man or the court that is responsible for acting in the name of the one people. The actions of individuals matter only insofar as they are assigned duties within the institutions of the people. And third, they had asked, What is the relationship between the individual wills of citizens and the collective will? Hobbes answered, They are not the same. Once the institutions of the people have been founded, three kinds of will exist. First, there are the wills of individuals. Second, there is the collective will of the people. But this is *represented* (to use more terminology that Hobbes made politically viable) on the world stage by a third will, that of the sovereign, whether monarch, court, or assembly. Citizens participate in the sovereign will, and make it part of their own will, by accepting what their institutions do for them, and by suppressing their own willing, contravening murmuring in discontent. Representation designates the psychological relationship that must be established between citizens and their sovereigns in order for the will of the people to exist. This is a relationship of repression: each citizen must accept that her political will exists virtually in the sovereign. Both the idealization of unanimity and the rejection of rhetoric shore up this habit of repression.

But what does "virtually" mean here? Hobbes is not far from the modern use of "virtual reality" to denote imaginary constructs that engage human attention to nearly the same degree as "reality." The word "virtually" admits that the people can exist only through an imaginative leap. Hobbes acknowledged that his sovereign would be "a creation out of nothing by human wit" (*EL* 2.1.1) and explained, "For the body politic, as it is a fictitious body, so are the faculties and will thereof fictitious also" (*EL* 2.2.4). After Hobbes had completed the theoretical restructuring of the people in *De cive,* one more task remained: his version of the people had to be not only conceptually coherent but also capable of capturing the imagination. In order for the will of the citizens to be represented by the sovereign institutions of the people, the people had to become a virtual reality. It would become a virtual reality primarily when citizens had cultivated the psychological attitudes toward their sovereign that Hobbes recommended. Now he had to determine what types of imaginative forms might cultivate the appropriate psychological orientations within the citizenry.

Hobbes's disgust with rhetoric, metaphor, and images reveals how crucial they are not only to his own argument, but also to any populist politics. His definition of the people, like anyone else's, can be stabilized only with figurative language. In *Leviathan* he employs both metaphor and image to convert his lengthy arguments about politics and the people into a neat symbol that citizens might assimilate easily, and with it a whole set of propositions about political life. As early as 1640, he had defined "the people" as a collective body "virtually contained in the body of the commonwealth or sovereignty." The organizing metaphor of *Leviathan* illustrates this idea. Leviathan, the sea monster in Job, is a symbol for the authoritative sovereign who has swallowed up all the citizens in a single, massive (and monstrous) body. But Hobbes was not content to engage his readers' imagination with arguments alone, nor merely with arguments plus metaphors; he also designed a frontispiece for *Leviathan.*

The frontispiece image of the Leviathan illustrates the idea of the

FIGURE 10. Leviathan, *frontispiece*

people as "virtually contained in the body of the . . . sovereignty."
Now at last, because it is imaginable even at the level of the image,
"the people" exists. A political buzzword "the people" has coalesced
finally into a dense and exceptionally stable concept. Hobbes had first
used description to stabilize the idea of "the people," writing, "when
the multitude is united into a body politic, [they] are a people in the
other signification, and their wills virtually in the sovereign." Then in
De cive he had turned to definition: "The people is somewhat that is
one, having *one will,* and to whom *one action* may be attributed." In the

definition the important metaphor of oneness is already beginning to surface. Then, in *Leviathan,* definition evolves fully into metaphor. "The people" becomes one in the body of the sea monster sovereign Leviathan. And finally metaphor evolves into image: a single figure, the sovereign, faces the reader; his body is composed of a multitude of individual figures who, backs turned toward the reader, direct their gaze at the sovereign's face. Before the inhabitants of the state of nature developed institutions to speak on their behalf, "they [were] as many and (as yet) not one." *E pluribus unum* is virtually a quotation of Hobbes. In 1589, George Buchanan invited his readers to imagine the whole people (*universo populo*) as coming together to overthrow tyrants. More than fifty years later, Hobbes responded that a multitude can come together as "the people" only if pictured in and through sovereign institutions.[18] Here at last is "the people."

What is the conceptual content of the image Hobbes relies on to make his argument effective? In an earlier draft of the image, all the members of "the people" faced outward, toward the reader (fig. 11).

By turning the citizens' gaze away from their equals and toward a superior, Hobbes transformed them into the people, as he defined it. The citizens all look alike but are isolated from one another by their attention to the sovereign's face. Contained within the body of Leviathan, they can act only through him. The published frontispiece illustrates our habit of focusing on institutional duties and of studiously ignoring one another. It implies that as long as citizens trust their institutions they need not trust one another, and that as long as sovereigns cultivate allegiance to institutions, they can ignore the subjective experiences of citizens. Citizens suppress disagreements, disappointments, and discontent, he realized, in order to preserve institutions that make them feel safe. They ignore the diverse effects on citizens of public policies. They do not try to see what citizens sacrifice for others, or where a public decision about the common good has produced resentment. They contentedly accept the institutional production of "oneness" as adequately representing their investment in the polity. Hobbes encourages his sovereigns to shore up this attentiveness toward institutions and blindness to fellow citizens by beating the drum of security. They could stabilize political life by shoring up citizens' commitment to their institutional duties and encouraging passivity in respect to personally or factionally held opin-

FIGURE 11. *Leviathan,* draft of the frontispiece

ions. Hobbes's frontispiece pointedly illustrates citizenly habits that remain fundamental today.

Now we have an explanation of why we are the way we are. Our citizenly bad habits originate in the effort to give the people integrity, and to secure that idea for politics.

There is, however, a weakness in Hobbes's way of imagining the people. The subjective reactions of citizens to public policies cannot be repressed without consequence, nor can they even always be suppressed. Even the strongest, most forceful institutions can neither totally repress distrust, as Hobbes hoped, nor keep minds from changing. Those subjective reactions determine, over the long term, whether political institutions remain trustworthy to citizens. Over time nega-

tive subjective feelings corrode the bonds among citizens and between the citizenry and their institutions. But if Hobbes's politics of
repression cannot solve the problem of distrust, what will? The challenge his work presents is this: if citizens want to acknowledge disagreement, distrust, and division, they must devise more muscular
habits of trust production than are typically found in human communities.

Is this possible?

7

Imperfect Pearls/Imperfect Ideals

THE PROJECT OF COLLECTIVE AUTOBIOGRAPHY led to the argument in chapters 5 and 6 that our bad habits of citizenship originate in an idealization of unanimity and a rejection of rhetoric, and that these commitments developed as part of the Hobbesian effort to stabilize the idea of "the people." Before I give a positive account of the citizenly habits necessary for generating trust, I need to respond to Hobbes's challenge. Can we bring disagreement and disappointment out in the open, and not destabilize a populist political order? This chapter develops a fuller account of the theoretical bases for an alternative to the pursuit of unanimity: political practices oriented toward making a democratic people whole, though not one, through techniques for generating trust even in contexts where agreement cannot be achieved.

I begin this positive account with a brief return to Habermas. My criticism of his commitment to an ideal of full agreement is not original, but I do not mean by it, as most critics have, that he has fallen into a naïve utopianism. The stereotypical realist critic expostulates, "Perfect agreement is impossible; why bother talking about it." Habermas and his defenders rightly respond that utopian ideals invigorate politics by establishing criteria with which to critique actual political practice. My objection is rather that the ideal of unanimity idealizes the wrong thing and fails to establish evaluative criteria for a crucial democratic practice—the attempt to generate trust out of distrust. Habermasian arguments idealize something that is already perfect (consensus), whereas we need ideals for improving things that are not yet good enough and will never be perfect (trust).

Let me offer an example of this distinction between ideals for perfect and for imperfect things. A few years ago fashion mavens stirred up a vogue for black pearls. With the trend came habits of connoisseurship, because two kinds of black pearls exist, the perfect and the imperfect. The former are perfectly spherical while the latter have hills and valleys on their surfaces. Nor is the surface shine quite as bright for the imperfect as for the perfect pearls. But which is more valuable? The imperfect pearl, for the other is synthetic. And although the imperfect pearls all have blemishes, some are thought to be better than others, and there are ideals about what counts as the best imperfect pearl. Most of all, it should have a deep glow from within rather than a surface sheen.

Theorists who base accounts of citizenship on an ideal of unanimity are more interested in generating ideals for the perfect than for imperfect pearls, for perfect agreement rather than for maximum agreement supplemented by practices for addressing remainders of disagreement and distrust. But preparing the way for agreement requires not merely universalizable arguments but also democratic techniques to engage citizenly subjectivity, to render political loss bearable, and to restore trust. Only with ideals to govern democracy's imperfections can we develop a satisfactory pragmatics of citizenship. We need ways to accommodate imperfections as they are, not render them to uniformity. Importantly, the move away from an idealization of consensus is neither cynical nor straightforwardly realist. In fact, orienting an account of citizenship on imperfection might be more idealistic than the aspiration to unanimity. What if, as some have argued about our personal lives, repression *is* the best way to deal with loss? Then the orientation on unanimity and oneness—which demands suppression of phenomena like disappointment and distrust—would be more "realistic," more coldly pragmatic, than an effort to develop ideal terms for describing practices that address such phenomena.

As we saw in chapter 6, Hobbes makes this argument for repression. His hardheaded view that the subjectivity of citizens can be ignored without penalty if institutions are sufficiently strong depends, however, on a strict separation between the multitude (or the mass of citizens) and their political institutions. He advocated a form of mon-

archy in which a citizen's relations to her fellow citizens would, theoretically, have minimal impact on her trust in institutions. But in a
democracy—and especially a multitiered, bureaucratic federal republic—governmental officials are to be encountered at every turn, and,
theoretically, they are fellow citizens and equals. To trust the institutions of one's polity is to trust those citizen officials. A democracy, like
any other popularly based regime, needs unitary institutions ("the
people" as one) that can act in the people's name and maintain the allegiance of the citizenry, but its citizens also need means of cultivating relationships among themselves that can nourish political trust.
Does every citizen need to trust every other citizen? Clearly not. The
goal of trust generation is merely to convert the multitude into the
"people as whole," a healthy but imperfect body that is able to pass on
a culture of trust generation across generations. Just as the universe is
a functioning organic complex full of heterogeneity, nonconformity,
and even mutually contradictory processes, but nonetheless a whole,
a democratic people should cultivate coherence from within heterogeneity. The development of practices for generating trust among citizens should supplement, not replace, efforts to maintain allegiance to
democratic institutions. And neither the cultivation of such trust nor
the promotion of allegiance to democratic institutions rules out a
simultaneous cultivation of intellectual skepticism about particular
policies promoted by fellow citizens or by one's political institutions.
The aim rather is to develop practices that support vigorous arguments about political disagreements by sustaining the relationships
that make it worthwhile to argue with others in the first place.

No doubt the project of devising ideals for things imperfect, like
trust, brings with it a host of subsidiary "imperfect ideals." For the
present I will focus on only two, the first being this one of wholeness.
It orients democratic practice toward the development of a people
that is not one or homogeneous but, despite its diversity, a coherent,
integrated body to which citizens willingly give their allegiance.
What would an ideal version of "the people as whole" look like?
Hobbes drew the frontispiece to *Leviathan* to help future generations
picture the people as "one" and in order to install the drive toward
homogeneity at the heart of democratic practice. How might we, in
contrast, picture the people as "whole"?

Trust-building requires that citizens turn their attention toward one another, and the Teenie Harris photo (fig. 12) serves as an illustration of the necessary attentiveness. Each musician's body is subtly attuned to the presence of the others, as all of them, preparing to sing, listen for the piano and cast the whole of their attention toward something invisible: the song. In politics the something invisible we look and listen for is the republic, or the *res publica,* which means the "public thing." As the musicians hold tight to each other in anticipation of the song, so too, once they have begun to sing, the musicians will hold to the harmonies and melodies of the piece they are singing. If they are good musicians, they will adapt to each other while also making accommodations for individual interpretations of the music. Each will have a sense of how his or her voice is supported by and supports the others. So too is the activity of attending to the "public thing" a matter of attentiveness to fellow players. To be the people as "whole," citizens do not need to spend more time in the public sphere attending to politics than they presently do, but they must learn to see and hear what is political in the interactions they already have with fellow citizens. Can we imagine them saying, "I pledge allegiance to the flag of the United States of America, the whole nation . . ."? They are asked to see customers, employees, employers, attendants as citizens, and to look out for how their participation in institutions—whether schools, churches, or businesses—implicates them in strangers' lives. Does the form of their connections to strangers render them trustworthy? The people as a whole is constituted of a multitude of citizens exchanging glances while holding firmly to the legitimate institutions of collective decision making.

The aspiration to wholeness (not oneness) is the first imperfect ideal that we need in order to develop a citizenship suitable to the post-1957 constitution.[1]

A second set of imperfect ideals prescribes techniques for engaging with fellow citizens' subjective experiences of politics in order to generate trust. What methods of speech are suitable for maximizing agreement while also attending to its dissonant remainders? The pursuit of such techniques takes us back, yet again, to the argument between Plato and Aristotle about rhetoric, for it has traditionally been the art that crafts just such imperfect ideals. Plato condemned it precisely because it operates on the terrain of the imperfect—with attention to emotion as well as reason, willing to accept persuasion

FIGURE 12. Photo by Teenie Harris, courtesy of the Carnegie Museum of Art, Pittsburgh, Pennsylvania

rather than knowledge for particular kinds of political and ethical questions. Rhetoric is just a "knack," he thought, like baking or doing makeovers, not a craft like medicine or legislation, for which there are absolute standards. As we have seen, Aristotle rejected the Platonic view. He even likened rhetoricians to doctors in pointed contrast to Plato.

In an interesting aside during a discussion of deliberation in the *Nicomachean Ethics,* Aristotle insists on that very equivalence. Arguing that "[w]e deliberate not about ends, but about means," he gives this example: "A doctor does not deliberate whether he is to cure his patient, nor an orator (*rhetor*) whether he is to convince his audience, nor a politician (*politikos*) whether he is to secure good laws (*eunomia*)" (3.3.11). He asserts parallels among health and good laws, two of the greatest goods on the Aristotelian scale of value, and also persuasion. The comparison suggests that rhetoric can secure a good as important to the life of the individual as health and as necessary to the life of the polis as good laws. When he puts rhetoric on a level with medicine and legislation, he does not, however, associate it with perfectibility but instead demotes medicine and legislation to the level of imperfection.

Rather than be put off by the idea that rhetoric and medicine are not perfectible, Aristotle argues that it is nonetheless possible to call them arts, provided one is willing to do without absolute principles and instead make use of generally valid rules:

> We must be content if, in dealing with subjects and starting from premises thus uncertain, we succeed in presenting a broad outline of the truth: when our subjects and our premises are merely generalities, it is enough if we arrive at generally valid conclusions. Accordingly, we may ask the student also to accept the various views we put forward in the same spirit; for it is the mark of an educated mind to expect that amount of exactness in each kind which the nature of the particular subject admits. It is equally unreasonable to accept merely probable conclusions from a mathematician and to demand strict demonstration from an orator. (*NE* 1.3.4)

In the *Rhetoric* he endeavors to determine the generally valid rules applicable to the imperfect art of persuasion. The analogy between medicine and persuasion grounds the argument of that text. In the first chapter, in a passage that distinguishes the sophist from the rhetorician, he writes,

> It is evident that the function of rhetoric is not so much to persuade as to find out in each case the existing means of persuasion. The same holds good in respect to all the other arts. For instance, it is not the function of medicine to restore a patient to health, but only to promote this end as far as possible; for even those whose recovery is impossible may be properly treated. It is further evident that it belongs to Rhetoric to discover the real and apparent means of persuasion. (*R* 1.1.14)

Just as a doctor aims to cure not 51 percent of her patients but all of them, so a legislator aims to make as many as possible of his laws decent, and an Aristotelian rhetorician aims not merely at a victory at the polls and a majority vote for her arguments, but rather at wholly persuading her entire audience.

But surely this argument that the rhetorician should be oriented toward consensus, not majoritarianism, sounds like Habermas? Significantly, a doctor aims not only to cure as many patients as possible but also to treat properly "even those whose recovery is impossible." So, too, a rhetorician seeks not perfect consensus but maximal agreement coupled with satisfactory treatment of residual disagreement and those emotions in which it is often registered: anger, disappointment, and resentment. A friend recently told me about a young doctor who, having set off to treat HIV patients, soon recognized that he hadn't been adequately trained for the job. His entire medical education had oriented him toward *curing* his patients, but he now found he had to learn instead how to *care* for them. That arguments about euthanasia, living wills, and hospice care can convulse our political world is no accident. Modern medicine, like Habermasian deliberation, is characterized by a drive toward perfection. But ever ongoing refinements of technology and treatment techniques cannot overcome all the limits of our imperfect power. The manifestations of limitation—death, on the one hand; disagreement or distrust, on the other—must be met with an ethical framework and treatment techniques that are proper to our limits. The switch of focus from oneness to wholeness, from idealizing unanimity to idealizing the proper treatment of disagreement, is analogous to this young doctor's switch from cure to care.[2]

The suggestion that we might draw our imperfect ideals for trust production from the art of rhetoric reasonably inspires worries about sophistry, manipulation, and propaganda. The analogy of the rhetorician to the doctor is useful, above all, in assuaging those worries. To say that doctors must know how to treat even the dying opens a set of problems. Should they assist suicides for those whose illnesses are incurable? Or should they simply judge when to shut off life support? Or should they do everything in their power to keep a person alive as long as possible? Or should they rather help people live well and then die with dignity? These questions all arise from the worry that concern about death with dignity may, albeit accidentally, encourage some doctors to commit murder. Worries about sophistry arise analogously from the fear that the use of rhetorical techniques to generate trust may lead speakers to exploit distrust and their ability to dissolve it. Doctors can be depended on to help the terminally ill live well only if their art is developed in accord with the norm that they treat the living and above all else do nothing to advance the cause of death. Similarly, the art of rhetoric, as distinct from sophistry, must develop norms whereby its practitioners think of themselves as treating distrust, and above all else wish not to increase its reach and power. What makes the sophist is not, as Aristotle says, the tools of the trade, but the intentions. Rhetoric, like any art, can be used ill, or well.

How, then, can we take this ideal of wholeness, and its accompanying ideals for trust production, derived from the art of rhetoric, and turn them into new habits of citizenship? Shortly, in part III, I will turn to this question and the effort to limn a new version of citizenship adequate to our post-1957 constitution. Before doing that, though, I'd like to point out that the faint glimmerings of an alternative to our present habits exist already, even in Hobbes's writing. Although he rejected rhetoric in his civil state, Hobbes, too, tried to discover the generally valid rules for the imperfect art for producing trust. His inhabitants of the state of nature originally come to consensus not because of institutions but because of their own interaction. They are a multitude in the state of nature until they establish a covenant, at which point they become the people as a whole, by Hobbes's own definition. They do not become the people as one until they invent institutions. This means that, strangely enough, we can already discern, albeit vaguely, the contours of the art of trust generation in Hobbes's writings if we investigate the habits of interaction that bring inhabitants of the state of nature into covenant with each other.

How, then, do the inhabitants of the state of nature generate trust?[3] We have to start at the beginning. Early in all his political texts, Hobbes argues that to make peace those who dwell in the state of nature must know one another's minds. Without speech "whereby men register their thoughts, recall them when they are past, and also declare them one to another for mutual utility and conversation . . . there had been amongst men, neither Commonwealth, nor Society, nor Contract, nor Peace" (L 4,1). The declaration that most effectively motivates agreement, he argues, "consist[s] merely in offering tokens of not resisting." That is, a citizen who foregoes opportunities to hinder someone else's will or to prevent the accrual of benefit to that person signals that his intentions are not harmful to his fellows (*De cive* 2.4). Trustworthiness is primarily a willingness to sacrifice some of one's own power for the sake of common agreement. He does not advocate that the weak passively accept the desires of the strong, but reminds all would-be peacemakers that they are answerable for the extent to which they permit their interests to impede the pursuits of others.[4]

As an example of behavior that threatens peace, Hobbes adduces the following speech: "What art thou to me; why should I rather do according to your than mine own will, since I do not hinder but you may do your own, and my mind?" This question endangers trust by making plain that the speaker's interests are compatible with disdain for fellow citizens. Our statements during negotiations always let people know where they stand with us, even if we do not mean them to, and he calls the remark, "What art thou to me?" a "speech, where there hath no manner of pre-contract passed" (*De cive* 3.4). When would-be peacemakers disclose their own interests, they must prove not only that these will not harm others, but also that those others figure positively in the peacemakers' own visions for the future. Martin Luther King, Jr., was exceptionally good at this: "I have a dream that one day on the red hills of Georgia the sons of former slaves and the sons of former slave owners will be able to sit down together at a table of brotherhood."[5] Citizens judge whether they will be disadvantaged by prospective collaboration on the basis of whether they believe themselves esteemed by their collaborators. The "pre-contract" tests interest by making public what one citizen is worth to another. Consensual agreements, Hobbes argues, can never be concluded but in conditions of avowed equality.[6]

Hobbes's emphasis on egalitarian expression comes out most clearly in his analysis of the political problems of his era. Observing that entrenched differences of position within the polity had led to insurmountably divergent opinions, he bemoans "the barbarous state of men in power, towards their inferiors"; and in "men of low degree," "sawcie behavior towards their betters." Marked social differentiation is the product of civil society, not of nature (*L* 15.21), he argues, and such differences are a bountiful source of strife: "When men arrogate to themselves more honour than they give to others, it cannot be imagined how they can possibly live in peace" (*EL* 1.17.1), and in *Leviathan* he writes,

> The question who is the better man, has no place in the condition of meer Nature; where (as has been shewn before) all men are equall. The inequality that now is, has bin introduced by the Lawes civill. If Nature therefore have made men equall, that equalitie is to be acknowledged: or if Nature have made men unequall; yet because men that think themselves equall, will not enter into conditions of Peace, but upon Equall termes, such equalitie must be admitted. (*L* 15.21; cf. *EL* 1.14.2, 1.14.12–14, 1.19.1, *DC* 1.3)

Hobbes analyzes politics by imagining civil society dissolved precisely because he despairs of people's moving toward peace from rigidly differentiated social positions (*De cive*, preface, 99). The state-of-nature metaphor builds into his argument about peacemaking the very specific proposition that perduring positions of advantage and disadvantage must be undone, or at least unsettled, before agreement can be brought out of war.[7]

But the metaphor is only the starting point in his analysis of what it takes to generate trust and peace. Simple equality of position generates fear, not trust, in his view. If inhabitants of the state of nature wish to convert distrust to trust, they must go beyond their natural equality by following some simple rules. He calls these the laws of nature. He would have spoken more accurately, though, had he called them laws of rhetoric, or trust production. His laws of nature frequently prescribe how distrustful people should communicate with each other. For instance, the ninth law of nature is that "equalitie [of all with all] must be admitted." Since "admitted" is synonymous to "acknowledged" or "confessed," the word underscores the fact that he is concerned more with the attitudes that the inhabitants of the state of nature display to their fellows than with what they are in their hearts and homes. Specifically here his concern is their avowals, linguistic representations of their subjectivity. *Elements of Law* prohibits, as a corollary to the ninth law, derision and contempt. He laments, "This law is very little practiced. For what is more ordinary than reproaches of those that are rich towards them that are not" (EL 1.16.11).[8] His other laws of nature in Leviathan include the following: (1) that people defend themselves; (2) that they be willing, when others are also willing, to lay down their right to all things; (3) that they perform their covenants; (4) that they display gratitude to those who give gifts; (5) that they strive to accommodate themselves to the rest; (6) that they pardon the repentant; (7) that they punish not for revenge but deterrence; (8) that they eschew pride; (9) that they eschew arrogance and the attempt to gain more than they are willing to give to others; (10) that they judge equally when serving as arbitrators; and (11) that they share what cannot be divided (L 14 and 15).

The majority of these laws prohibit or encourage certain kinds of display.[9] The fourth law explicitly enjoins shows of gratitude, but the other laws too encourage people to disclose to one another what they are to each other. In eschewing pride, inhabitants of the state of nature will not present themselves to others as their superiors. If they are to pardon the repentant, there must be a display of repentance on the part of the wrongdoer and of pardon on the part of the judge or jury. Pardon differs from forgiveness largely in this requirement of publicity. Similarly, citizens who punish for deterrence, not revenge, must disclose the reasons behind the punishment, for deterrent and vengeful motives are not otherwise distinguishable. Hobbes, unlike Habermas, specifies the interactions in which interlocutors must think rhetorically—with an attention to audiences—in order to generate reciprocity.

But what does thinking rhetorically imply about the practice of citizenship? Hobbes sometimes summarizes his prescriptions as specifically requiring displays of equity, justice, and gratitude (L 26.8). Occasionally he calls these three phenomena natural virtues, occasionally good manners, or simply the way to peace.[10] The equation of good manners to virtue and the disposition to peace underscores the point that his laws of nature finally enjoin sociability. He writes, in a passage in Elements of Law that has parallels in Leviathan,

> The sum of virtue is to be sociable with them that will be sociable and formidable to them that will not. And the same is the sum of the law of nature; for in being sociable, the law of nature taketh place of the

way of peace and society; and to be formidable is the law of nature in war . . . the former consisteth of actions of equity and justice, the latter consisteth in actions of honour. (*EL* 1.17.15)[11]

Sociability, not rationality, produces agreement, and consists particularly of equity. In *Elements of Law* Hobbes defines equity as "that habit of nature by which we allow equality of nature; arrogance the contrary vice" (1.17.14). Since to "allow equality" is to acknowledge it, equity is a habit of rhetorical display, and we have come full circle. Agreement is possible when people are sociable, which means "when they are equitable," which means "when they allow equality."[12]

This circularity might seem a weakness, if one ignores the fact that Hobbes's laws of nature highlight areas of policy in which equality is most important. They pertain to situations that involve citizens in admissions of what they are to each other. These laws identify areas of public policy that raise issues of mutual esteem. His focus is especially on blame and punishment (which draws attention to the criminal justice system), on social systems of benefaction and injury (here attention is drawn to issues of social justice, taxes, and welfare), on intense competition (which draws attention to the labor market), and on promise-keeping. Not surprisingly, our most divisive current political issues fall squarely under the purview of Hobbes's laws. Debates over the death penalty, imprisonment, and the severity of punishments for drug-related crimes directly concern laws six and seven (that the repentant should be pardoned and that punishments should be carried out not for revenge but for deterrence). Debates about unemployment, welfare, taxes, affirmative action, monetary policy, and other social justice issues trigger laws four and nine (that one display gratitude to those who give gifts and that one eschew the attempt to gain more than one is willing to give to others). Concern about hate speech and crimes bears on laws eight and nine (that one eschew pride and arrogance; or, as Hobbes puts it in *Elements of Law*, derision and contempt).

Debates over these issues are politically divisive not only because they are substantively difficult but also because they give citizens superb opportunities to reveal what their fellow citizens are worth to them. Unfortunately, most of us frequently fall short in such moments. Citizens most need to "allow" the equality of their fellows in respect to issues like these, but too often they fail at exactly this, not understanding that their disagreements have as much to do with reciprocity and issues of mutual esteem as with the substantive issue under discussion. Although Hobbes's laws of nature establish communicative norms, these clarify not reasons (as Habermas would like) but relationships. One simple rule covers all these laws of nature. This is the proverbial "commandment of mutual charity" that you do not to others what you would not have done to yourself (L 15.35; 30.13). This law becomes a critical test for key areas of policy.

The signal discovery behind Hobbes's laws of nature, then, is this: *Reciprocity does not merely aid the conclusion of agreements that are achieved primarily through reason. Instead, it is one of the substantive questions at stake in all disputes within a consensually based political community.* But having made this discovery, Hobbes then foreclosed the possibility of cultivating within citizens a culture of reciprocity. He abandoned the political possibilities inherent in citizenship for authoritarianism, replacing his habits of trust generation with the invention of which he was most proud: the perfectible political science of "that great Leviathan, or rather (to speak more reverently) of that *Mortal God* to which we owe, under the *Immortal God,* our peace and defence" (L 17.13).

Scholars often characterize the argument of *Leviathan* as resting on a piece of illogic. Hobbes describes a state of nature so deadly, so poisoned, that all inhabitants should expect a quick death. Yet he expects unanimity to arise nonetheless and state institutions to be erected on the basis of this consensus. Most scholars doubt that adherence to his laws of nature would generate the unanimity Hobbes seeks. And they are right. The rules of rhetoric cannot generate perfect consensus; they only identify the means of persuasion while also preparing to treat residual disagreement properly. The transition from a state of nature where a few, some, or even all of the inhabitants act in accord with his laws of nature to a moment of unanimity followed by the Leviathan marks a theoretical shift in Hobbes's argument from an effort to develop ideals for the imperfect art of trust generation to an attempt instead to create a perfectible art of politics.

Hobbes knew that the cultivation of habits of trust generation is an ongoing task and that it is impossible ever to generate bonds of trust so firm that perpetual stability is assured. The first difficulty of an imperfect art is that one must be committed to it in perpetuity, if one wants visible results. The second difficulty is that the citizen who turns away from the ideal of unanimity and toward the imperfect must be like a doctor who thinks about life and also paradoxically about death, about curing but also about treating the incurable, for this too is life.

And why treat dissenters properly? Why not just forget about them? Because the process of negotiating differences allows for social stability, and the alternative is civil war, whether in major or minor keys.

PART THREE: NEW DEMOCRATIC VISTAS

8

⤳

Beyond Invisible Citizens

NOW AT LAST IT IS TIME TO TURN to the truly difficult question. In what new habits should we clothe ourselves?

In writing the preceding chapters on the political imagination, I discovered some facts about our political lives that I knew unconsciously but did not fully admit: that our benefits derive not merely from our own hard work or even luck but also from the sacrifices of strangers; that our fixation on perfect consent assuages problematic (but ordinary) psychological needs without adequately educating us in democratic citizenship; that our best taught habit of citizenship is "don't talk to strangers"; that precisely this habit allows us to ignore how strangers bring us benefit; and, most important, that 1957 was a year of reconstitution, which has left us still with a political challenge: how to invent a citizenship of trust generation. Now I return to my political home, and it looks different.

What is this political "home"? It's built out of interactions with strangers, and is visible not only when I watch congressional hearings on C-SPAN but, more important, when I observe how the passers-by interact on the street: what is each giving up in order that the others may live better? How exactly does the whole of society look from the different perspectives of each of these people? Are we developing forms of citizenship adequate to the post-1957 constitution? Because street corners do produce answers for me—epiphanic political knowledge—I feel I have traversed the same terrain by a different conveyance, as did the protagonist in Ralph Ellison's *Invisible Man.* In his odyssey from naïf to mature citizen, the Invisible Man grows hep to the difficulties of democratic life and his epiphanies begin to come on subway platforms. He says of three young African Americans,

> What about those three boys, coming now along the platform, tall and slender, walking stiffly with swinging shoulders in their well-dressed, too-hot-for-summer suits. . . . It was as though I'd never seen their like before. . . . I got up and went behind them. . . . Do others see them, think about them, even those standing close enough to speak? . . . They were men out of time. . . . Men out of time, who would soon be gone and forgotten . . . but who knew (and now I began to tremble so violently I had to lean against a refuse can)—who knew but that they were the saviors, the true leaders, the bearers of something precious? The stewards of something uncomfortable, burdensome, which they hated because, living outside the realm of history, there was no one to applaud their value and they themselves failed to understand it. (440)

The young men carry their value within them: the heavy truth that democracies need to establish consent despite an inability to address everyone's interests equally. Their skin, although it teaches us nothing about their personal experiences, conveys a general history of the United States. Like the protagonist of *Invisible Man,* we stand now on some such platform, surveying others and wondering how to respond to the ornery, ordinary difficulties of democratic life; how to deal justly despite this inability to address everyone's interests to the same degree.

Although I wanted to provide in parts I and II a diagnosis of our current situation, I cannot now in part III offer some simple policy solution to democracy's difficulties. They're irresolvable; we have rather to learn how to live with them. This is where and why citizenship comes in. In this final section, rather than promote a policy, I will track some political thinkers who have dropped clues about the political aspirations and techniques that may suit efforts to deal with the inevitability of sacrifice, loss, and distrust in democracy. I will weave their fragmentary observations into a narrative about the citizenly techniques needed for generating trust.

At the start of this story is the subject of sacrifice. What criteria can distinguish legitimate from illegitimate sacrifices? Which political practices help one to cope with loss? In this chapter, I turn again to

Ralph Ellison, this time to his novel, *Invisible Man,* where he analyzed sacrifice most thoroughly. The protagonist, a twenty-something African American, journeys from a childhood in a segregated Southern town to an early adulthood in New York, where, first as a laborer and then as an operative for the Brotherhood party, he discovers the difficulties inherent in democratic practice. After assorted personal travails, he falls down a coal chute into a cellar, from which he narrates his life story. We learn that he has learned how inescapable is sacrifice in democratic life and has also prepared a response to this fact. The novel helps us toward a guiding, if vague, political aspiration and also to some preliminary techniques for a trust-generating citizenship.[1]

The Invisible Man starts his life story by recollecting his grandfather's deathbed words:

> Son, after I'm gone I want you to keep up the good fight. I never told you, but our life is a war and I have been a traitor all my born days, a spy in the enemy's country ever since I give up my gun back in the Reconstruction. Live with your head in the lion's mouth. I want you to overcome 'em with yeses, undermine 'em with grins, agree 'em to death and destruction, let 'em swoller you till they vomit or bust wide open . . . Learn it to the young 'uns. (*IM* 16)

Although he had lived in the Jim Crow South, where he had never been able to vote, the grandfather was insistent: even the invisible never leave politics; they remain always actively engaged in their polities even if no one notices. His claim to subversive agency, however, inevitably also reports on a problem of impotence. Ellison often suggested that the experience of African Americans living under Jim Crow was a neat metaphor for the basic impotence that dogs all democratic citizens. Segregation, he thought, revealed in the starkest terms a basic feature of democratic politics, namely, that some lose out to the benefit of others. He closes his novel by having his protagonist remark to his audience, "Who knows but that on the lower frequencies I speak for you?" (581). Almost all democratic citizens often feel like powerless sovereigns. The grandfather's riddle about political agency should be relevant to everyone.[2]

This is a perplexing idea. In what sense do the dominated have any agency? And what does it mean to "agree" someone to "death and destruction"? In what sense is the riddle an analysis of the political agency of all citizens? The Invisible Man returns repeatedly to his grandfather's last words as he slowly comes to recognize the significance of sacrifice first to his own political experience and then to all democratic life, and then also slowly formulates a style of citizenship in response. He makes several attempts in the novel to define the political agency of invisible citizens, and with each one, he wins for himself a critical truth about democracy. They add up to the basis for a new citizenship.

His first try at self-reflection comes when, as a teenager, he thinks about the agency available to him in the segregated South. He has few words to explain his sufferance of segregation, but he endures for the sake of achieving a greater part in American democracy. He understands that being a citizen in democracy means that consent, autonomous action, and a willingness to follow the polity's laws are attributed to him. He hopes to be the next Booker T. Washington and believes that following the rules will get him there. But at the same time he does not want to follow the laws of the Jim Crow South. How then, when he lives by rules he does not wish to obey, can he call himself a consenting citizen? Even as a youth he needs an answer. He describes his stance then as one of humility, which he calls "the secret, indeed the very essence of progress" (*IM* 17). When he gives a high-school graduation speech on the subject, it is so well received that he is invited to repeat it before a gathering of the town's prominent white men. On the appointed evening, the town's eminences are all drunk and lecherous; they maul a stripteaser, and then turn to the entertainment they expect from "the shines." Only after being forced to participate in a battle royal boxing match with nine other boys is the Invisible Man finally allowed to give his address. Amid yells, laughter, and humiliation, he begins his paean to, of all things, humility.[3]

As the context for his speech has shifted, so too has his memory. Instead of reciting his text on his own "social responsibility," the Invisible Man resoundingly commits himself to "social equality." Ellison writes, "The laughter hung in the sudden stillness. I opened my eyes, puzzled. Sounds of displeasure filled the room. . . . 'Say that slowly son!'" Realizing his mistake, with a flutter of fear, he retracts his desire for "equality," affirms his commitment to "social responsibility," and finds himself rewarded. The men give him a scholarship to a local black college. The pressure on the Invisible Man has led him to reveal, for a brief moment, the question raised by his focus on humility: How does social responsibility, obedience to laws and norms, relate to social equality or the ability to use common institutions to accrue benefit in the social and private sphere? Does the one not, in a democratic society, promise the other?

Ellison's focus is on the unseen political actions of invisible people. In the eerie moment when the Invisible Man replaces the phrase "social responsibility" with "social equality," Ellison proposes that hidden responsibilities and obligations underwrite democratic peace. The Invisible Man averts violence to himself by publicly committing himself to "responsibility." His audience vaguely senses that some gift is involved in the resulting release of tension. Wrongly, they think it is theirs: "We mean to do right by you, but you've got to know your place at all times," they say (31). But his slip of the tongue reveals that he already has an intuitive sense of the agency hidden behind his mask of humility: he is being humble *in exchange* for future goods. He conceives of his humility as an instrument for achieving social and political benefits within a political order that he naïvely hopes is indeed based on his fellow citizens' recognition of their reciprocal responsibilities.

As the novel progresses, the Invisible Man repeatedly suppresses his opinions and desires in the hope of advancement, and eventually realizes that not only does his "humility" get him nowhere, but neither does anyone see it or, beneath its mask, him. He becomes increasingly aware that his willingness to put aside his personal desire for social equality in order to gain access to the democracy's institutions of power has been abused precisely by not being recognized for what it is: an act (a gift and also more than that, for it also involves an assumption of loss) and not merely, like humility, an aspect of character. What he recognizes, but no one else does, is sacrifice: "the destruction or surrender of something valued or desired for the sake of something having, or regarded as having, a higher or more pressing claim; the loss entailed by devotion to some other interest" (*OED*).[4] He discovers that those who are dominated and peaceable in any political order should be seen as philanthropists, agents in this regard, toward those who dominate them. This discovery of the centrality of sacrifice leads to the realization that democratic citizenship consists primarily of reciprocity.

But surely the claim that those who are dominated are in fact philanthropists is perverse. Mere discovery of the place of sacrifice in politics does not explain the relationship between it and political agency. What if sacrifice has been thoroughly disconnected from reciprocity and the same people give things up all the time without anyone reciprocating? Can their gifts still be considered examples of political agency? The discovery of the place of sacrifice in political life is a major theme of the central narration in the novel, but the long narrative section is flanked by a prologue, in which the Invisible Man explains why he is narrating his life history, and an epilogue in which he draws some conclusions. Although the prologue comes at the beginning of the novel, it represents the protagonist's views on his world *after* he has already had the experiences he is now about to relate; it gives his reasons for sharing his experiences with a broad audience. The epilogue, in contrast, represents his opinions after they have been changed by the experience of narrating his life history. Whereas his youthful self-reflection led to the discovery of the inevitability of sacrifice, the prologue and epilogue represent his more mature second and third attempts to think through the meaning of democratic citizenship in conditions of severe impotence. Each contains another account of the political agency open to invisible citizens.

In the prologue, the Invisible Man explores the agency available through criticism. He relates how, being bumped in the dark and cursed by a stranger, he beat the man within an inch of his life; he reflects on his actions: "I can hear you say, 'What a horrible, irresponsible bastard!' And you're right. I leap to agree with you. . . . But to whom can I be responsible and why should I be when you refuse to see me? . . . Responsibility rests upon recognition, and recognition is a form of agreement" (14). Ellison equips the Invisible Man with the idioms of a political theorist—agreement, responsibility, and recognition are his terms. His protagonist is willing to act responsibly, adhering to law and social custom, provided that his acts and restraint are recognized as a gift other citizens have requested for their own good, and which they agree to reciprocate. His invisibility results from the refusal of those around him to take up his offer of reciprocity. They abdicate responsibility.

This logic leads to an unnerving conclusion. He finally decides, about the man who bumped him in the dark, that "I was the irresponsible one; for I should have used my knife to protect the higher interests of society. . . . All dreamers and sleepwalkers must pay the price, and even the invisible victim is responsible for the fate of all. But I shirked that responsibility" (14). As the Invisible Man (ironically) sees it, his real responsibility is to end the refusal of the sleepwalkers to engage in norms of reciprocity.[5] Their indifference to the gift of democratic responsibility endangers citizenship. Invisible citizens see these failures of reciprocity more clearly than do those who perpetrate them; the invisible in particular have a duty to be critics and to challenge these mistakes. The word "criticism" comes from the Greek *krinô* for "to separate good from bad," and can be associated with cutting.[6] The critic *is* someone who uses a knife, maybe even "acutely," pruning or sacrificing a branch here or there for the sake of a better whole. When the Invisible Man says, "I should have used my knife to protect the higher interests of society," he turns critic but also transforms himself from a giver to a taker of sacrifices. He too desires to sacrifice others; the sinister side of democracy lives in his own heart.[7]

Bumping into strangers in the dark is a figure for democratic citizenship. But putting the knife in is a metaphor both for criticism and for taking sacrifices from those who have not volunteered them. In its second sense, this latter figure warns citizens of those moments when they impose sacrifice on others. But the knife's first sense designates a second form of citizenly agency. All ordinary interaction with strangers is structured by rituals that shape life within our democracies. Every interaction or bump in the dark is an opportunity for criticism of and intervention in those rituals. The Invisible Man expands his account of political agency to include not only the making of sacrifice, but also the commitment to criticize severely myopic accounts of citizenship. His metaphors will surface ten years later in Martin Luther King's descriptions of nonviolence as "a powerful and just weapon. It is a weapon unique in history, which cuts without wounding and ennobles the man who wields it. It is a sword that heals."[8]

We have followed the Invisible Man to the development of two preliminary hypotheses: first, his most youthful proposition that those who have been dominated actively sacrifice for others; second, the intermediate claim that the dominated should "use the knife" on others—to criticize or sacrifice those who are misguided as to political responsibility. Neither hypothesis, though, solves the riddle of the grandfather's injunction to "agree 'em to death and destruction." The first focuses all on agreeing as a source of political agency, but ultimately makes a mockery of it, turning citizenship into an acquiescent step-and-fetch-it routine. The second hypothesis focuses all on destruction, turning citizenship instead into violence and hatred, and "caring not what pain one causes others." Moreover, both hypotheses pertain only to the dominated; they do not explain the responsibility that applies to all democratic citizens. A solution of the riddle that can combine agreement with destruction will come only when the Invisible Man theorizes forms of citizenship that can belong to everyone—the former dominators as well as the formerly dominated. In the epilogue, he proposes a third type of political agency, open to all citizens: namely, the ability to invent new forms of citizenship.

He achieves the discoveries of the epilogue, however, only after refining his terms concerning sacrifice; a healthy mode of citizenship, he comes to see, must lie somewhere between giving sacrifices without reciprocation and taking them from others without a concern for reciprocity. Both of these extremes turn citizens into scapegoats, a concept that Ellison develops in his essays with reference to lynching. In scapegoating rituals particular citizens are expelled from the city in order to expiate a common guilt. African Americans living under Jim Crow were ultimately scapegoats, not philanthropists, and if the Invisible Man had killed the man who bumped him in the dark, that man too would have been a scapegoat. Ellison gives the Invisible Man a chance to consider the problem of the scapegoat in the novel's most explicitly political discourse.

For decades, readers of *Invisible Man* have assumed that in it the Brotherhood party is a stand-in for the American Communist Party, with which Ellison briefly flirted. It isn't. Ellison often irritably brushed off the claim that his portrait of the Brotherhood party was a send-up of communism and, in his critical essays, also frequently suggested that the party instead represented, simply, democracy. When the Invisible Man joins the Brotherhood party as its Harlem spokesman, he is the equivalent of any new democratic citizen who expects to play a part in public decisions.[9] He works hard, on behalf of the party, to organize the neighborhood around housing issues, but exactly when he has brought the neighborhood to its highest pitch of commitment,

the Brotherhood switches its focus away from Harlem. The Invisible
Man is neither included in policy deliberations nor even forewarned
of the change. In his anger, he confronts Hambro, his tutor in Brotherhood doctrine, who admits, "It's unfortunate, Brother, but your
members will have to be sacrificed" (501). Here Ellison at last brings
the Invisible Man face-to-face with what has, throughout the novel,
kept him running and accepting loss in pursuit of an elusive gain: the
repeated requirement that he sacrifice. "Sacrifice?" the Invisible Man
says, "You say that very easily" (501).

At last the Invisible Man is obliged to think hard about what it
means to invoke sacrifice in political discourse, and eventually the
conversation with Hambro results in his elaboration of three criteria
for distinguishing legitimate from illegitimate sacrifices. Beginning a
dialogue between them, Hambro responds:

> "The interests of one group of brothers must be sacrificed to that of
> the whole."
>
> "Why wasn't *I* told of this?" I said.
>
> "You will be in time, by the committee—Sacrifice is necessary
> now—"
>
> "But shouldn't sacrifice be made willingly by those who know
> what they're doing? My people don't understand why they're being
> sacrificed. They don't even *know* they're being sacrificed—at least not
> by us . . ." (502)

Any use of the term "sacrifice" in political discourse introduces problems of agency: the word can mean either the giving or the taking of
sacrifices. The grammatical distinction between Hambro's use of the
passive voice—"your members will have to be sacrificed"—and the
Invisible Man's reference to the *making* of sacrifices by choice and
with foreknowledge accurately registers the conflict here. Scapegoats
are sacrificed by others; a hero chooses her sacrifice and thereby gains
honor from other citizens who acknowledge that she, and not they,
have borne the worst of it. The term "gift" does not have a semantic
range wide enough to capture the losses involved in democratic politics; it is inadequate to the task of "honoring" those whose gift is to
absorb loss. Here already are two of the three criteria for distinguish-

ing legitimate sacrifices: first, a legitimate sacrifice is made voluntarily and knowingly; second, democratic responsibility consists of an agreement to honor the voluntary sacrifice.

Hambro refuses to acknowledge the importance of these criteria and continues to argue:

> "All of us must sacrifice for the good of the whole. Change is achieved through sacrifice. We follow the laws of reality, so we make sacrifices."
>
> "But the community is demanding equality of sacrifice. We've never asked for special treatment."
>
> "It's inevitable that some must make greater sacrifices than others . . ."
>
> "That 'some' being my people . . ."
>
> "In this instance, yes."
>
> "So the weak must sacrifice for the strong. Is that it, Brother?"
>
> "No, a part of the whole is sacrificed—and will continue to be until a new society is formed." (502–3)

Hambro hopes that sacrifice will produce a new and internally consistent society; he is engaged, figuratively, in a ritual purification through a scapegoat.[10] In response, the Invisible Man asks whether those who sacrifice can be kept within the community so that society becomes different but not new. Losses do not disappear but are retained in the fabric of society; this must be acknowledged. The first two criteria for establishing the legitimacy of sacrifice—that they must be voluntary and honored—also establish a framework for mourning processes that can eventually reconstitute trust.

The Invisible Man articulates one last criterion for determining legitimate sacrifices, which brings us back to the central point: sacrifice becomes illegitimate when one party regularly sacrifices for the rest. The weak have been incorporated into the democratic polity only when they are in an equal position to request sacrifice from others; "equality of sacrifice" is the third criterion of legitimacy. The Invisible Man learns that Hambro is merely cynical when the latter remarks, "I thought that you had learned that it's impossible not to take advantage of the people. . . . The trick is to take advantage of them in their own best interest." The Invisible Man realizes that Hambro "didn't have to deal with being both sacrificer and victim; . . . he didn't have to put the knife blade to his own throat" (506). Reciprocity tests and sets limits to sacrifice and, combined with the democratic promise that one can choose one's own sacrifices, should establish the distinction between sacrifice and scapegoating. Those who promote sacrifices for others should also expect to bear them themselves, but the Brotherhood's policies separate decision about sacrifice from the experience of it. Democracy, in contrast, should distinguish between those who give up their interests consensually and suffer something they understand and those who do not, between sacrificers and victims; the democratic objective should be to reduce the category of victim to insignificance.

Properly undertaken—with foreknowledge, consent, and the prospect of honor—a democratic sacrifice opens a covenant so that those who benefit from a sacrifice see themselves as recipients of a gift that they must not only honor but also reciprocate. Veterans are due just this recognition in the United States, by force of law but also by custom. But similar practices of recognition should also apply to the more prosaic sacrifices of our ordinary political world. Sacrifices draw people into networks of mutual obligation and in so doing have the capacity to rejuvenate political relationships. This they can do, however, only if accompanied by the questions asked by the Invisible Man: Who is sacrificing for whom? Is the sacrifice voluntary? Is it honored? Will the sacrifice be reciprocated?

How sacrifices are handled affects the ability of a democracy to maintain institutional allegiance and trust among citizens. When Hambro refuses to discuss equitable sacrifice, the Invisible Man's party commitment disintegrates; he feels the Brotherhood changing "to water, air" (503). Similarly, citizens, confronted with a politics that does not address the distribution of burdens within the citizenry, disengage from politics and abandon the polity. In the conversation with Hambro, the Invisible Man realizes that the Brotherhood has no room at all for brotherhood with a small "b." His disillusionment is significant because he has directed great energy to trying to understand the "brotherhood" his party supposedly represents. He seeks to understand an "unnamed something" that resides in his voice as "a living proof of Brotherhood" (420), "*that something* for which the theory of Brotherhood had given me no name" (453). With the exposure of Hambro's hypocrisy, the always unnamable, hard to understand, brotherhood becomes substanceless, no addition to the world. Distrust is born in the conversation between Hambro and the Invisible Man. This suggests that, for those who can properly acknowledge sacrifice, and so avoid Hambro's hypocrisy, brotherhood will *not* change into air and water, but will remain "some thing," even if it stays unnamable. Proper acknowledgment of sacrifice preserves trust.

The Invisible Man has discovered a new political aspiration for himself. Unlike Hambro, he seeks practices of reciprocity that democratize sacrifice and develop "something like brotherhood" into a real feature of citizenship. Ellison believed that intimate and personal practices such as love and friendship hold resources for dealing with democracy's difficulties. In his own voice, he argued that "[t]he way home we seek is that condition of man's being at home in the world, which is called love, and which we term democracy" (*CE* 154).[11] The conversation on sacrifice between Hambro and the Invisible Man provides a powerful reason for taking this new aspiration seriously, for their conversation is followed by the overwhelming riot scene.

Soon after the Invisible Man leaves Hambro, riots break out in Harlem. He makes it uptown only after things are really jumping. First he accidentally joins up with an arson party; then he finds himself fighting Ras, the black nationalist; finally, he is shot superficially, and while being chased by a group of white men, falls into a coal chute and passes out. There the epiphanic climax of the novel comes in the form of a wild, vivid dream-vision of castration:

> *I lay beside a river of black water, near where an armored bridge arched sharply away to where I could not see. And I was protesting their holding me and they were demanding that I return to them and were annoyed with my refusal. . . . But now they came forward with a knife, holding me; and I felt the bright red pain and they took the two bloody blobs and cast them over the bridge, and out of my anguish I saw them curve up and catch beneath the apex of the curving arch of the bridge, to hang there, dripping down through the sunlight into the dark red water. And while the others laughed, before my pain-sharpened eyes the whole world was slowly turning red.* (569, emphasis in the original)

Sixty pages earlier in the conversation about sacrifice Hambro had coldly said, "I'm sorry but your members will have to be sacrificed." That pun on "members" is the mother of the dream, which turns out to be the last word on the conversation between Hambro and the Invisible Man.[12] The dream is also the last word on the riot scene, and with it Ellison links what he has discovered about sacrifice to large-scale political events. The riot, as an answer to the conversation, tells how existentially and politically bracing are ordinary citizens' experiences of loss and sacrifice. If we assimilate the riot scene to the dream, and take the surreal riot and dream sequence to originate in the Invisible Man's earlier personal experiences of sacrifice, the end of the novel makes a powerful statement about the psychic pressures of democratic life. Brotherhood is an antidote to these.

The novel reminds us of a point discussed in chapter 4: sacrifice is ubiquitous in democratic life, and democratic citizens are by definition empowered only to be disempowered. Democratic citizenship requires rituals to manage the psychological tension that arises from being an often powerless sovereign. The democracy in which the Invisible Man lives had adopted castration as its solution, and that in itself suggests the severity of stress felt even by the dominators. Through that ritual, some citizens were made to bear the marks of the impotence with which all the rest were also afflicted. They became apotropaic off-scourings in a ritual of extreme purification. But some future democracy may, Ellison is hopeful, one day find healthy rituals to manage the distribution of burdens and benefits. All citizens, and not only the invisible, would benefit from a politics of brotherhood that could minimize such psychological stress.

In the epilogue, the Invisible Man uses these insights about sacrifice, brotherhood, and democratic psychology as the foundation for a new approach to citizenship. He returns to his grandfather's riddle with a solution, at last:

> I'm still plagued by his deathbed advice. . . . Could he have meant—
> hell, he *must* have meant the principle, that we were to affirm the principle on which the country was built and not the men, or at least not the men who did the violence. Did he mean say "yes" because he knew the principle was greater than the men? . . . Or did he mean that we had to take responsibility for all of it, for the men as well as the principle, because no other fitted our needs. . . . Or was it, did he mean that we should affirm the principle because we, through no fault of our own, were linked to all the others in the loud, clamoring, semi-

visible world? . . . "Agree 'em to death and destruction," grandfather had advised. Hell, weren't they their own death and their own destruction except as the principle lived in them and in us? And here's the cream of the joke: Weren't we *part of them* as well as apart from them and subject to die when they died? (574–75; emphasis in original)

The Invisible Man deliberates (democratically arguing with himself) on how best to fulfill his commitment to democracy. Can he affirm democratic principles while harboring hate in his heart for particular people? Or does citizenship inevitably implicate our attitudes toward strangers? Do we fail as citizens if we hate other citizens? What is required of our interactions with strangers, given that "through no fault of our own, [we are] linked to all the others in the loud, clamoring, semi-visible world"? In weighing his democratic responsibilities, he comes to a breakthrough:

> Was it that we of all, we, most of all, had to affirm the principle, *the plan in whose name we had been brutalized and sacrificed*—not because we would always be weak nor because we were afraid or opportunist, but *because we were older than they in the sense of what it took to live in the world with others* and because they had exhausted in us, some—not much, but some—of the human greed and smallness, yes, and the fear and superstition that had kept them running? (547, emphasis added)

Something in the African American experience of sacrifice, he argues, has brought extra knowledge about the nature of democracy— "we were older than they in the sense of what it took to live in the world with others." This knowledge could be the basis of a new approach to citizenship. Back then to the grandfather's riddle.

"Agree 'em to death and destruction," the old man had said. Be "spies in the enemy's country." The Invisible Man's commitment to brotherhood seems to militate against espionage or duplicity, but this depends on how one plots the geography of the enemy's country and describes the nature of the injustice that characterizes it. Take the segregated South as an example. If exclusion is the basic injustice perpetrated by segregation, the segregating regime is a fundamentally sound political order, but for the unfortunate exclusion of black people. Then the charge that one should "agree 'em [those who are included in the public sphere] to death and destruction" seems an injunction to destroy a fundamentally healthy public sphere, and a refusal of brotherhood. If, however, one sees that segregationist regime in terms of domination, as Ellison did, the matter is otherwise. The dominated are inside the political sphere already ("Weren't we *part of them* as well as apart from them?"), with its two complementary forms of citizenship: one for the dominators and one for the dominated. The political cultures and forms of citizenship belonging to both groups are diseased. The target of the covert action is, therefore, not a fundamentally healthy order but rather a corruption within a failing polity. To "agree 'em [segregationists] to death and destruction" is to kill the segregationist within any given citizen off, in order to allow that citizen to be reborn as a full democrat.

But how on earth is "agreeing" supposed to bring about the sort of destruction that is really a transformation? The grandfather's sense of the subversive power of apparent agreement is traditional in African American culture: the paradox of agreeing to death invokes a characteristic trickster strategy. How does it work? First, the grandfather knows that his riddling counsel suits the U.S. enlightenment political system, threatened as it is by its paradoxical racist sophistry. The way to engage the issue of racism in the United States is to begin by agreeing—to the rights of humanity; that way leads to cultural self-contradictions and so, in the ideal, to political transformation. But the grandfather's second insight is more subtle. He realizes that those who agree, in the face of violence and domination, cast aggressive acts into the starkest relief by allowing them to expend their full force. Those who are agreeable in this way show up violent citizens for what they are, and force witnesses to the spectacle to make a choice about whether to embrace or disavow the violence. This was the effect of the Elizabeth Eckford photograph, and Ellison saw the techniques of activists like Martin Luther King, Jr., who "became overtly political through the agency of passive resistance," as serving precisely this purpose (WNJ 360).

Here it is crucial to understand, as Ellison did, that the modes of citizenship of the dominators and the dominated are not comprehensively diseased; each also retains some healthy elements. For instance, something in the African American experience of sacrifice, the Invisible Man argues, has brought extra knowledge about the nature of democracy. The "agree" in the phrase "agree 'em to death and destruction," stands in for an instruction to the Invisible Man to overemphasize the fundamentally healthy elements of the citizenship of subordination—the ability to agree, to sacrifice, to bear burdens in order to force contradictions in the citizenship of the dominated, until this citizenship caves in upon the rottenness of its inherent ills. From Ellison's perspective, the central question for an effort to craft new citizenly techniques, then, is how to integrate into one citizenship the healthy political habits of both the dominators and the dominated. Such an integration—and, importantly, it is integration or blending, not assimilation—is the response to injustice he advocates. It heals by destroying and destroys by healing. The effort to "agree 'em to death and destruction" should heal those who suffer from deeply embedded habits of injustice—both the dominators and the dominated—by letting their diseased habits kill themselves off.[13]

The best way to explain Ellison's suggestion that the healthy elements of malformed modes of citizenship can be used as political weapons is to consider again the epigraph to this book: "This society is not likely to become free of racism, thus it is necessary for Negroes to free themselves by becoming their idea of what a free people should be" (WNJ 356). The remark underscores the fact that even the dominated have forms of citizenship that contribute to the stability of the polity; if they change their own habits, the structure of the polity will be obliged to shift around them. The remark also admonishes all of us—for, as democratic citizens, we are all Negroes—that only citizens who recognize that domination breeds forms of citizenship suitable to it can undo its legacy and develop alternative habits for interacting with strangers that befit freedom and mutuality. As Elizabeth Eckford knew, citizens must have new habits to slip into if they are not to revert to yesterday's patterns. The invisible can exercise their own political agency precisely by converting the wisdom derived from their experience into the material from which to refashion the meaning of citizenship for everyone. All democratic citizens possess the agency of inventiveness.

To achieve such inventiveness is the great ambition of the epilogue to *Invisible Man*. As the Invisible Man says, "Yes, but what *is* the next phase?" (576). Here, in the epilogue, he presents his own most specific conclusions about the techniques needed for a passage toward a more democratic form of citizenship. Though he will be too vague, he is clear on one point: citizens must transform their habits of seeing, thinking about, and dealing with sacrifice and loss. Turning to exhortation, he makes these suggestions:

> Whence all this passion toward conformity anyway? Diversity is the word. Let man keep his many parts and you'll have no tyrant states. . . . America is woven of many strands; I would recognize them and let it so remain. It's "winner take nothing"; that is the great truth of our country or of any country. Life is to be lived, not controlled; and humanity is won by continuing to play in the face of certain defeat. Our fate is to become one, and yet many—This is not prophecy, but description. (577)

The Invisible Man's discovery that no political decision can be perfectly good for everyone has led him to the complementary conclusion that any policy will look different from the diverse perspectives of all the citizens. Though the polity lives under one law, it is as if it is many laws: "Our fate is to become one, and yet many." The question for Ellison, then, is how a politics of diversity (he stressed this term as early as 1952) can ensure that the winner of an argument "takes nothing," especially when some people remain unconvinced by the outcome of debate. "Take nothing" seems to mean that nothing should be taken that would endanger the continuance of the process. We should hark back to the discussion of Hobbes's laws of nature in chapter 7. Remember, he outlined types of interaction (about punishment, honor, and benefaction) where winners are too often apt to take so much as to prevent future cooperation. The injunction to "take nothing" also reminds winners that they can think creatively, even in their moments of victory, to invent alternate ways of satisfying those concerns that have been pushed to one side in the decision that resulted in their own gain. Parliamentary procedure closes discussion by deciding a winner. The conversation might have one additional step after the vote: an initial conversation on how, in the future, the community might address the concerns of those who have lost out in the present. The problem is not how a citizen can be a good loser in the political process (which has often been discussed), but rather how to move beyond the idea of the zero-sum political game to a conception of reciprocity so fluid that even a winner doesn't expect to stay a winner for long.[14]

Democratic citizens, Ellison frequently argued in his essays, need habits of "antagonistic cooperation."[15] As we have seen, the Invisible Man argues for a system of reciprocal sacrifice guided by four questions: Who sacrifices for whom? Are sacrifices voluntary? Are they honored? And are they reciprocated? These questions constitute the substance of a citizenship guided by solidarity or brotherhood. Ellison hopes for a form of democratic politics that might convey the wisdom of friendship into politics. Antagonistic cooperation involves admitting that the participants' interests diverge and then tussling over them, like friends, with the instruments of agreeability. Forward-looking citizens, like King, could use their political habits of sacrifice and agreeability, which already contain some of the elements of political friendship, to destroy political enmity and expand the reach and depth of a citizenship based on brotherhood. But above all else, Ellison proposes as central techniques that citizens learn to see the intricacy of their relations with strangers and in every possible instance convert their struggles with them into "winner take nothing" situations.

In the end then, the Invisible Man aspires to brotherhood, and proposes techniques for attending to the intricacy of our world, and reciprocity among citizens. If we addressed his questions about sacrifice, would we, in fact, have a foundation for a new citizenship?

Not quite.

"Ah," I can hear you say, "so it was all build-up to bore us with [some] buggy jiving. How can modes of citizenship developed by the dominated at one particular moment of crisis yield techniques for all democratic citizens? And isn't brotherhood vague, touchy-feely, and also, as the French revolutionaries proved, dangerous?" The skeptic has a point. Nor are the ideas of "winner take nothing" politics and a discourse for interrogating sacrifices any less vague. Have Ellison, and his invisible citizens, really taken us beyond where we were?

9

Brotherhood, Love, and Political Friendship

IS ELLISON'S "BROTHERHOOD" a reasonable political aspiration? In fact, "friendship" feels like a pretty tired-out term when introduced to political analysis. Who's going to listen to anyone who says, "Why can't we all just be friends?" Is there any point in trying to rescue friendship? In fact, I think it must be rescued, if we are to revitalize political insights that are fundamental to democratic, as opposed to aristocratic or oligarchical, practice.

Political theorists of different periods have often pointed to "something unnamable" as the ideal for relations among citizens. Ellison finally settled on a metaphor to define his vision: "The way home we seek is that condition of man's being at home in the world, which is called love, and which we term democracy" (*CE* 154). Hannah Arendt also fell back on metaphor in *Human Condition* (1958) when she argued for a citizenship based on respect: "Yet what love is in its own, narrowly circumscribed sphere, respect is in the larger domain of human affairs. Respect . . . is a *kind of 'friendship'* without intimacy and without closeness" (243; emphasis added). For her such respect—a mutuality that conveys a commitment to equality and shared decision making—is the prime enabler of democratic political activity. An agile shadow, like Ellison's "brotherhood," it can be arrested only by metaphor and simile. It is love, but in a different context; it is like friendship.

Hobbes, like the others, could not divine a single name to capture citizenly relations:

> There is yet another passion sometimes called love, but more properly
> good will or CHARITY . . . in which first is contained that natural
> affection of parents to their children, . . . as also that affection where-
> with men seek to assist those that adhere unto them. But the affection
> wherewith men many times bestow their benefits on strangers is not
> to be called charity, but either contract whereby they seek to purchase
> friendship or fear, which maketh them purchase peace. (*EL* 1.9.17)

In contrast to Ellison and Arendt, Hobbes reduces citizenship to fear
and divorces self-interest from altruism, as if the two were inherently
opposed motives.

Is Hobbes right to sever self-interest and altruism? Or do self-
interested political relationships need friendship? Like Ellison and
Arendt, Aristotle argued a counter case: "If men are friends, there is
no need of justice between them whereas merely to be just is not
enough—it is also necessary to be friends" (*NE* 8.1.4). The philosopher John Cooper interprets this remark that justice on its own is not
enough to mean that strict legality cultivates a hard sensibility that
must be softened through the cultivation of friendly relations with
fellow citizens. He writes, "The sense of justice, understood as respect for fairness and legality, is compatible with a suspicious, narrow,
hard, and unsympathetic character. . . . The sentiment of political
friendship in short, transforms what might otherwise be hard and
narrow forms of all the virtues."[1] But when Aristotle argues that
friendship, too, is necessary, he means necessary for politics, not for
personal virtue. As we shall see, it is not the emotions of friendship
that are relevant to politics but rather its core practices. Friendship, he
claims, has something to offer to politics that even justice does not.
In what sense can friendship substitute for justice? Where does it go
beyond it? These are the central questions of this chapter.[2]

Like Ellison and Arendt, Aristotle argued for the interchangeabil-
ity of friendship and successful citizenship. In the famous discussion of
the virtues in books 2–4 of the *Nicomachean Ethics,* he discusses liber-
ality, magnanimity, courage, and so on, but then a less frequently noticed political virtue appears. This one concerns interaction, speech,
and living together with strangers and acquaintances (*homilia, logoi,
suzen,* 2.7.13 and 4.6.1–9).[3] Specifically, it is the ability to "behave with
propriety" toward them. Like the others, this virtue too is a matter of

hitting a midway point between two extremes. Whereas a courageous person, for instance, hits a midway point between cowardice and rashness, citizens who behave with propriety toward strangers avoid acting, on the one hand, like acquiescent people who accept everything and "think it a duty to avoid giving pain to those with whom they come in contact" (*NE* 4.6.1–2) and, on the other, like domineering people who "object to everything and do not care in the least what pain they cause" (Ibid.). The central virtue of citizenship, then, is a midway point between acquiescence and domination.[4] When Aristotle wants to name this virtue, he too can't. "To it," he says, "no special name has been assigned, though it most closely resembles friendship. It differs from friendship in not possessing the emotional factor of affection for one's associates" (4.6.5). He draws the analogy between citizenship and friendship so far as to conclude, "In every constitution, friendship is as extensive as justice" (8.9.1). Friendship achieves what justice does.

What exactly is justice and what does it achieve?

Aristotle makes attempts on it from several angles, defining it in the *Nicomachean Ethics,* comparing and contrasting just and unjust regimes in the *Politics,* and proposing utopian visions of just cities in both the *Nicomachean Ethics* and the *Politics.* In the definition, he emphasizes the practices that constitute justice; in the comparisons, the outcomes of justice, and in the utopian vision, the problem that justice solves. It is necessary to lay these out, in a short section of exegesis, if we are to understand fully his link between justice and friendship. Once I have laid out the basic terms of Aristotle's account of justice, we will turn back to the question of friendship.

Aristotle famously defines justice as comprising both "universal" virtue and also one "particular" virtue. Justice in its universal aspect is the ability to act in accord with all the virtues: temperately, bravely, liberally, magnanimously, and also justly, in the particular sense of not taking more than one's fair share (*to ison*) and resisting the desire for "unfair gain" whether of money, honor, or something else (*NE* 5.2.6–12). Since his word for "fair," *to ison,* also means "equal," particular justice, or justice as fairness, is also the ability to manage equality properly. When he divides particular justice itself into two types, each consists of a different approach to this task.

Distributive justice, the first type, organizes the allotment of public goods—honor, money, property. It depends on a "geometric" or proportional notion of equality. For instance, two people get an equal amount to eat for dinner when each is served a portion in proportion to his appetite. Although one diner may get a larger serving than another, each will have been treated equally provided that in each case the serving matches the appetite. Every type of regime has its own principle of desert for deciding how to make proportional distributions: aristocracies, for instance, assign greater benefits to nobly born citizens. Aristotle advocates instead an approach in which people receive benefits from the public store equivalent to what they have given to it, and he consistently argues, for instance, that the rich should contribute proportionally more wealth to the public store and receive proportionally more honor in return. Honor is the good that the poor have to give.

The second type is "straightening-out justice." It ignores the public distributions that set all citizens in relation to one another geometrically and instead straightens out the private transactions that have gone bad between two people. These transactions may have been entered into by the victim either voluntarily, as in contracts and business deals, or involuntarily, as in theft, assassination, false witness, assault, murder, maiming, and abusive language (*NE* 5.2.12–13). Typically scholars have interpreted Aristotle to be recommending retributive punishment, whereby a wrongdoer suffers pain equal to what she has caused. In fact, the task of straightening-out justice is broader. Whereas distributive justice protects proportional equality, the straightening-out type focuses on arithmetical equality, or strict equivalence, whereby everyone simply gets the same quantity of whatever good is being distributed. Take the right to vote as an example. These days one cannot give out more or less of it, but only give it or not. Nor in contemporary democracy is the right to vote distributed in proportion to anything else; every adult gets one vote, even though one voter may be baser and another smarter.

Aristotle explains how arithmetic equality factors into straightening-out justice thus:

> It makes no difference whether an estimable man [*epieikes*] has defrauded an insignificant man [*phaulon*] or whether an insignificant man an estimable man, nor whether it is an estimable or insignificant

man that has committed adultery; the law looks only at the nature of the damage [*tou blabous*], treating the parties as equal, and merely asking whether one has done [*ho men . . . adikei*] and the other suffered injustice [*ho d' adikeitai*], whether one inflicted and the other has sustained damage. Hence the unjust being here the unequal, the judge endeavors to equalize it: inasmuch as when one man has received and the other has inflicted a blow, *the suffering* [to pathos] *and the doing* [he praxis] *of the deed are divided unequally* [dieiretai . . . eis anisa]. And the judge endeavors to make them equal by the penalty or loss [*zemiai*] he imposes, taking away the gain [*kerdous*]. (5.4.3–4; trans. modified slightly; emphasis added)

Every citizen deserves an autonomy equal to that of other citizens, but a crime leaves one person as a "doer" and another as a "sufferer." Straightening-out justice is responsible both for restoring and for preserving this equality of autonomy. Agency is the good it distributes according to the principle of strict equivalence.

As a set of practices, then, Aristotelian justice involves, first, managing an equal distribution of benefits and burdens and, second, protecting citizens' agency or autonomy. Equality and freedom are the objectives of this justice, but these are not the only outcomes of such practices. It's time to turn to Aristotle's comparisons of just and unjust regimes in the *Politics* for a closer look at the outcomes of just practices.

The discussion in the *Politics* emphasizes the importance of practices compatible with those discussed in the *Ethics*. Just regimes, for instance, govern according to the rule of law, which fends off arbitrariness and so protects the equality and freedom of citizens (*NE* 5.6.4–6; *P* 3.4.7, 4.9.1–6, 7.13.1–4).[5] And just regimes are governed in the interest of the people, not the ruler. But the most important point of comparison between just and unjust polities turns on their divergent outcomes. The best city makes its citizens virtuous, but there is a second, often overlooked point. The legitimate ruler rules *willing* and therefore free citizens/subjects; the tyrant rules *unwilling,* enslaved subjects (*hekontes* vs. *akontes: P* 3.9–10). To be ruled willingly is to have consented to obey (*boulomenos peitharkhein*) as opposed to having been forced to submit (*biazesthai*) (3.10.10). Practices for dealing with benefits, burdens, and autonomy in accord with principles of equality win as their reward the consent and allegiance of the governed. The just practices of the *Nicomachean Ethics* are therefore meant to achieve not only equality and autonomy but also consent and stability.

But why does Aristotle care about consent? For what problem are peace and stability evidence of a solution? The central problem of politics, conflicting desire, becomes visible just when it is resolved into the vista of utopia, and so I turn now to Aristotle's utopian descriptions. Interestingly, he brings friendship and justice together precisely here. Each is a practice invented as a response to the fundamental human difficulty of conflicts of desire.

Among the utopian states in the *Nicomachean Ethics* is the timocracy. In it equal citizens of perfect virtue rule and are ruled in turn (8.10.1–6, 8.11.5). Among them, concord obtains:

> Concord is not merely agreement of opinion, for this might exist even between strangers. Nor yet is agreement in reasoned judgments about any subject whatever, for instance, astronomy, termed concord; . . . Concord is said to prevail in a city when the citizens agree concerning their interests [*peri tôn sumpherontôn*], choose the same things [*tauta prohairontai*], and act on their common resolves [*prattosi ta koinêi doxanta*]. Concord then refers to practical ends, and practical ends of importance, and able to be realized by all or both parties. . . . Men are not of one mind merely when each thinks the same thing (whatever this may be), but when each thinks the same thing in relation to the same person . . . for thus all parties get what they desire [*houto gar pasi gignetai hou ephientai*]. . . . Concord appears therefore to mean friendship between citizens . . . for it refers to the interests and concerns of life [*peri ta sumpheronta gar esti kai ta eis ton bion anêkonta*]. (9.6.1–2)

The distinguishing feature of the ideal city is not so much agreement as the universal satisfaction of desire. The problem with imperfect worlds is not diversity of opinion but that this diversity necessitates the uneven satisfaction of citizens' wishes. Disappointment and frustration, not mere rational disagreement, are at the heart of politics. The objective of justice is to manage desire and its consequences.

In Aristotle's utopian timocracy the solution to conflicting desire is simple homogeneity. Everyone gets what he wants because everybody wants the same thing. The Greek for concord, *homonoia*, literally means same-mindedness. Everyone wants the same thing because all the citizens have one character. They are all perfectly virtuous:

> Now concord in this sense exists between good men, since these are of one mind both with themselves and with one another, as they always stand more or less on the same ground; for good men's wishes [*boulemata*] are steadfast, and do not ebb and flow like the tide, and they wish for just and expedient ends, which they strive to attain in common [*koinêi*]. (9.6.3–4)

Habermas tried to discover deliberative practices that might, theoretically, achieve perfect agreement, but Aristotle argues that unanimity is a conceptual possibility only if a set of identical citizens can also be conceived. Character is partly a matter of habituating experiences, he argues, and so a theorist of perfect agreement must expect these too to be identical throughout the citizenry, if his ideal is to have any real force. To desire consensus is to have begun to fantasize about a city of brothers, which is exactly what Aristotle calls his timocracy. His utopia flaunts its status as fantasy.

In the *Politics*, Aristotle does propose methods for cultivating homogeneity, arguing that governments should educate their citizens to virtue. But he also acknowledges, even in the *Politics*, the impossibility of a perfect city and the need for ideals for real cities, full of people of only ordinary ethical stature. The description of the timocracy as a city of brothers likewise qualifies his case for homogeneity (*NE* 8.11.5). It is an admission that an entire population of good men is an impossibility—as unlikely to gather as one woman is to give birth to an entire population. And how likely is a group of brothers to get along? Sibling rivalry was not trivial in the Greek imagination. Think of the two brothers, Eteocles and Polyneices, whose deaths initiate the action of the *Antigone*. They were supposed to share their father's throne, but one tried to stay in office for more time than he had been allotted. Out of their rivalrous self-interest came a battle in which both died. Real brothers and real polities, too, with diverse and less than virtuous citizens, Aristotle admits, will be persistently troubled by problems of rivalrous self-interest or, in Greek, *pleonexia*.

Our standard translation of *pleonexia* is "greed," but in fact it means simply "wanting more than"—more than someone else, more than what one deserves, more than is consistent with concord in the city.[6] This idea that rivalrous self-interest, or "wanting more than," is the basic problem of any human collectivity explains why Aristotle likes to think of both friendship and citizenship in terms of the relations between brothers. For him, brothers are exemplary friends, and this is not, ultimately, because they are like each other but because their relationships, especially, are plagued by rivalrous self-interest, and they can remain brothers only if they overcome it.

Pleonexia, the problem of "wanting more than," is not only an elegant description of sibling rivalry; it is also the basic problem that necessitates justice and legal systems. Citizenship, like brotherhood, is plagued by rivalrous desire, which, manifest in politics, can be solved neither by breeding brothers nor ultimately by cultivating virtue.[7] Polities use law to restrain rivalrous self-interest. Friendship introduces a different technique for solving this problem. Friends know that if we always act according to our own interests in an unrestrained fashion, our friendships will not last very long. Friendship teaches us when and where to moderate our interests for our own sake. In short, friendship solves the problem of rivalrous self-interest by converting it into equitable self-interest, where each friend moderates her own interests for the sake of preserving the relationship.

Aristotle's figure of the brothers idealizes not only politics but also friendship. "Friendship" was a broader category for him, as for all Greeks, than it is for us, covering not only companions who are not blood relations but also familial bonds like brotherhood and the father-son and husband-wife relationships. It included, too, the ties among members of a comrade group and among families that habitually played host to one another. In building a utopia out of brothers specifically, and not merely good men, he suggests that friendship itself, as distinct from virtue and homogeneity, offers resources for dealing with the problem of conflicting desire. No matter what size the community, or how virtuous, it must negotiate conflicting desires and their attendant disappointments and resentments. Friends do this routinely, even if actual brothers are often the most rivalrous of friends.

Justice and friendship are analogous in that each is a potential solution to the problem of conflicting desire; both friendship and justice cultivate habits of resolution. Aristotle's parallel between justice and friendship implies that political consent should resonate with the goodwill that arises in our successful friendships.

Significantly, friendship and virtue are separable for Aristotle. In his analysis, there are ethical, pleasure, and utility friendships. Only the first involve virtue. In ethical friendships, each party has achieved all the virtues; the friends unite out of mutual esteem and goodwill, which blossom into love. In pleasure friendships, they unite only for the pleasure to be had from interaction. Finally, utility friendships are profit driven, and these friends need not feel goodwill nor even pleasure. Importantly, Aristotle makes these distinctions among types of friendship only to blur them, and I will do the same here, providing an explicit explanation of the blurring toward the end of the chapter. Although pleasure and utility friends have not achieved virtue either independently or in conjunction, they do nonetheless establish functioning collaborations, and succeed at bringing the techniques of friendship to bear on rivalrous self-interest. Friendship can arise, Aristotle believes, even in contexts where greed prevails, not virtue. Utility friends may feel neither love nor goodwill, but they do experience consent; they already have a foot in the realm of politics.

Citizens are precisely such utility friends (*NE* 8.9.1–6).[8] As we saw, Aristotle argued that good citizenship amounted to interacting with strangers in ways that look like friendship even if, since they lack the emotional charge, they don't feel like friendship. In positing the category of the utility, or political friend, he suggests that the core practices of the best friendships can be separated from the emotions of love and goodwill and be distilled into habits for resolving rivalrous self-interest into consent in any context—whether friendly, commercial, or political. Contemporary writers about practical political arts like negotiation similarly propose a set of techniques for generating consent that might be equally useful in both friendship and politics. Roger Fisher and William Ury, authors of the bestselling book on negotiation techniques, *Getting to Yes,* write, "Every day families, neighbors, couples, employees, bosses, business, consumers, salesmen, lawyers, and nations face this same dilemma of how to get to yes without going to war" (xi). They remind us that our friendships work best when we and our friends have learned both how to negotiate conflicting desires (for instance, about what movie to see or where to have dinner) and also how to respond to betrayals of trust, such that both parties can restore their commitment to the relationship. They argue that the same simple insights apply to politics. As if to prove how similar are the techniques of friendship and politics, they market their book with endorsements from both personal column writer Ann Landers and former secretary of state Cyrus Vance.[9]

The core practice Fisher and Ury isolate is, once again, a midway-point mode of negotiation between domination and acquiescence. Like Aristotle's "political friend," the ideal negotiator in *Getting to Yes* is halfway between the "soft negotiator" who "wants to avoid personal conflict and so makes concessions readily in order to reach agreement" and the "hard negotiator" who "sees any situation as a contest of wills in which the side that takes the more extreme position and holds out longer fares better" (xviii). Friends are distinctively able to resolve conflicts of interest without recourse to domination; in seeking out the practical core of friendship we aim to find the basic elements of a non-dominating, nonacquiescent approach to interaction.

What, then, is friendship's core activity? Is friendship mainly talk? Is it mainly companionship? These are the answers people give most often when I ask them this question about friendship's core. Or do its main activities resemble the techniques of justice? Let us turn straight to an examination of friendships in contexts bereft of affect in order to see what remains after the emotion is withdrawn.

Aristotle isolates precisely such emotionless relationships when he speculates about the proper extent of a friendship network:

> But should one have as many good friends as possible? Or is there a limit of size for a circle of friends as for a city? 10 would not make a city and 100,000 is too much; though perhaps the proper size is not one particular number, but any number between certain limits. So also the number of one's friends must be limited, and should perhaps be the largest number with whom one can constantly associate [*suzên*] since living together is the most friendly thing [*philikôtaton*]. . . . Persons who have many friendships and are hail-fellow-well-met with everybody are thought to be friends of nobody, except politically [*plên politikôs*]: I mean the sort of people we call obsequious. (*NE* 9.10.3, 6)

With the last sentence, Aristotle distinguishes the intimacy of ethical friendships, which limits the number of our friends, from political relationships, which require no real intimacy and so can extend to the size of the city. The danger of pursuing something like friendship in political relationships is that one can fall into obsequiousness. This, indeed, is how people ordinarily understand the idea of political friendship, he suggests. But then he continues with a crucial rider: "It is true that one may be political friends to many people and not be obsequious but truly equitable (*hôs alêthôs epieikê*)" (9.10.6).[10] Here his argument harks back to his earlier discussion of the virtues where the citizen who hit the mean between obsequiousness and domination achieved something like friendship in his interactions with strangers. Now it turns out that to get political friendship right, to hit that mean, one must be equitable. At last we have a name for the practice that lies between domination and step-and-fetch-it acquiescence. Equity is friendship's core.

What, then, are equity's elements? First, for a political friendship understood in this rich sense to flourish, friends must feel that their relationship rests on equality: each must believe that the relationship's benefits and burdens are shared more or less equally; each friend needs equal recognition from the other; and each needs an equal agency within the relationship. Aristotle approvingly quotes a Greek proverb that runs, "Friendship is equality" (*philotes isotes*) (*NE* 8.5.5; cf. 8.8.5). Granted, he does not always mean that an equivalent to political equality obtains within all friendships. Father-son relationships, for instance, are defined by "geometric" equality, and in them fathers are superior to sons. In accordance with the proportion that fathers are greater than sons, they should give their sons the greater benefits, and in exchange sons should give them the greater portion of honor and power (*NE* 8.11.1–3; 8.12.5–6). In contrast, friendships among brothers rest entirely on "arithmetic" equality: each brother should receive an equal amount of power, honor, and material benefit (*NE* 8.6.7, 8.11.5).[11]

Notably, such negotiations over how to distribute power, honor, and material benefit are precisely the province that Aristotle assigns to his two types of particular justice. Friends learn how to negotiate such distributions with habits of reciprocity, but polities, he thinks, should employ distributive and "straightening-out justice." His ideal political regime of brothers achieves arithmetic equality, but real cities, he thinks, will inevitably distribute honor and material resources proportionally, and not according to strict equivalence. They will, though, distribute agency according to strict equivalence. They should follow the principles of justice to combine geometric and arithmetic equality so that the overall distribution achieves parity and all citizens have equal agency. If one citizen gets a lot of one good, she gets less of another. Although the rich will give proportionately more in money to the common good and the poor will give more honor, both rich and poor should have the same degree of agency and autonomy (*NE* 8.14.1–4). The important point here is that friendship's basic habits for establishing equality of material benefit, recognition, and agency do exactly the same work as justice. For this reason, friendship can seem like a substitute.[12] Friendship manifests itself in conversation and companionship, but the core practices that are necessary for a relationship to count as friendship are practices to equalize benefits and burdens and power sharing. Strangers can converse, or even hang out with each other, but if they don't act equitably toward each other, or are unwilling to share power with one another, they don't count as friends.[13]

But friendship goes beyond justice, too. The hardest part of friendship is not establishing a decent equality of benefits and burdens but preserving equal agency among all parties. As we have seen, ethical friendships are not troubled by conflicts of interest because, in their perfection, all the friends want the same things. But in all other relationships, friends have conflicting desires; if one is satisfied, another will not be: "A friendship whose motive is utility is liable to give rise to complaints for here the friends associate with each other for profit, and so each always wants more and thinks he is getting less than his due, and they make it a grievance that they do not get as much as they deserve and want" (8.13.4). Insofar as friends think they do not get what they deserve, they believe that a just equality in outcomes has been violated. But when they simply do not get what they want, they feel diminished agency. This latter situation is more common and so more difficult to solve. Friendship does not, however, accommodate the notion that agency and autonomy consist of having total control over one's actions, or of always getting one's way. Friends learn that limits on their agency can be compatible with a full sense of autonomy; they develop an extremely sophisticated approach to the relationship between agency and autonomy. To understand clearly how friends approach agency and autonomy, we must reconsider friendship's basic act: reciprocity.

Scholars typically describe reciprocity as a practice by which friends preserve parity in the distribution of both benefits and burdens over time.[14] But reciprocity also, and more importantly, allows friends to preserve equality of agency. In his discussion of utility friendship, Aristotle outlines three different types of reciprocal exchange that can make a utility relationship work. They differ not in how they achieve a parity of benefits but in how they handle each party's desire for control. He calls two of these types of reciprocity "legal" and one "ethical":

> Friendship based on utility may be either ethical or legal. . . . Such a connexion when on stated terms is one of the legal type, whether it be a purely business matter of exchange on the spot (from hand to hand) [*ek cheiros eis cheira*], or more liberal [*eleutheriôtera*] in respect to time, though still with an agreement about the reciprocal exchange [*ti anti tinos*]. . . . The ethical type on the other hand is not based on stated terms, but the gift or other service is given as to a friend [*hôs philôi*], although the giver expects to receive an equivalent or greater return. . . . One ought not to make a man one's friend if one is unwilling to return his favors. (*NE* 8.13.5–9)

Utility friends may bargain, simultaneously exchanging things from hand to hand; they may contract for an exchange on stated terms whereby one party provides the first service and the other returns it later. Both of these are legal types of reciprocity. Or, turning to ethical reciprocity, friends may make exchanges over long time periods without depending on stated terms. In all three types of reciprocity equality of benefits and burdens is established by straightforward exchange, although in the ethical relationship the friend who gives first can reasonably expect to receive in return even a bit more than he gave. Presumably this is because, in giving without requiring stated terms, he has also compromised his control, making himself vulnerable to the other party and diminishing his autonomous power to satisfy his own interests. The extra gift he receives repays his sacrifice of control.

The main difference between the three types of reciprocity is the level of vulnerability and the diminishment of agency to which the parties expose themselves. The barter exchange from hand to hand best expresses what's at stake: not equality merely but the desire of both parties to feel secure in their agency and in their ability to satisfy their own desires. Trust consists primarily of believing that others will not exploit one's vulnerabilities, and that one's agency is generally secure, even when one cedes some elements of it to others. In ethical exchanges, friends trust that their elected vulnerability will not permanently affect their general power to satisfy their own desires. But even hand-to-hand bargaining involves a modicum of trust that neither party has an overwhelming desire to master the other. Reciprocity, Aristotle argues, is the bond of the city because "it keeps people from feeling like slaves" (*NE* 5.5.6). His account reveals the shortsightedness of Habermasian disavowals of bargaining. Bargaining is not fundamentally different from the ethical act of coming to agreement; it is a first attempt at friendship and agreement in contexts where trust is shallow.[15] Bargainers have at least agreed not to violate each other's sense of agency.

Friendship limits a friend's agency and yet nonetheless generates consent and the experience of autonomy. In this regard, friendship is, in Aristotle's view, a model for how political freedom, properly understood, also works. Thus he writes,

> There is little or no friendship between ruler and subjects in a tyranny. For where there is nothing in common between ruler and ruled, there can be no friendship between them either, any more than there can be justice. It is like the relation between craftsman and tool, soul and body [or master and slave]: all these instruments it is true are benefited by the persons who use them but there can be no friendship nor justice towards inanimate things; indeed not even towards a horse or an ox, nor yet towards a slave as slave. For master and slave have nothing in common: a slave is a living tool, just as a tool is an inanimate slave. Therefore there can be no friendship with a slave as slave, though there can be as human being: for there seems to be some room for justice in the relations of every human being with every other that is capable of participating in law and contract [*ton dunamenon koinonesai nomou kai sunthekes*], and hence friendship also is possible insofar as one is human. (*NE* 8.11.6–7)

Autonomy no more consists of getting one's own way all the time in the political realm than in the sphere of friendship. It consists instead of getting one's way in concert with others, and as modified by them. Friends have different purposes and hopes, and yet they somehow yoke these in ways that preserve not only equality but also each friend's security in his autonomy. Practices of reciprocity coalesce in politics in the form of law and contract.[16] But it is friendship's ability to achieve ethical, and not merely legal, exchange that outpaces justice. The friend who gives something to another without stated terms makes a sacrifice, and when Aristotle at last defines the equitable man, he is "one who from practice and habit does what is equitable and does not stand on his rights unduly, but is content to receive a smaller share although he has the law on his side" (*NE* 5.10.8). He frequently repeats this: a friend disregards his own interest (9.8.2); he will surrender (*proêsetai chrêmata*) wealth and power for friends and country, confident that the honor he receives instead is the greater good (9.8.9). Ethical reciprocity begins with an act of sacrifice, and this is crucial to politics. No political order can meet the requirement that every collaborative decision be a perfect bargain for all parties, for "life is not long enough to repay all debts in utility and pleasure friendship" (9.10.2). Politics thus constantly opens exchanges that remain open for difficult lengths of time, or even forever, and nothing but ethical reciprocity can make such delay bearable. Friendship makes such ethical forms of exchange possible by ensuring that social contexts are shaped by equitable, not rivalrous, self-interest.

What exactly is equitable self-interest? Aristotle explains the idea by arguing that friends are "second selves" to each other. Friendship is the extension of one's interests to include someone else's in ways that annihilate loss:

> In being a friend to their friend, friends care for their own good. For the good man in becoming dear to another becomes that other's good. *Each party therefore both loves his own good and also makes an equivalent return by wishing the other's good.* (*NE* 8.5.5; emphasis added)

One wishes a friend well for one's own sake, because the friend and the friendship have become part of one's self, and when we give things up for the sake of preserving the friendship, we discover that disappointment and consent are existentially compatible phenomena. "[I]f friendship extends the self, then one is not so much sacrificing oneself, as acting in the interests of this new extended self."[17] In most circumstances, there should be limits to what one is willing to give up, but this does not obscure the basic point. Sacrifice is friendship's fundamental act, and a crucial political one in that it is the only action that reconciles agency and autonomy with not getting what one wants. Whereas rivalrous self-interest is a commitment to one's own interests without regard to how they affect others, equitable self-interest treats the good of others as part of one's own interests. Rivalrous self-interest creates the conflicts of agency that drive the main engine of politics, but equitable self-interest resolves them.

Equity thus entails giving in the public sphere, but there is more to be said about the equitability that characterizes friendship. Clearly, friends don't keep chits recording exactly who owes what to whom. Instead, when friendships successfully endure over time, it is because friends have developed heightened capacities for attending to what each is giving to the relationships and where each needs to repay a gift. Citizens, too, need to cultivate such habits of attention in respect to their fellow citizens. Equity entails, above all else and as in friendship, a habit of attention by which citizens are attuned to the balances and imbalances in what citizens are giving up for each other.

Here we must also confront the counterintuitive idea that citizens who give often and generously to other citizens may be distrusted, despite their equitability. Precisely because they are in a position to give more to other citizens than others give to them, they also often have the power to avoid making themselves vulnerable before strangers. They may be willing to give money or recognition to other citizens, and may do so frequently, but without giving them real power. They may have laid claim to a moral high ground, on account of their gifts, and to immunity from criticism that in itself provokes distrust. A friendship cannot survive if one friend insists on controlling all decisions, for friendship entails self-exposure.

Citizens who act like political friends not only befriend others, making sacrifices for them; they are also willing to ask those others for favors. It's important for us to remember that friends are people to whom we are willing to be in debt while also knowing that we must acknowledge and repay our debts.[18] Citizenship combines equitable flexibility and a developed discourse of reciprocity with real habits of power sharing. What counts as power sharing will differ with context, but anyone who wishes to cultivate trust across boundaries of distrust must aspire to bring people on either side of the relevant boundary into shared decision making with each other.

How do citizens develop equitable self-interest? Ethical friends achieve their second-self relationships, and develop equitable self-interest, because of emotional attachments; family members do so because of homogeneity and blood loyalty. But what about utility friends? Aristotle writes of their bond:

> All friendship as we have said involves some version of community [*koinoniai*]; the difference between families and comrades [*ten hetairiken*] on the one hand and citizens on the other is that the latter seem to be more in the way of a partnership [*koinonikais*] founded as it were on a definite agreement [*homologian*]. . . . In families the relationship comes not from agreement but from sameness. They are parts of themselves; one's offspring is a second self. (*NE* 8.12.1)

Utility friends develop their relationship on the basis of agreement. They are busier than brothers, needing to negotiate not only specific conflicts but also the continuance of their relationships. That they will inevitably seek the continuance of political relationships is one of Aristotle's biggest claims.

He argues that we human beings live in political communities not by accident but because we desire to share our lives with strangers (*suzên*) (*NE* 9.10.3; *P* 1.1.12, 3.4.3).[19] Living together "does not mean feeding in the same place, as with cattle, but conversing and communicating thoughts and plans" (*NE* 9.9.10) for the purpose of achieving some benefit in common (*to koinêi sumpheron, P* 3.4.2; cf. *NE* 8.9.4). That unnamed virtue, which is like friendship but without the emotional charge, is excellence precisely at living together with strangers. This excellence is motivated by our own desire to live with—and ultimately not merely to eat beside but to talk to—those strangers. Insofar as the preservation of the polity is in a citizen's interest, so too is it to her benefit to cultivate second-self relations even with strangers. For my own long-term good, *because I desire to continue living among strangers,* the self-interest that marks my regard for my fellow citizens should be equitable, not rivalrous.

Now we can see how friendship extends beyond justice. It contributes to politics two things that justice cannot. First, friendship cultivates a habitual expertise at the only practice that converts rivalrous into equitable self-interest. Sacrifice is the only act that might convince others to abandon legal for ethical forms of reciprocity and to seek suppler means than strict barter to preserve autonomy. A signal sacrifice, like Elizabeth Eckford's, declares a context of equitability, not rivalry, to obtain; her gift was one of faith. Second, friendship develops an awareness that our interests, properly understood, include a desire to preserve key relationships. Among these, the political bond especially requires active and constant rejuvenation. Character friendships are long-lasting, but utility relationships are not:

> Friendship between good men is alone proof against calumny; for a man is slow to believe anybody's word about a friend whom he has himself tried and tested for many years; and with them there is mutual confidence in the incapacity ever to do each other wrong, and all the other characteristics that are required of true friendship whereas in other forms of friendship [those of utility and pleasure] nothing keeps such things from happening. (*NE* 8.4.3)

In utility friendships trust is impermanent. The relationship must fight against the corrosion of the ethical type of reciprocity into the minimalist, legal hand-to-hand type. Only friendship teaches citizens how to start over again with symbolically significant acts that regenerate trust where it has disintegrated. Aristotle writes that the Athenians set up a shrine of the Graces, the goddesses of charitable giving, in a public place, to remind men that it is a duty not only to repay service done to one, but also to take the initiative in doing a service oneself (*NE* 5.5.6). Someone like Elizabeth has to go first.

Friendship thus turns out to be not merely a metaphor for citizenship but its crucial component. Why, then, have theorists been so tentative in positing a single name for good citizenship? The trouble is that citizenship engages so many human faculties and so diversely. It is not mere membership in a polity. It is not acting justly only, but also equitably. To do this requires (a) an *orientation* toward others, a recognition how and why we have an interest in their good; (b) *knowledge* that rivalrous self-interest is the basic political problem for democracy; (c) *habits* as flexible as friendship for distributing benefits and burdens with a view to equality and autonomy; and (d) a *psychological state* that in politics is called consent, but in other contexts, goodwill.

The pull to draw analogies between citizenship, friendship, and justice derives from an instinctual recognition that these are three of the most complex, and also rewarding, of human activities precisely because all three try to convert rivalrous into equitable self-interest. Only friends fully succeed at converting rivalry into equitability; wherever such a conversion occurs, people become friends. Only the idea of friendship captures the conjunction of faculties—the orientation toward others, knowledge of the world, developed practices, and psychological effects—that must be activated in democratic citizenship if it is to succeed. Finally, friendship goes beyond justice by teaching us something that legal justice on its own cannot. Friendship is conceptually important because our experience of it teaches us that self-interest comes in a variety of types, ranging from the rivalrous self-interest of brothers who kill each other for the father's throne, to the equitable self-interest of friends who have secured their relationship. There is no such single thing, self-interest, as some economists pretend. An orientation toward wealth maximization is only one of several varieties.[20]

Indeed, when we talk about self-interest as if it comes only in the rivalrous form, and as if legal systems are all we need to manage it, we are giving law too much credit for maintaining the social bond. The legal system does not on its own restrain, and cannot on its own manage, the problem of rivalrous self-interest. Aristotle's biggest philosophical claim about politics is that our political relationships with fellow citizens are no different from friendships. If we always act according to our own unrestrained interests, we will corrode the trust that supports political bonds. When political scientists, economists, and politicians argue that, if every citizen simply pursues her own self-interest without reservation, the common good will result, they make a sad mistake. No consensually based form of social organization can, over the long term, sustain relationships of cooperation in the face of unrestrained self-interest. The self-interest that marks a citizen's regard for her fellow citizens must necessarily, if it is to serve her well, be equitable. Our real social capital problem is simply that we have come to believe that self-interest comes only in one form, namely the rivalrous variety, when, in fact, it inhabits a spectrum from rivalrous to equitable. Any effort to cultivate friendship preserves a valuable cultural understanding of that spectrum.

Once again, the guilty party behind our modern tendency to reduce the notion of self-interest to its rivalrous variants and to elevate law as the only tool necessary for dealing with the problem is Hobbes. As we saw at the start of the chapter, he reduced citizenship to fear and set self-interest in opposition to charity. His strong distinction between self-interest and altruism was crucial to his effort to certify institutions as capable of solving the problem of distrust without any help from citizenship: if political bonds rest only on self-interest and fear, and not more broadly on practices like friendship, politicians, working within institutions, can sustain them simply by manipulating the baser human drives. But modern politics and its repeated and, if anything, proliferating experience of civil war has proved Hobbes wrong. Institutions cannot on their own solve the problem of rivalrous self-interest in the polity. There too, if citizens wish to secure the social bond that constitutes their polity over the long term, it is crucial to seek cultural habits based on equitable, not rivalrous, self-interest.

The cultivation of a cultural orientation toward equitable self-interest requires three things: first, recovery of the idea that self-interest comes in a variety of forms; second, recognition that preserving the political bond is in every citizen's interest; and third, an understanding that only equitable forms of self-interest can sustain the political bond, or any form of social bond. These are the philosophical claims that must anchor any cultural form in which the generation of trust is to be prioritized. They are in fact the ideas that already anchor friendship's core practices of equity and power sharing, and indeed, as transposed to our interactions with strangers, these habits of political friendship, equity, and power sharing are what give equitable self-interest, and the ideas behind it, living shape in the public world.

Friendship is the bond of the city, as Aristotle argued, and political friendship is not merely a serviceable aspiration, but a crucial one. Citizens who adopt it commit themselves to pursuing liberty and equality simultaneously, and to resisting accounts of politics that insist that commitment to one requires short-changing the other. (At present we are in more danger of losing the commitment to equality than the commitment to liberty.) Since most people spend more time practicing friendship than any other activity, getting better at it as they grow older, many of us have a rich intuitive knowledge of what maintains consensual relationships. But how on earth can the techniques and expertise of friendship be conveyed into the rivalrous realm of politics?

Rhetoric, a Good Thing

WHAT NEW HABITS, finally, should we adopt? I think we need a citizenship of political friendship. The phrase designates both a set of ideas and some core habits that might guide our relations to the strangers with whom we share our polity. I discussed the ideas implicit in political friendship in the last chapter; now I turn to the habits. How can the expertise of friendship be brought to bear on politics?

I begin with a simple thought. Remember that Aristotle had described political friendship as differing from ordinary friendship in "not possessing the emotional factor (*aneu pathous*) of affection for one's associates" (*NE* 4.6). This Aristotelian virtue of public life, concerning proper interaction with strangers, looks like friendship even if it doesn't feel like it, since an emotional charge is missing. Political friendship is not mainly (or not only) a sentiment of fellow-feeling for other citizens. It is more importantly a way of acting in respect to them: friendship, known to all, defines the normative aspirations. One doesn't even have to like one's fellow citizens in order to act toward them as a political friend. There is a very easy way of transforming one's relations to strangers. We might simply ask about all our encounters with others in our polity, "Would I treat a friend this way?" When we can answer "yes," we are on the way to developing a citizenship that is neither domination nor acquiescence. When the answer is no, we have not escaped our old, bad habits.

Beyond this simple question, there exist several other specific techniques for cultivating political friendship. It is time to turn to the imperfect ideals for trust production crafted in the rhetorical tradition. I find important aids to inject friendship into citizenship in Aristotle's *Art of Rhetoric*. That book is neither a guide to manipulation nor a superficial manual of style, but rather a philosophically subtle analysis of how to generate trust in ways that preserve an audience's autonomy and accord with the norms of friendship. Notably, he begins his treatise with the overarching point that a speaker must remember that it is the business of the audience to judge, not to learn (1.1.6). Here he invokes a distinction from the *Nicomachean Ethics* between the understanding of the judge and of the student. A judge's understanding operates in the field of opinion, where each must make her own decision; a student's understanding is to be led to truth by a teacher (*NE* 6.10.3–4). Rhetoric is the art not of rousing people to immediate or unthinking action but of putting as persuasive an argument as possible to an audience and then leaving actual choices of action to them. But let me provide some background on the *Art of Rhetoric,* that is, on the book itself, before I turn to its substance: the art of trust production.

In the *Nicomachean Ethics,* Aristotle had defined the art of politics as involving two distinct sciences: legislation, which deals in general, prescriptive rules, and judgment, which concerns the actions to be taken in particular cases (6.7). It is seldom noticed that the *Politics* concentrates only on legislation and primarily on constitutions, ignoring the subject of deliberation other than to affirm its importance and to argue that the many will typically judge better than a single individual. Aristotle left the study of judgment, and of the speeches that lead up to it, to the *Rhetoric.* Judgment is not merely the second political science but also, according to the *Rhetoric,* "that for the sake of which rhetoric is used" (2.1.2; cf. 1.1.10).[1]

Decisions that cannot be automatically determined by simple reference to the law, and that are ultimately a matter of judgment, are carried out in the realm of "equity," as Aristotle calls it. Equity is not merely that quality of character which aids conflict resolution among friends and friendly citizens; it also names the arena of public decision making where resolutions can be achieved only when citizens and politicians establish conditions in which adversaries can yield. Aristotle's account of the relationship between law and equity requires that judgments issuing from communal deliberation be compatible, like the rule of law, with the consent of citizens, whose equality and autonomy they protect.² The quality of the citizenly speech preceding a judgment will determine whether citizens can make their equity decisions justly.³

What kind of persuasion is compatible with legitimate consent? Interestingly, Aristotle's discussions of consent also identify the varieties of legitimate persuasion. He describes those who have consented to obey in legitimate regimes with the Greek phrase *boulomenoi peitharkhein*. This term, *peitharkhein*, has the word for persuasion, *peithô*, in it; the phrase *boulomenoi peitharkhein* therefore identifies people who obey because they wish (*boulomenoi*) to obey on the basis of having been persuaded. He also uses the term *peitharkhein* to talk about the operations of the soul, and this other usage delimits precisely the kind of persuasion that is compatible with consent.⁴ "The irrational part of the soul has two parts," he writes, "one that is vegetative, and one that shares the rational principle to the degree of being amenable to it and persuadable by it [*peitharkhikon*] even as we say one consents [*logon echein*] to the speech of father and friends and not as in mathematics" (*NE* 1.13.18). This description of one part of the soul consenting to another part has within it two different models for understanding the nature of persuasion: it may be equivalent to the speech either of father to child or of friend to friend. The former establishes a hierarchical relationship between speaker and audience, the latter a relationship of democratic equality. As it turns out, the hierarchical model is nowhere to be found in the *Rhetoric* as example, explanation, or justification for the art of rhetoric; persuasion is treated solely as the speech of a friend. For instance, Aristotle remarks that those who are stronger than others force people to do things (*anagkazo, kreissous*), but friends persuade each other (*peithoi, philoi*) (*R* 2.19.9–10). Masters (*kurioi*), in contrast—and fathers were masters in ancient Greece—use a combination of force and persuasion. To be fully a "persuader" and not a master or aggressor, one must address oneself to others as a friend and democratic equal.⁵

And which others, exactly, should one address this way? Aristotle asks his students to imagine speaking to an audience consisting of people from diverse economic classes and with varying abilities, educations, and experiences. They are even to imagine that their audiences include people who envy or dislike them as well as people who believe slanderous lies about them. Finally, the art pertains not only to public life but to every citizen's daily interactions. "Everybody," he says, "has in a manner a share in both rhetoric and dialectic since everyone, up to a certain point, endeavors to criticize or uphold an argument, and to defend himself or to make accusations" (R 1.1). The *Rhetoric* is in fact a treatise on talking to strangers. At last, we have hit upon some useful clues as to how to do that.

To understand trust, one must begin with distrust. Two types of it trouble politics. First, there is the distrust that arises from the instability of political events, and the difficulty that any of us has in trying to judge facts, causes and effects, and the relations of past and present to future in the political realm. Second, there is interpersonal distrust, or distrust of one's fellow citizens themselves. This arises from a citizen's uncertainty about how others' interests will affect his own vulnerabilities, and about how other citizens will see the relationship between their interests and his own. In order to dispel the first sort of distrust, which is caused simply by factual uncertainty, a speaker must give his audience good reason for trusting his facts and factual analyses. He must prove to his audience that his proposals to resolve particular problems are most likely to navigate future obstacles successfully. This is the first challenge a speaker faces. The problem of interpersonal distrust introduces three more challenges. A speaker must try to bring an element of predictability to the unstable world of human relations; he must tackle negative emotions like anger and resentment and try to convert them to goodwill; and above all else, he must prove that his approach to self-interest is trustworthy. In meeting these three challenges, the speaker addresses the ethical status of the proposed policy.

This distribution of effort—in which 75 percent of the work of political conversation is directed toward generating interpersonal trust among citizens—already makes the important point that in every political discussion, audiences are always judging not merely the pragmatic political issue under discussion—say, the most cost-effective way of providing health care—but also a speaker's commitment to developing relations among citizens and forms of reciprocity that justify trust.[6] Decisions about how to handle health care must be satisfying on these grounds too. Logic, understood technically as demonstrative argument, is on its own insufficient to bring debate to a successful close in the deliberative forum. In fact, language equips us with three distinctive capacities for meeting the challenges of distrust. They are our capacities (1) to make logical arguments, (2) to convey character, and (3) to engage the emotions of our audience. A speaker's display of character or her response to an audience's emotions does not involve her in irrational speech. Aristotle's important point is that reason, properly understood, extends beyond arguments about natural facts (say, historical or physical facts), and even beyond arguments about universal or universalizable principles. Reason extends beyond such subject matter as can be handled by demonstrative logic and also has the job of helping us draw conclusions about how people are likely to treat others. These are conclusions about human probabilities. What is the probability that a speaker is telling the truth when she introduces facts to support her arguments? Is another speaker likely to act in accord with the general principles he espouses? How likely is it that the fear that still another speaker inspires accurately anticipates some evil that may come from her proposal? A speaker's words, all of them, including those used in her logical arguments about facts, causes, and effects, also provide information about a speaker's reliability and about whether circumstances obtain to justify particular emotions. This information about probabilities also belongs to the domain of reason, regardless of whether the words that convey it are part of a logical syllogism crafted by the speaker. Even words dropped casually into speech can trigger syllogisms in the listener. I offer a crude example that makes the point easy to see. An audience member who hears a slur against her ethnic group will distrust the speaker, and her distrust rides on the following syllogistic thought: "Speakers who use ethnic slurs are not likely to take the interests of the slurred group to heart; the speaker has just made a slur against my group; she is therefore not likely to take the interests of my group to heart." The project of persuasion depends on speakers' recognizing the rationality involved in ordinary, human judgments about the probable behavior of others.

How, then, do our three speech capacities—to make logical arguments, to convey character, and to engage emotions—combine to dispel both the distrust caused by factual uncertainty and interpersonal distrust? When I raise this question to students, they often leap excitedly to the conclusion that we use demonstrative logic to deal with factual uncertainty and other speech techniques to convey character and respond to our audience's emotions. If only matters were so tidy! In fact, demonstrative argument can do relatively little about a lack of factual clarity. Take the case of a country facing decisions about whether and how to go to war. More often than not, even when it has made its irrevocable decision, facts, probabilities, and likelihoods remain murky. Regardless of how logical (in the technical sense) are the arguments for or against war, which are inevitably strung together from only the few facts that can be publicly agreed upon, they will not in themselves convince an audience that a speaker has an accurate, credible analysis of the future. In political controversies, there will always be logical arguments for a counterposition, on the basis of exactly the same facts. In this circumstance, no amount of logical argument will determine which speaker to trust. Audiences will turn to assessments of character, and so our capacity to convey our habitual mindsets turns out to be directed not merely at concerns about interpersonal relations, but also at the distrust arising from factual uncertainty. But in what sense is character relevant to this type of distrust?

People trust those who have the ability to make astute, pragmatically successful decisions in contexts of uncertainty and who can convey that practical levelheadedness through speech (*R* 2.6.17; cf. 2.6.21). Just as one prefers to be a passenger in a car whose driver processes large amounts of information quickly and can navigate an efficient, safe path through a world of constantly changing obstacles, so too one finds speakers persuasive who convey competence at practical reason in political affairs. For Aristotle, competence at practical reason is a character virtue—*phronêsis* in the Greek.[7] And how does one know someone has this ability? For Aristotle, character virtues are a matter of habit. If a policy advocate has previously made nine good proposals out of nine attempts, the likelihood is that his tenth will also be good. A speaker who wishes to convince his audience that his policy proposal is likely to bring practical success would do well to find ways of conveying to his audience that he does have such habitual competence. This is not so much a matter of reciting one's record as of recounting at least some of the thought process involved in one's previous successful proposals. The point is to display to an audience that one's habitual thought processes lead to pragmatically successful endeavors. The question of character arises here to prompt an assessment not of a speaker's personal morality in general, but only of the probable efficacy of his proposals. Where logic cannot dispel the distrust that arises from uncertainty about the future, arguments from character often can. Character judgments, when they focus on evaluating a speaker's competence at practical reason, are assessments of probability as to whether the proposed policy is likely to achieve success.[8]

This is not the only way that character affects persuasion. Clearly, audiences will distrust a speaker whose policy proposals are merely practicable. A proposal to save public funds by ceasing to collect garbage from the homes of the elderly may be practicable but meets obvious ethical objections. In conveying his character, a speaker reveals not only his decision-making habits but also the ethical commitments that guide his treatment of other people. This draws us away from the issue of factual uncertainty and into the area of interpersonal distrust. Much more might be said, and Aristotle does say much more, about how to dispel the distrust arising from factual uncertainty, but since my concern in this book is indeed with interpersonal trust, I turn now to that issue.

Once again, there is no neat correlation between our three different speech capacities and the types of distrust. In fact, a speaker's logical arguments are central to how she conveys her character, and this for two reasons. Aristotle recommends that speakers construct the logical element of their argument around general principles. His term is "maxims," and he offers as an example the proverb that "the true friend should love as if he were going to be a friend forever" (*R* 2.21.14). For Aristotle, the principles one espouses express character. Demonstrative argument about general principles brings to the fore a speaker's ethical commitments concerning the treatment of others, allowing an audience to assess these principles easily and to decide whether they render a speaker reliable. But the use of general principles has another important effect too.

In advocating the use of maxims, Aristotle seems close to the Habermasian argument that speakers should always try to convert their opinions into universal or universalizable terms in order to test whether those arguments are good for everyone. In fact, he is less interested in universality than in the value of general principles for social stability. In using maxims, an Aristotelian speaker does not so much check whether her position is good for all as draw herself into a contract with her audience in order to stabilize the future (the responses of her audience will tell her whether the principles are good for other people, too). Speakers who use universal principles—a language of eternity—indicate a willingness to fashion rules in the present that they too will have to abide by in the future; perhaps those rules will compromise those very speakers' interests in the future. This does not mean that a community's principles are set in stone after a public debate—only that those who have proposed particular principles have committed themselves to being judged by them at some future point, should other citizens choose to return to them. In using a language of eternity, and thereby accepting the possibility that her fellow citizens may one day use her own principle in cases where she will lose out, a speaker helps bring predictability to human relations and also accepts some degree of vulnerability before her fellows. In short, she embraces a rule-of-law approach to politics whereby decision-rules are decided in advance of the appearance of the cases to be decided by them, and she offers her audience an opportunity to set the content of those predetermined principles. The best test of a policy proposal is whether the principles on which it is based are consistent with the terms on which citizens can live together. Speakers who use generalizable rules draw a rule-of-law ethos beyond institutions into ordinary interactions and help bring predictability to human relations.

An example of the role of logical argument in clarifying ethical commitments, as distinct from factual claims, can be found in events surrounding the U.S. invasion of Iraq. Prior to March 2003, when the U.S. invaded in its first-ever application of the doctrine of preemptive strike, which the administration had put forward in its 2002 foreign policy statement, citizens and pundits debated whether Iraq had weapons of mass destruction, and whether there was a connection between Iraq and the terrorist group Al-Qaeda. These were fairly fruitless arguments. The facts, had we been able to reach public agreement about them, would have mattered, but logical argument itself was unable to achieve factual clarity on these issues. On the contrary, these arguments generated ever-increasing levels of confusion about the pertinent facts. In contrast, citizens debated very little about whether the doctrine of preemptive strike is compatible with a democratic way of life, let alone the terms on which it might be compatible. If citizens and politicians had wanted to produce political stability, this question should have been at the center of the debate. Logical argument often cannot clarify the facts of uncertain political situations, but it can always provide a public airing of communal standards and reinforce a rule-of-law culture.

A rule-of-law ethos cannot, however, simply be equated with a fixation on rules; it entails a more fundamental commitment to social predictability and to a limited but acknowledged vulnerability of citizens to each other. A rule-of-law ethos can therefore be drawn into ordinary relations even without the use of maxims or general principles. The events of the U.S. invasion of Iraq yield two odd, but useful, examples here. The British, important allies to the U.S., had been assigned the job of securing Basra, and in the war's immediate aftermath, generally did a much better job than the U.S. military in cultivating trust among hostile Iraqi citizens. Many commentators pointed this out, and attributed the British success to their army's experience with hostile civilians in Northern Ireland.[9] Trust-generation, the commentators suggested, is a cultural habit.

What, then, did the British do to try to bring peace out of war? Upon capturing the headquarters of the ousted Baath party, they allowed local civilians to ransack it, contrary to standard procedure to halt all looting. The British soldiers had found a way to show symbolically that the arbitrariness of the ruling Baath party no longer held sway in Basra; not only were the British now in charge, but things would be counter to what they had been. In permitting the looting, the British allowed an exception because it confirmed a rule, and so the aim of this lawlessness was, ironically, to establish a rule-of-law ethos. Also, at a point when U.S. soldiers were still decked out in full armament, the British wore soft berets and shed their body armor, accepting some vulnerability to make the point that the time had come for peace. Both gestures—the blow struck to arbitrariness and their elected vulnerability—revealed a sophisticated relationship to rhetoric and display; both symbolic acts astutely conveyed the character of a rule-of-law culture, and in so doing might have served as foundation stones for rule-of-law institutions.

In the end, though, the British efforts at trust-generation had less success than anticipated. Similarly, even a speaker who has managed to deal with factual uncertainty, who has convinced his audience that his core principles are sound, and who has found ways to cultivate a rule-of-law ethos, has by no means yet faced his most difficult challenges. He must still tackle negative emotions like anger, fear, and resentment. At the core of such emotions are problems of self-interest. Envy, indignation, and the like are often judgments on an important matter: do a speaker's interests clash or harmonize with those of his audience?

Many commentators have taken Aristotle's willingness to discuss the political impact of emotions as proof that rhetoric inevitably disintegrates into a sophistic manipulation of the passions. But, on the contrary, he frames his arguments by criticizing speakers who "warp" (*diastrephein*) their auditors by rousing them to anger, envy, and pity. Also, he repeatedly insists that speakers prepare their audiences emotionally "in a certain way" (*poion tina kai ton kriten kataskeuazein*), and then casts his discussion of the emotions as an analysis of goodwill (*eunoia*) and friendship (*philia*), saying, "It is necessary, with these discussions about the emotions, to take up the subject of goodwill and friendship" (*R* 2.1.7). The "certain way" in which audiences should be prepared is such that they are ready for the possibility that goodwill and friendship can arise between them and other citizens.

I want here to be precise about the role of each of these terms, friendship and goodwill, in the project of trust production.[10] Aristotle takes care to distinguish friendship, and also hatred, from the emotions. Both are habitual dispositions, or sets of practices for interacting with others, not passions.[11] Significantly, he concludes his discussion of friendship and hatred by remarking, "It is evident, then, from what we have just said that it is possible to prove (*apodeiknunai*) that men are enemies or friends, or to make them such if they are not; to refute those who pretend that they are, and when they oppose us through anger or enmity, to bring them over to whichever side may be preferred" (*R* 2.4.32). This is the only passage in the discussion of the emotions that states what rhetoricians need to accomplish when they engage with the emotions, and the possibility of generating (or destroying) friendship is just what's at stake. Goodwill is the pivotal emotional element of this work, because it is an emotion that can arise between strangers and that paves the way for friendship. But to get to goodwill and then to friendship, a speaker needs to work principally with negative emotions.

The emotions, as Aristotle defines them, are pleasures and pains (*lupai*) that, as they change, affect men's judgments (*kriseis*) (R 2.2.1). These pleasures and pains mark moments when people's interests are either satisfied or left unfulfilled, and so emotion registers the effects of loss and sacrifice on politics. "All men rejoice when their desire comes to pass and are pained when the contrary happens; so that pains and pleasures are signs of their interest" (R 2.4.3). A speaker who seeks to inspire trust must be especially concerned with the pains, or losses. In the *Rhetoric,* Aristotle investigates ten specific emotions: anger, fear, shame, charity, pity, indignation, envy, emulation, mildness, and confidence. Notably, all but the last two are pains, or sympathetic responses to the pains of others. Nor are the two exceptions, mildness and confidence, pleasures exactly. Mildness is only the absence of pain (R 2.3.12), and confidence is the absence of the particular pains that characterize fear. Recognizing that anger, fear, and the other negative emotions on the list are the critical political passions, Aristotle teaches his speakers to deal with the impact of feelings of loss on politics by converting the negative emotions into these other two, mildness and confidence. This conversion is prior, even, to any effort to inspire the positive emotion of goodwill. How can such a conversion be accomplished? A question for our time.

Emotions have conceptual structures, as Aristotle argues; this is what makes it possible to intervene in them. Anger, for instance, differs from indignation in that the first arises when one gets less than one thinks is one's due; and the second, when someone else gets more than what one believes to be her due. People are talked into their feelings of loss insofar as their assessments of what they are owed rest on ideas about what is due to whom within their polity, and such ideas derive from discourse.[12] They can, therefore, be talked out of them. One can counteract the anger, for instance, by proving that no slight occurred, or that it was unintentional. One can assuage fear by revealing or creating safeguards. And for a range of the negative emotions, one can draw on the techniques of mourning.[13] As Aristotle anatomizes the conceptual content of the negative emotions, he constructs a very precise taxonomy of political vulnerability. Speakers who succeed at dealing with the play of emotion in politics find ways to minimize that experience for others. But a speaker can begin the process of turning negative emotions first into mildness and then into goodwill only if she takes the time to identify precisely which ones buoy up the distrust she intends to disarm. Which emotion is the problem precisely? Having answered this question, the speaker can then engage the conceptual content particular to that emotion.

Importantly, the negative emotions are pains that register not merely objective, but also "apparent," losses, to use Aristotle's terminology. Speakers always have to deal with exactly how painful a given proposal *appears* to their audience, regardless of their own beliefs about how much suffering their proposals in fact inflict. Citizens' idiosyncratic perceptions of events and beliefs about their due and that of others within their polity determine the intensity of their feelings of loss. Democratic citizens are obliged to recognize that even the subjective experience of loss is politically significant, for it establishes the extent of any given citizen's consent to a polity's policy. Although we may wish it otherwise, citizens can negotiate loss and generate trust only on the shifting ground of subjectivity.[14] This does not mean that apparent losses and real losses should be treated in the same way. The first step in dealing with apparent losses is to make the case that the loss is only apparent. If citizens can be convinced on this account, the real pain they feel in respect to their apparent loss should shift in its nature; citizens would then deal with the remaining pain felt by their fellows on the terms necessary to it, whether through mourning techniques, techniques of reassurance, or other psychologically relevant responses.

Public negotiation even of apparent pains is crucial to democratic deliberation because it gives a community an opportunity to address inconsistencies in how different citizens think benefits, burdens, recognition, and agency should be distributed within the polity. Since these are the basic topics of justice, it is in addressing, and trying to resolve, negative emotions, that a citizen-speaker contributes most to refining his polity's account of justice. Only by addressing negative emotions with a view to generating goodwill can a citizen find the seeds of improved citizenly interactions and a more democratic approach to the problem of loss in politics. Citizens must, then, cultivate their capacities to identify the particular emotions at play in respect to any given political question as well as refining their understanding of how particular emotions can be dealt with. Here I have named only the emotions to which citizens must especially attend: anger, fear, shame, charity, pity, indignation, envy, emulation. Each has its own conceptual structure and requires a logical response fitted to that structure. For now, I leave it to citizens to study the particular content of each of these emotions independently, or with Aristotle.

Once a speaker has converted negative emotions to mildness, the next task is to convert mildness to goodwill. Goodwill is not friendship proper but only its first root. It blossoms into friendship only after it becomes mutual (*NE* 8.2.4, 9.5.3). The actual production of goodwill therefore involves two steps. A speaker must display her own goodwill to an audience, and then must inspire reciprocal goodwill in them.

How can a speaker prove his own willingness to befriend his fellow citizens? Here, since any willingness to be friends involves a desire to enter into real, and not merely juridical, peer relationships with one's fellow citizens, we return to the topic of freedom and equality. To prove that one speaks as a friend one must demonstrate a commitment to the equal autonomy of all citizens. As we saw, Aristotle began his treatise with the overarching point that a speaker must remember that it is the business of the audience to judge, not to learn. In essence, if a speaker is to know that his audience consists of judges rather than of passive and submissive students, he must check that the audience is not simply suffering in silence while being told what to do. It is evidently to this end that Aristotle recommends that speakers be willing to let anybody whom the people choose judge their speeches (*R* 3.16). Citizens who are political friends do not stray into patronizing their fellow citizens. They are willing to share power with their audiences and to make themselves vulnerable to them. This was the important message of the soft berets worn by the British in Iraq. They chose unnecessary, conspicuous vulnerability in order to prove themselves trustworthy. In political deliberation, Aristotle requires that citizens accept being vulnerable before the judgment of *any* of their fellow citizens, even those of diverse social classes and backgrounds.[15]

The requirement that speakers submit to the judgment of any randomly chosen audience member has another important effect, too. It forces speakers to ask themselves whether their narratives will seem to everyone a convincing account of reality. The willingness to be judged by anyone whatsoever cultivates in citizen-speakers the regular habit of checking how different proposals look from perspectivally differentiated positions within the citizenry. This habit is crucial to generating trust, because citizens generate goodwill when they can prove that they are concerned to address the whole citizenry and not merely the 50 percent plus one whom they need to carry a vote. This technique helps reduce the play of negative emotions in politics by anticipating and avoiding them. The speaker who checks how a proposal will look from all the perspectivally differentiated positions within the citizenry explores the problem of loss in advance of the imposition of losses on particular people, and deals with it directly. Citizen-speakers should be vigilant not to induce a feeling of political vulnerability in their audience; and to deal effectively with negative political emotions, they must both anticipate how their proposals will sound to their diverse fellow citizens and also develop their willingness to be judged by any fellow citizen.

Again, I will offer a small success story that reveals the connection between anticipating negative political feelings by listening to the whole of one's audience and successfully dealing with those emotions. In 2002 Los Angeles hired, as its chief of police, Bostonian William Bratton who was credited with "licking" crime in New York during his time as police commissioner there from 1994 to 1996. When he got to LA, he decided to tackle gangs, and to quote the *Economist*, immediately "declared 'war' promising to take back the streets" (March 22–28, 2003, 30) This was his mistake. When he began to cultivate his "many constituencies," talking to rich folk in restaurants but also spending time at churches and with neighborhood organizations in Central Los Angeles (as the city has renamed notorious South Central), the people in Central L.A. told him "that talk of 'war' was not a good tactic." One makes war only on those with whom one will not share a polity; to declare war on a neighborhood or set of citizens is tantamount to banishing them. The point of the term is to intimidate and produce political vulnerability. Bratton rightly dropped the term and as a result has gained some trust to make his job easier. The *Economist* concluded its report by saying, "If Mr. Bratton is to win the approval of LA's honest citizens, he will have to teach his officers the lesson he learned himself—less war and more jaw" (ibid.). To provoke or assuage people's sense of vulnerability is learned behavior. Cops, too, learn how to succeed or fail at trust production, and public diplomacy is as necessary at home as abroad.

Now, to the final, crucial question. Having proved her goodwill toward her audience, how does a speaker also inspire others to feel goodwill? Here the main challenge is to prove that one's approach to self-interest is trustworthy. This is the most fundamental element of trust generation and the task that Aristotle prioritizes. Above all else goodwill springs up, he argues, in response to a display of equity (*epieikeia*) (9.6.4). As we have seen, an equitable person displays the generosity of friendship and is "content to receive a smaller share although he has the law on his side" (*NE* 5.10.8). Here we are again, at the need not only for flexibility but even for sacrifice. Equity is the core of friendship and also of trust production. A speaker's equitability shows that her own interest in preserving her community has led her to moderate her other interests. This display allays an audience's distrust of the speaker's self-interest, from which all of the most politically corrosive distrust arises. The British in Basra are said to have captured a high-ranking Iraqi officer in the middle of the street with a crowd of boys around. They found beside him in his vehicle a significant stash of Iraqi cash. Rather than turn it in to their own officers, according to standard procedure, the soldiers distributed the cash to the boys. They were buying them, yes, but the soldiers were also showing that their own self-interest did not extend so far as to override the boys' self-interest. The soldiers were advertising themselves as people who employ equitable, not rivalrous, self-interest. This is the basic move required for generating trust.

Of course, we have already encountered a significant example of this move. As we have seen, an exemplary sacrifice, like Elizabeth Eckford's, declares a context of equitability, not rivalry, to obtain. Aristotle has a word for the ability to be good at such acts of equity. It is *suggnomê*. Usually translated as forgiveness, *suggnomê* more literally means "judging with" (*NE* 6.11.1). "Forgiveness" captures only the form of equity that operates in the judicial realm, when a prosecutor requests or a judge imposes a lesser penalty than the law allows. "Judging with" in the deliberative context is less forgiveness than the ability sometimes to argue for or to accept a decision that, to some degree, goes against one's own interests or is even less than one's due. Speakers need not shed their private interests when they advocate policies, but they must prove that they have in the past been and will again in the future be willing to accept decisions that benefit themselves less than others.[16] If a speaker openly takes less than his legal share now and then, he will generate goodwill in his audience. The key to generating trust is, above all else, an ability to prove that one governs one's life by equitable, not rivalrous, self-interest.

But the game of generating trust does not end with that sacrifice. If all else fails and a citizen is unable to talk his audience around to mildness and confidence, he can always make a signal sacrifice. Indeed, in contexts where trust has completely disintegrated, someone has to go first, as did Elizabeth. No single act of sacrifice can, however, complete the work of generating trust until its audience reciprocates. To quote Aristotle again, "A friend is one who befriends and *is befriended in return,* and those who think their relationship is of this character consider themselves friends" (*R* 2.4.7; emphasis added).

Political friendship must be reciprocal, and Elizabeth Eckford's sacrifice was at last converted from a symptom of domination into an act of equity only when it became clear that her fellow citizens around the country would reciprocate her self-sacrifice by accepting changes to their political regime. Had they not reciprocated, people in positions like Elizabeth's would have had further grounds to distrust their fellow citizens.[17] People who offer up sacrifices do not do it for nothing; they always aim to engage equitable reciprocity, and at the very least, like Jepthah's daughter, implicitly expect to earn honor, gratitude, and respect.

Aristotle might, with his stress on equity, friendship, and reciprocity, seem to set even more utopian standards for his speakers than do the deliberative democrats of chapter 5, but, to the contrary, his recommendations are embedded not in an argument about what citizens *ought* to do, but instead in an argument about what democratic persuasion demands for success. No decent judge, he argues, would consent to an argument in which a speaker does not establish a rule-of-law ethos, display equity, and cultivate goodwill in addition to making logical arguments. His rules for persuasion also constitute a theory of the grounds for reasonable consent, and so his *Art of Rhetoric* is as much a guide for listeners, who give or withhold their consent, as for speakers.[18] Equity comes into existence in the interaction between speaker and listener.

Equity is so important to Aristotle because no agreement can ever be equally good for all citizens, reconciling all their various interests and outlooks. No political decision can garner ardor from every citizen. To make consensus politics possible, democratic citizens need ways to consider those communal decisions that do not go in their favor as nonetheless decisions to which they can consent. The idea that one consents even to those decisions that go against one's own interests, out of political friendship for the good of the other, makes such decisions products of an autonomous choice for everyone, and not tyrannical constraints on one's freedom. Rhetoric, understood as the art of talking to strangers as equals and of proving that one has also their good at heart, inspires the trust that provides a consent-based regime with the flexibility needed to garner, from citizens of diverse backgrounds, consent to decisions made in uncertainty.

A final, surprising twist remains, however, before this account of the techniques for producing trust is complete. Aristotle encourages his citizens to cultivate goodwill, but in his view, goodwill does not arise "in friendships of utility and pleasure," the two lowest and least taxing levels of friendship (NE 9.5.1). Yet citizens are, in fact, utility friends, by his own account. Has he set us to pursuing a phantom?

No. We have sought an appropriate goal. Aristotle places the effort to cultivate goodwill at the center of his art of talking to strangers because it matters what kinds of aspirations citizens have. Citizenly relations are not stable but change over time. Sometimes trust is increasing, or at least being renewed; sometimes, instead, it is corroding. A polity will never reach a point where all its citizens have intimate friendships with each other, nor would we want it to. The best one can hope for, and all one should desire, is that political friendship can help citizens to resist the disintegration of trust and achieve a community where trust is a renewable resource. But to accomplish this, citizens must set their sights on what lies beyond their reach: goodwill throughout the citizenry. If they do, here and there citizens who were perfect strangers to each other will become friends simply by acting as if they were friends. More important, however, even in the vast majority of cases where citizens do not become intimates, they will at least have achieved a guiding orientation that will help make them more trustworthy to each other. Our aspirations determine the nature of the failures amid which we have to live.

We have, at last, found a new mode of citizenship in friendship understood as not an emotion but a practice. One can use its techniques even with strangers and even in the absence of emotional attachments, as in utilitarian friendships like business relations and most other relations among citizens. Political friendship consists finally of trying to be *like* friends. Its payoff is rarely intimate, or genuine, friendship, but it is often trustworthiness and, issuing from that, political trust. Its art, trust production, has long gone by the abused name of rhetoric. Properly understood, rhetoric is not a list of stylistic rules but an outline of the radical commitment to other citizens that is needed for a just democratic politics. The rest is a set of suggestions about how to turn those commitments into real politics. At this point, we might as well equip ourselves with a list.

In order to generate trust, a speaker should
— aim to convince 100 percent of her audience; if she finds herself considering rather how to carry a majority, she is acting in a fashion that over the long term will undermine democracy;
— test herself by speaking to minority constituents whose votes she does not need;
— once she has found the limits of her ability to persuade, she should think also about how to ameliorate the remaining disagreement and distrust;
— "separate the people from the problem" by (i) developing external standards and universal principles for assessing problems and (ii) recognizing that dealing with the people means engaging with specific features of their subjective situation;
— be precise about which emotions are at stake in a particular conversation;
— seek to transform conditions of utility into experiences of goodwill;
— recognize that reciprocity is established over time and that enough trust has to be generated to allow this process to proceed;
— recognize that the most powerful tool for generating trust is the capacity to prove that she is willing to make sacrifices even for the strangers in her polity;
— be aware too that she is trustworthy only if she can point to a *habit* of making sacrifices for strangers and not merely to a single instance;[19]
— recognize that where there is no trust, a great sacrifice will be necessary to sow the first seeds of trust, which can develop only

over time through repeated interactions in which citizens have opportunities to test each other;
— give her audience opportunities for judging (accepting or rejecting) her arguments;
— be willing to have any member of the polity respond to her arguments.

In order to prepare the way for the generation of trust, a listener should
— separate a speaker's claims about facts from the principles on which her conclusions are based; assess both;
— ask whether a speaker has a history of making pragmatically correct decisions;
— ask who is sacrificing for whom, whether the sacrifices are voluntary, and honored; whether they can and will be reciprocated;
— ask whether the speaker has spoken as a friend;
— insist on opportunities to judge political arguments;
— judge.

Here then are some new habits to try on.[20] Rhetoric is relevant not only in the halls of the legislature and in the courtrooms but wherever any stranger has to convince another of anything. Any interaction among strangers can generate trust that the polity needs in order to maintain its basic relationships. If citizens keep in mind these guidelines for speaking and listening to their fellow citizens, they will import the expertise of ordinary friendship into the political realm, and political friendship will grow out of that. Political friendship thus generated sustains a democratic polis by helping citizens to accept decisions with which they may disagree. But friendship must be mutual.

Self-sacrifice serves the political purpose of enabling and legitimating agreement only when citizens act generously toward other citizens exactly because they know that at some point they will find themselves befriended in return. If one citizen or group repeatedly lives with less than its legal share, political friendship has been violated, or has never existed. Indeed, decisions that impose continuous sacrifice are based not on persuasion but on force and are therefore illegitimate. Since democratic citizenship entails turn-taking at displays of equity, democracy will be stronger for cultivating in citizens an ability to talk to strangers in ways that support taking turns.

And yet . . . again the skeptic's voice rises: one can employ practices like these in the supermarket, at the movies, in airports, at bus stands, at the workplace. But why should one believe that they will have an impact? One might even teach rhetoric to kids. But aren't the words of politicians the only ones with power to transform our world? In what sense can ordinary citizens be said to be powerful? How can their techniques of political friendship have real political effects?

II

Epilogue: Powerful Citizens

"DON'T TALK TO STRANGERS!" That is a lesson for four-year-olds. Eyes that drop to the ground when they bump up against a stranger's gaze belong to those still in their political minority. If the experience of the most powerful citizen in the United States is any guide, talking to strangers is empowering; the president is among the few citizens for whom the polity holds no intimidating strangers. Presidents greet everyone and look all citizens in the eye. This is not merely because they are always campaigning, but because they have achieved the fullest possible political maturity. Their ease with strangers expresses a sense of freedom and empowerment. At one end of the spectrum of styles of democratic citizenship cowers the four-year-old in insecure isolation; at the other, stands the president, strong and self-confident. The more fearful we citizens are of speaking to strangers, the more we are docile children and not prospective presidents; the greater the distance between the president and us, the more we are subjects, not citizens. Talking to strangers is a way of claiming one's political majority and, with it, a presidential ease and sense of freedom.

· · ·

Talking to strangers has not been the traditional way of claiming one's political majority. During much of the last century, the other option for most citizens was to assimilate into the "white majority." Countless immigrants of assorted ethnic backgrounds and speaking diverse languages found that this was the route not to political maturity exactly but at least to a satisfying sense of security. At the very least, assimilating into the white majority increased one's chances of being trusted by other members of that majority, and trust, as social capital, is very easily converted into material security.[1] "This country gives you the chance to become a very highly respected citizen, become wealthy or succeed," wrote a man born in a European slum in a letter to the editor published in the *Los Angeles Times* on September 13, 1957, alongside a letter on the Little Rock desegregation crisis. For the path into the majority to be visible, the country also needed a visibly permanent "minority group" or long-lived opposition group of low political status.

The growth of de facto and de jure segregation of people of color throughout the first half of the twentieth century served many purposes and had many damaging effects, but among them was the solidification of the ideas of majority and minority. The use of the term "minority" to refer to an individual person rather than to that percentage of a group which loses a vote is a modern invention—more particularly, a U.S. invention.[2] This usage is possible only when a minority voting group appears to be permanently in a position of reduced political power, for otherwise it would be senseless to refer to an individual as a "minority"; in a fluid democracy any citizen may be one day in the minority, and the next in the majority. But used thus, to designate an individual, the term "minority" names someone at whom a member of the majority can look and know that that "minority" probably has less power in the polity, all in all, than she does. For the first half of the twentieth century, African Americans were invisible as individual democratic agents because they were so very visible as less than that. To become a member of "the majority" was to acquire the privilege of looking at others as permanent minorities.

Strength and confidence issue from this kind of claim to political majority, but not freedom. This idea of political majority that entails assimilation depends on the visible apartness of minority citizens, and it takes work to keep a set of citizens apart so that they see themselves, over the long term, as a unified, oppositional group. But maintaining the apartness of minority citizens means also that majority citizens have to stay away from them. This approach to political majority sets limits on where majority citizens can go and to whom they can speak. In the twentieth century, this segregation of majority citizens was enforced less by laws than by an indefatigable psychological policing that constantly reminded them that their claim to political majority depended on their remaining apart and distinct from "minorities." The continuing power of this isolation is evident in that white Americans rarely think of themselves as related by ancestry to black Americans, whereas I wonder about every white person I meet in the United States with the last name of "Allen." The prison is not small for those citizens who continue to choose assimilation to achieve political majority, but it is confining still. The traditional method of achieving political majority depends on a fear of strangers.

. . .

When the United States was reconstituted between 1954 and 1964, its redirection toward integration began the long, slow end of its durable minority group. To dissolve the durable minority would, however, also disband the durable majority. When Schlesinger and others lament the "balkanization" of the U.S. citizenry, they register only the passing of the "white majority," which had long erased differences among a variety of Eastern European, as well as other "white," ethnicities via the opposition to "black." We are not experiencing the end of social bonds, but only, at last, the small first death tremors of the ideas of "the majority group" and "the permanent minority." But disbanding the idea of the majority group also strips many citizens of that feature of their identity that has always provided them with their most stable, if unacknowledged, source of social and political security.

A letters-to-the editor page from the September 12, 1957, *Chicago Tribune* nicely captures the psychological complexities of the project of integration. The letters mostly respond to the issue of school desegregation in Arkansas, with two exceptions. The first anomalous letter concerns the safety of children. A fifteen-year-old girl had been murdered, and the letter-writer advises her compatriots that "[t]his crime and many other crimes against girls would be avoided if parents did not allow teen-age daughters on the streets alone at night." Most notable about the page is the movement in theme from one letter to the next. An editor laid it out, choosing the order for the letters, constructing the rhythms and patterns in the imagination of hypothetical citizens reflecting on integration in September 1957. The thematic movement is from thoughts on integration, to worries about personal security, to further meditations on integration, to more anxiety about personal security. You could call it a nervous tic.

The first letter responds to a *Tribune* editorial criticizing Arkansas's

Governor Faubus for using his state's National Guard troops to keep the Little Rock Nine out of Central High. The second letter, entitled "Integration in Chicago," responds to another editorial from a few days earlier, entitled "Chicago's Record in Race Relations." This letter-writer takes up the editorial's claim that "a Negro can walk anywhere in Chicago and not be molested," and advocates the expansion of this freedom of movement for Negroes. "That is not much of an achievement. If whites would like to aid the so-called Negro problem, they could do so quickly just by letting qualified Negroes live in the vacant apartments all over the city. One Negro family in a block is not going to hurt anybody." Right after this letter, about the free movement of Negroes through formerly segregated space, we get the letter about children's safety. And the letter about teaching children not to go out alone at night and, implicitly, not to talk to strangers, is then followed by a letter disputing the claim that Negroes can go anywhere in Chicago unmolested. "Mayor Daley has never, to our knowledge, used even the moral force of his office to suggest to the perpetrators of racial violence that their conduct is vile, unlawful, and ungodly." Then, the final letter on the page takes up the topic of "Travelers Aid" and "helping travelers in trouble." Like the letter about protecting children, this one registers worries about personal security in public spaces.

The idea of integration that recommends letting "Negroes live in vacant apartments all over the city" produces the anxiety and insecurity expressed in the letter about keeping kids off the streets. And then the movement repeats itself. The editorial organization of the letters reveals this social logic: once Negroes can leave their ghettoes and go anywhere safely, the beginning of the end of the permanent minority, and so of the permanent majority, is at hand; the security these social ideas had always provided to many citizens was shaken by this horizon of expectation. When Negroes can go anywhere, those who wish, even unconsciously, to maintain the psychological security that comes from being a member of the permanent majority have to limit the ambit of their own movements. To keep their sense of well-being, they have to set themselves apart.

The *Oxford English Dictionary* dates to 1951 the use of the word "minority" to refer to an individual; neither the 1953 edition of the *American College Dictionary* nor the 1961 *Webster's New World Dictio-*

nary registers this meaning of the word. This usage is a product of the end of de jure segregation; it reflects a development from a legal to a psychological defense of the idea of the permanent majority.[3] For many citizens, the beginning of the end of that majority has brought a diminishment of the power and security that they or their parents once experienced. This feeling of diminishment is based, however, not on real reductions in power or safety, but on the disintegration of those psychological props that had long provided a fake, but satisfying, sense of security.[4] The remarkable retreat to gated communities, SUVs, and now Hummers is not a response to real crime rates but rather to the psychological effect of lost social certainty. Those who claim their political majority with such psychological props get at best the security of the fearful, and not the self-confidence of a mature democrat.

. . .

I advocate talking to strangers as a healthy path to political majority and seek to cultivate modes of citizenship that provide citizens with the security and self-confidence of full-fledged political agency. I have offered only a sketch of political friendship as a timely mode of citizenship, but in the process I have tried to undo two notions currently credited as common sense. First, citizenship is not, fundamentally, a matter of institutional duties but of how one learns to negotiate loss and reciprocity. Second, unrestrained self-interest does not make the world go round but corrodes the bases of trust. In fact, self-interest ranges through a myriad of forms from rivalrous to equitable. The ability to adopt equitable self-interest in one's interactions with strangers is the only mark of a truly democratic citizen, and to employ the techniques of political friendship would be to transform our daily habits and so our political culture. Can we devise an education that, rather than teaching citizens not to talk to strangers, instead teaches them how to interact with them self-confidently?[5]

Urban planners have long understood that architectural designs affect whether spaces feel safe enough for citizens to speak to each other. Taking Ellison's *Invisible Man* as a guiding spirit, Marshall Berman describes his ideal "open-minded" public plaza, square, or mall thus:

> It would be open, above all, to encounters between people of different classes, races, ages, religions, ideologies, cultures, and stances to-

ward life. It would be planned to attract all these different populations, to enable them to look each other in the face, to listen, maybe to talk. It would have to be exciting enough and accessible enough (by both mass transit and car) to attract them all, spacious enough to contain them all (so they wouldn't be forced to fight each other for breathing space), with plenty of exit routes (in case encounters get too strained), and adequate police (in case there's trouble) kept well in the background (so they don't themselves become a source of trouble).[6]

Berman realizes, as did Aristotle, that most of us take positive pleasure from living among strangers. They are, more often than not, a source of wonder to us, and wonder is (as Aristotle put it) the beginning of philosophy. Strangers help feed the human desire to learn. Nonetheless, strangers also raise fears that are sometimes justified; security is and always will be a real political issue. How should we handle it?

These days our instinct is to vote for more police or, as in the Berman quotation, secret police. Yet experience suggests that, while strengthened penal regimes enhance cooperation when people distrust each other, they also destroy trust where it already exists.[7] Berman does not, nor would any other urban planner, rely exclusively on police to make a space feel safe enough for fruitful interactions among strangers; open public space in a police state is, paradoxically, an oxymoron. Any city-dweller knows that streets are safer the more they are occupied by ordinary folk, and in recent years urban planners have designed benches, fountains, lighting systems, maps and well-marked pathways, making spaces both inviting and easy to leave, in order to encourage us out of our houses and back to interaction. What is true of urban planners applies also to all democratic citizens. If we rely too heavily on police oversight to shape our public spaces, we fail at our jobs. We will have acquired modes of citizenship appropriate to a police state, and so will have undermined the very ideas of public space, and also of democracy. Like urban planners, citizens, too, have a panoply of instruments, other than policing, available for creating a public life worthy of a democracy. How can we now find modes for interacting with strangers that simultaneously enhance security and improve the quality of our interactions?

First, there are small steps to help achieve a basic sense of physical

safety. An urban planner builds exit routes into public space. An ordinary citizen can move through her world with heightened attentiveness to exits and options and determine which spaces are safe
enough for talking to strangers. An urban planner tries to build watchful eyes into the background of urban space. An ordinary citizen can
develop greater sensitivity to who is where around him and to
whether there are enough trustworthy eyes nearby to provide a safe
opportunity for conversation with a stranger. There will be times
when one needs to cross the street for safety's sake; the question is
how one does it. On a street late at night, when there aren't other
watchful eyes around, it's better to cross sooner, rather than scurrying
away at the last minute; it's better, if possible, to change one's route,
instead of simply crossing to the other side. Our methods, even of crossing streets for safety's sake, signal to others what we think of them.
One needs to display to strangers, as much as possible, that one is willing to give them the benefit of the doubt, and one must present oneself, too, such that one earns the benefit of their doubt. To cross early
is to leave open the possibility that one has crossed for reasons unre-
lated to the stranger's approach; that possibility gives the stranger a
chance not to take personally the fact that one has crossed the street.
Democratic trust depends on public displays of an egalitarian, well-
intentioned spirit.

I wish in no way to minimize everyone's need for security from
violence but am also convinced that we have resources available to
achieve security that extend well beyond policing. These resources
reside in how we interact with strangers, for we can turn these interactions themselves into a source of strength. Through interaction,
even as strangers, citizens draw each other into networks of mutual
responsibility. Engage a stranger in conversation as a political friend
and, if one gets a like return, one has gained a pair of watchful eyes to
increase the safety of the space one occupies. Engage a stranger in
conversation across a racial, ethnic, or class divide and one gets not
only an extra pair of eyes but also an ability to see and understand parts
of the world that are to oneself invisible. Real knowledge of what's
outside one's garden cures fear, but only by talking to strangers can
we come by such knowledge. Wisdom about the world we currently
inhabit generally can't be gotten from books, because they can't be
written, or read, fast enough. Strangers are the best source. Take

Socrates as an example. He gave living form to the injunction "Know thyself" by talking freely with anyone, Athenian or foreign, he came upon. A direct approach to curing one's fear of strangers would be to try especially hard to engage in conversation those strangers who come from worlds and places one fears.

I am no stranger to frightening personal attacks but have found ways of increasing my sense of security as I move about public spaces to such a degree that strangers are now for me a remarkable source of pleasure, and not fear. Beyond that, they are a source of empowering knowledge that enables me to move through the world freely and to roam widely. This personal self-confidence is one of the great rewards of claiming one's political majority by talking to strangers.

.   .   .

Political self-confidence is the other great reward. Citizens have powers to affect their world that extend well beyond their ability to dial 911. The cultivation of an ethos of political friendship depends on citizens' recognition of these powers, and their commitment to employ them, rather than police, to shape their environments.

.   .   .

Why should one believe that political friendship can affect politics and not merely an individual's personal experience of the public realm? As political candidates know, each interaction with a stranger holds the seeds of a transformation, and each of us already has far more political power within our grasp than we acknowledge or allow. For that matter, all democratic citizens, even nonvoters, are already more engaged in politics than they realize.

The bills of federal and state legislatures are not the only laws that structure life. A host of publicly binding decisions—some written, others customary—arise from public institutions like schools, churches, media outlets, and businesses to set the terms of our cohabitation. Political representation occurs not merely when Congress-folk gather. I recently heard a flight attendant ask "those *lucky* people in first class" to put away their footrests. Anyone who offers citizens narratives of who they are, how their political world works, and what its structuring principles are acts as a representative, and such representation is carried out not only in schools, churches, and businesses, but also in newspapers, movie theaters, and even airplanes. Our participation in assorted institutions, like our choices about what to read and watch and how to speak about ourselves, shapes our political world. Insofar as a commitment to political friendship might change our institutional choices and our communal narratives, it would also transform our politics.

Let me put us in step a final time with the Invisible Man, who came to a similar understanding of the parochialness of law and representation. After his arrival in New York, his search for work, and a disastrous stint at a paint factory, he wanders lost in thought through Harlem's wintry streets until an eviction scene startles him out of himself. An elderly couple and all their belongings have been ejected into the snow. When he sees, amid their stuff, a photograph of the couple in their youth, "look[ing] back at [him] as though even then in that nineteenth century day they had expected little, and this with a grim unillusioned pride that suddenly seemed to me both a reproach and warning" (*IM* 271), he is inspired to give his first speech to the general public. He argues for conformity to the law and, wanting to keep the angry crowd from attacking the police, he tries to provoke his audience to think about law's place in democracy. As he does so, he realizes that citizens establish rules for themselves in moments of enforcement, like the eviction, as well as of legislation. When his first call for acquiescence to the law fails, he switches tactics, shouting out that, in accordance with the law, the crowd should undertake a cleanup campaign to "clear . . . the sidewalk of junk," by putting the elderly couple's possessions back in the house. He has suddenly understood law's fluidity and seen an opportunity to reinvent social forms even within law's confines. The crowd takes him up on this proposal, and so his imagination thwarts a simple move to violence by reinterpreting, even if euphemistically, legal possibilities.

The Invisible Man's reinterpretive work engages the officers too. The crowd's anger at them had surged when an officer had refused the old woman's request to go inside with her Bible for just long enough to pray. I. M. shouts to the angry crowd:

> Look at them [the officers] but remember that we're a wise, law-abiding group of people. And remember it when you look up there in the doorway at *that law standing there with his forty-five.* Look at him, standing with his blue steel pistol and his blue serge suit, or one forty-five, you see ten for every one of us, ten guns and ten warm suits and

ten fat bellies and ten million laws. *Laws* that's what we call them down South! Laws! And we're wise and law-abiding. . . . How about it Mr. Law? Do we get our fifteen minutes worth of Jesus? You got the world, can we have our Jesus? (*IM* 278; some emphasis added)

Little laws, and not just constitutional ones, construct the world. In this scene, an invisible citizen proposes a renegotiation of losses and benefits in a moment of enforcement. He affirms law in general—the existence of collective agreements that turn conflicting narratives into a common world—but denounces a particular distribution of loss and benefit ("You got the world, can we have our Jesus?"), and invites the officers to join an experiment in imaginative reciprocity. Their flexibility about fifteen minutes of prayer might at least acknowledge a general need to reconsider how goods and harms are distributed in the polity. But the officers, who stand before the crowd as "the law," falsely claim to have no opportunity for judgment. Once again they refuse to allow the old woman into the house to pray: "'I got my orders, Mac,' the man called, waving the pistol with a sneer" (*IM* 278). Soon after, however, the police send in a riot call. A white man helping to move the furniture back into the house responds, "What riot? There's no riot," and the officer tells him, "If I say there's a riot, there's a riot." The officer then admits that his own judgment factors into the production of law. His phone call represents the world and establishes policy.

Law finally becomes what it is—in on-the-ground experience—through the interactions among citizens. In Mark Warren's words, "[e]ven the most explicit set of laws or administrative rules is almost always insufficient to organize a collective action. Ultimately, collective action depends upon the good will of the participants, their shared understandings, their common interests, and their skilled attention to contingencies."[8] Law is not an *artifact,* or made object, that embodies the one will of the people once and for all, but a *practice* in which any and every citizen may be involved at any moment, through deliberation, legislation, or enforcement. As citizens deal with the contingencies attendant on law's enforcement, they renegotiate loss and sacrifice constantly. This is the core activity of the practice of law.

Since negotiating loss comes neither easily nor instinctively, citizens' success at it depends entirely on whether they have built up habits for it. Citizens who cultivate their own desire to prove themselves trustworthy to others, and who develop into habits the techniques for doing this, will acquire the rich reservoirs of political imagination that are needed for generating democratic agreement amid strife. Cultural abilities at trust cultivation within a citizenry intersect with more formal political procedures in this regard. They vastly increase the number of possible solutions imagined in any dispute. If the officers in the eviction scene had desired to prove themselves trustworthy, or had understood that cultivating trust would make their own jobs easier in the future, they would have let the old woman into the house to pray. The modicum of trust implied by this gesture might at a later point have facilitated a more substantive political discussion between police and residents. Instead, the police reduced the possibility of future conversation.

Political friendship (which finds its tools in the art of rhetoric) cultivates habits of imagination that generate politically transformative experiences out of ordinary interactions among strangers. Herein lies its power. To be a good rhetorician, one must see oneself as strangers do. The effort to do so entails understanding how one is implicated in strangers' lives, and how calculi of goods and ills look different from other experiential positions. Ellison argued, "I believe . . . that unless we continually explore . . . the network of complex relationships which bind us together, we [will] continue being the victims of various inadequate conceptions of ourselves, both as individuals and as citizens of a nation of diverse people" (CE 523).[9] If democratic citizens ignore the intricacy of their relationships, they will constantly produce public decisions that obscure the truth about what citizens demand of each other. Such decisions rest on domination more than justice, and over time blindness to patterns of imposition corrodes political legitimacy. Political friends remain attentive to the losses and benefits that constantly circulate through the citizenry, and they remain vigilant that this circulation not settle into patterns of domination that precipitate distrust. To develop a cultural habit of such friendship would transform our political world.

. . .

Whether any one citizen who makes political friendship an individual habit will noticeably affect our political world in the near term depends entirely on that citizen's ability to imagine ways to extend the impact of her political friendship beyond her particular interactions with other citizens. I began this book by directing our political attention away from institutions and toward habits of citizenship, but when a citizen wishes to cultivate her dream citizenship throughout the polity she is obliged to confront institutions once again. Institutions are ossified versions of particular patterns of human interaction, and they inevitably extend the reach and force of the cultural norms around which they are shaped. A shift in how people interact will inevitably also transform their institutions, just as when the snail changes direction, its shell turns too. But the cultivation of new cultural habits is not the only way to reorient institutions. They can also be reconfigured by intentional policy; a body constituted to amplify the effect of one set of norms in the world may reconstitute itself so as to amplify another set of norms. A citizen who wishes to extend the reach of her own practice of political friendship will have to engage with the institutions in which she participates. Do they act like political friends? If not, what might bring them closer to that ideal? I return to Ellison's wise remark that "[t]his society is not likely to become free of racism, thus it is necessary for Negroes to free themselves by becoming their idea of what a free people should be." All citizens who desire to live in a democracy that has slipped the shackles of domination and acquiescence must embody their idea of what a free people should be. This means pushing the institutions that one inhabits to embody this norm too, for they are extensions of our selves, as is the shell to the snail.

. . .

How, then, might a citizen undertake the construction of political friendship? Perhaps we should begin modestly. Aristotle drew some tentative conclusions about the size of a community in which one can act as a political friend. He concluded that the maximum number of people with whom one can actively be political friends is 99,999 fellow citizens. What if we did (with an ironic wink) take this number seriously? How would it be practical to be a political friend to 99,999 other adults, even those living in our own vicinity? First, one would require maps and recent census figures in order to figure out the geographical boundaries around one's home or place of work that enclose 99,999 adults. And then the citizen would have to get down to the business of political friendship at a minimum in this terrain. She could call it her "polis."

Let me take myself as an example. I work at the University of Chicago and live nearby in a neighborhood called Hyde Park (51st to 59th Streets, Cottage Grove to Lake Michigan). My colleagues, neighbors, and I also consider a second upper-middle class neighborhood, directly to the north, South Kenwood (47th to 51st Streets, Drexel to Lake Michigan), as part of our own neighborhood. But Hyde Park and South Kenwood don't come close to having 99,999 adults. A small portion of my neighbors might also consider a poorer neighborhood to the south, Woodlawn (60th to 67th, Cottage Grove to Lake Michigan), as part of our own neighborhood, but even this boundary does not embrace the 99,999 adults that Aristotle thought even ancient polis dwellers could handle. We think the ancients drew tight boundaries around small communities made up entirely of "their own kind of people." In fact, we may draw even tighter boundaries around ourselves. We are at least less likely to interact meaningfully with strangers than were the ancient Athenians.

The extended boundaries of our own polis of 99,999 adults would include not only Hyde Park, South Kenwood, and Woodlawn, but also several neighborhoods poorer still: directly to the west and across a very large and frequently empty park, the very poor Washington Park and Englewood neighborhoods; to the north and west, North Kenwood and the southern half of Bronzeville and the bottom third of the Robert Taylor Homes housing project; and then, to the south, the northern sections of the Park Manor neighborhood (which one must cross an interstate to reach), and the northern half of the Grand Crossing neighborhood (which one must cross another boundary, the Oakwoods Cemetery, to reach). Here, then, is my polis. How do I act as a political friend within it?

First, I must develop contexts in which to interact with the other members of my polis, for these do not exist. Just by drawing a map of it, I have realized that what my neighbors and I typically recognize as our own neighborhood is in fact separated from the other parts of our polis by freeways, major traffic arteries, train tracks, one large cemetery, and empty parks. Soon I learn, too, with a little historical research, that these boundaries were carefully considered by an earlier mayor, Richard J. Daley, to keep Chicago neighborhoods racially segregated.[10] My own university helped construct these boundaries.[11] A commitment to political friendship, even in respect only to the 99,999 other adults living in my immediate vicinity, requires that I cross geographical, racial, economic boundaries, and challenge the habits of action and mind that my political order and its major institutions have cultivated for nearly half a century; these habits have been fostered since exactly the point when the major institutions of my polis first had a significant opportunity to invent new, integrationist forms of citizenship. There have been glimmerings of a new citizenship. St. Claire Drake and Horace Cayton's *Black Metropolis* (1945) is one of the products of Hyde Park scholars who have faced the challenge I am describing, and the University of Chicago, too, has itself sometimes pointed to an alternative path, for instance, insofar as it has trained some of the twentieth century's most important African American sociologists.

But simply traveling around my polis, learning more about it, talking to the strangers in it, and learning the manifold lessons they have to teach are not enough. In their daily activities, citizens can interact with strangers according to the norms of political friendship and begin to develop reservoirs of trust to sustain political reciprocity, but this nascent interpersonal trust will never mature into full-blown political friendship unless it is given serious political work to do. The military has been the best place for generating interracial trust in the United States precisely because it so often requires people who don't trust each other to take responsibility for one another's lives.[12] In the civilian world, citizens have gotten fairly good at collaborating in musical and athletic exchanges, but when it comes time to share institutional power across racial lines our cooperative skills frequently break down. Yet the techniques of political friendship generate the richest trust when they are exercised in contexts of mutual vulnerability. Citizens, too, like soldiers, must take risks together in shared decision making with real consequences, if they wish to solidify a politics based on political friendship. If the powerful institutions of the polis have carved up the territory so that different groups within the region have their own domains and are rarely involved in power-sharing activities with others, there is little hope for developing extensive trust in the region. At this point, the citizen who desires to extend the reach of political friendship would do well to catalog the powerful institutions within his polis. There will be churches, schools, businesses, and political networks that offer opportunities and resources to reweave the relationships among citizens by establishing contexts for shared decision making. He should advocate the invention of a power-sharing body to his own institution and try to identify those issues—whether social, economic, or political—that affect the quality of life for everyone in the polis, proposing these as especially important areas of discussion for any power-sharing body.

Again, let me take myself as an example. The one institution with which I work daily is the University of Chicago. Can one speak of a relationship that binds a university to those who live around it? What is its relationship to the other institutions in the polis? As it happens, the institutions of my polis have divided up the territory, each cleaving to its own domain. In my own desire to live according to norms of political friendship and to cultivate trust among citizens within and beyond my polis, I want to reorient my own institution's habits for interacting with strangers. I might propose some boundary-crossing policies to my university as part of an argument that it has a remarkable opportunity to help develop modes of citizenship suitable to their new post-1957 Constitution. As do we all.

. . .

In fact, I *will* propose policies of political friendship, addressing a challenge to the university community in general but particularly to its central faculty governing body, the university senate, in which the president and provost of the university are members ex officio. Call this challenge a first sketch for a utopia; it describes ideals in terms of concrete realities. It is by no means a comprehensive set of policy proposals, but rather exemplifies (I hope) the imaginative habits of political friendship. Here goes.

. . .

To Members of the Faculty Senate:
This country was reconstituted between *Brown v. Board of Education* (1954) and the Civil Rights and Voting Rights Acts (1964–65). Nearly fifty years have gone by and we haven't yet managed to develop for this new era modes of citizenship to supplant domination and acquiescence. At this juncture, our habits of citizenship need reconstitution more than our laws. Each of us confronts a choice be-

tween fostering new modes of citizenship and, by doing roughly nothing, allowing old forms of citizenship to persist. What is the next phase?

The events of 1957 and of the whole civil rights movement revealed, to those who cared to look, that citizens of the United States have deeply ingrained bad habits: we evade straightforward consideration of when and where public policy asks some citizens to sacrifice for others; we have little interest in cultivating habits for generating trust; we idealize unanimity rather than aspiring to maximize agreement while also dealing frankly with disappointment, anger, and resentment. Our most deeply ingrained lesson in citizenship is "Don't talk to strangers." We, the faculty, have opportunities to embody political friendship instead by converting the university into a visible, public model of that citizenship.

This country's postapartheid reconstitution did not occur elsewhere, distant from the university. Nor is any place in this country innocent of these changes. The University of Chicago did its part to affect the course of integration by inventing, in response to the changing racial makeup of its neighborhood, a program of "urban renewal" that was intended by city, state, and federal governments to serve as a model throughout the country.[13] What exactly happened? What role has the university assumed for the still ongoing period of integration?

In 1940 fewer than 4 percent of the residents of the university's immediate neighborhood, Hyde Park–Kenwood, were African American. In 1950 African Americans were 6 percent of the population; in 1956 that figure was 36 percent (*PUR* 21). Despite myths to the contrary, the socioeconomic structure of the neighborhood did not change dramatically; roughly 20,000 lower-income whites left and were replaced by roughly 23,000 lower-income African Americans (*PUR* 27–38). Despite myths to the contrary, the increase of African American residents in Hyde Park–Kenwood was not accompanied by rising crime rates. The neighborhood had indeed experienced a perceived increase in crime rates (actual data is difficult to come by) prior to the community's changes in the racial makeup, and residents had thought of their neighborhood as having become a "victim area" that had since the 1930s attracted criminals from other parts of the city (*PUR* 30–31). A handful of fairly dramatic crimes in the early

1950s led the university to establish in 1952, with community consent, the South East Chicago Commission (SECC), which was charged to "organize the total community in order to stabilize it and prevent further flight from the area. Its more specific program [was] to fight crime . . . and begin a long-term project of neighborhood planning and improvement" (*NPUC* 7–8). As a result, from 1952 to 1957, the years of the greatest demographic changes, crime rates dropped steadily in Hyde Park–Kenwood. And, finally, despite still other myths to the contrary, the demographic changes did not cause a mass exodus of university faculty from the neighborhood—with the exception of minor outmigrations by members of the medical school and the administration (*PUR* 32–36).

Many in the university community believed the myths, however, and the look of the community did change dramatically during these years, because of the presence of people of color with different habits and tastes, and also because of profiteering landlords, who took advantage of the pressure on the housing market caused by the migration of African Americans into the city. (After years of neglect during World War II, many buildings were converted into overcrowded rooming houses without adequate facilities and maintenance.) Even a University of Chicago sociologist, writing a history of urban renewal in 1961 from a perspective guardedly in favor of "interracialism," used the language of pest control to describe the situation, implicitly revealing the effect the changes had on him: "The community's southern border zone, the Midway, surrounded by university-owned land, did not lend itself to use as an invasion route" (*PUR* 20); "The invasion did not by 1956 make serious inroads on the population elements that set the tone for Hyde Park" (*PUR* 33).

From 1952 to 1954 members of the SECC worked to develop a plan for urban renewal that would preserve the community "from the infiltration of blight from the broken and disintegrated sections of the old inner city adjacent to it" (SECC 2) and, in March 1954, two months before *Brown v. Board of Education,* the mayor of Chicago, Martin Kennelly, "formally announced the inauguration of the 'first real demonstration of a program intended to reverse the trends toward deterioration which characterized older communities in most U.S. cities'" (SECC 1). Only in 1961 would a university official finally acknowledge that the subtext had always been integration, and the country's reconstitution. "Until we Americans have learned to re-build and prevent slums, restore beauty to our cities, and provide ed-ucation and social opportunities to people who have not had them—largely because of the color of their skins—we will not have justified the faith of those who laid the foundations of our nation. . . . We must keep up the effort, for if we succeed we will have established a pattern for the rest of the nation to follow." So wrote George Beadle for his inauguration to the chancellorship of the university in May 1961, a month before he would also become president of the SECC, the body that was primarily responsible for conceiving and bringing to maturation the project of urban renewal. What, then, was the pat-tern that the university and the SECC, together with city, state, and federal governments, established for integration?

The creation of the SECC initiated the division of the city of Chicago into a multitude of neighborhood development corpora-tions, each taking as its mission the protection of its own neighbor-hood, quite frequently from the communities neighboring it.[14] Well before other neighborhood development corporations sprang up, on the model of the SECC, the leaders of that organization had already achieved state and federal legislative victories that made development corporations a remarkably powerful instrument for controlling a com-munity (*NPUC* 14–15, *PUR* 84–88). New laws and amendments to old ones that were advocated by the SECC resulted in the follow-ing situation:

Any three citizens and residents of a neighborhood could organ-ize a private corporation, with capital of not less than $1000, to carry out a redevelopment plan. The corporation had to prove that it would be working in an area of at least two acres in which at least 20 percent of residential dwellings were in dilapidated structures. Dilapidation included "obsolescence, faulty arrangement or design, lack of ven-tilation, light, or sanitary facilities, excessive land coverage, deleteri-ous land use or layout or any combination of these factors" (SECC 48). Once a territory had been designated as a development zone, the private development corporation, if it could acquire 60 percent of the property in that area or the consent of 60 percent of the property owners to its development plans, acquired right of eminent domain over the other 40 percent of the property in that zone. The private development corporation could exercise that right of eminent domain to acquire and destroy buildings and resell property even to private developers.[15]

Eminent domain powers (which we typically think of as enshrined in the Constitution) to allow federal and state governments to pursue projects for the public good are, in Illinois, available in an especially vigorous form to private parties even to this day.[16] They were strengthened to this degree to help Northern cities cope with the effects of looming civil strife in the South and the rising prospect of integration. The Federal Housing Act, yet another important political decision of 1954, made substantial subsidies available to neighborhood development corporations for the exercise of those eminent domain and redevelopment powers. The SECC began by seeking $3,149,379 of federal funds and $1,574,690 of city and university funds for the first phase of the renewal program (SECC 124). By 1956, the federal government had approved $25,835,000 of federal funds for the project (NPUC 20), demolition had begun, and the neighborhood looked "like Berlin immediately after the late war," to quote the university's chancellor (NPUC 23). By 1957 the university had spent $5,325,000 of its own funds (NPUC 25), and the initial phase of operations had moved 4,519 people from a 48-acre area (SECC 95; NPUC 15). By 1958, a complete urban renewal plan was finally approved at federal, state, and local levels, after "bitter controversy." The plan covered 591.4 acres, of which 101.2 were to be cleared, which entailed demolition of 5,941 living units in the area. By this point, federal monies granted to the project had risen to $28,312,062. Throughout, the SECC steered decisions about which buildings to condemn and how to rebuild.

The other arm of the SECC's activity was law enforcement. In 1952 the commission decided that its "interest in law enforcement would not involve vigilante activities or the employment of private investigators. Attention would, rather, be directed to detailed, ongoing statistical analysis of police performance in the area, with particular attention as to the adequacy of the manpower assigned, offenses occurring, arrests made, and the percentage of crimes solved" (NPUC 8). Yet by 1955 the SECC had hired two full-time private policemen (PUR 82), and in the 1960s the university established its own police force to patrol the Hyde Park–Kenwood neighborhood with powers equal to those of the city police. A citizenship of distrust requires dismal expenditures, and the annual budget for the force now reaches into the millions.

In the 1950s and 1960s the university thus established a pattern for dealing with integration that had force at its core. The university community, not well integrated in the 1950s, was willing to accept integration in its neighborhood provided that it had nearly total control over the terms, establishing how traffic patterns would flow, what sort of businesses would be permitted and where, which parts of the neighborhood would be available for lower-income residents, and how to arrange the look and functions of public spaces. A "biracial" middle- and upper-class community that has achieved low crime rates and that successfully avoided "becom[ing] all-Negro, like surrounding areas," by relocating lower-class whites and African Americans out of the neighborhood has resulted from these efforts (PUR 45–46); so too has a culture of distrust now several decades old. Members of the university community were willing to share space with strangers (or at least a certain minority percentage of strangers), and were generous to this degree. But they were unable to share power. The university had approached integration without accepting the prospect of the mutual vulnerability of white and black to each other's influence. Friendship cannot flourish on such ground. It is no surprise that the university has enduring problems recruiting African American students from Chicago, or that the neighborhood remains biracial more than integrated.

Lately, however, the university has begun to move in a new direction, at last seeking to create trust and to dissolve old boundaries: by starting charter schools in immediately surrounding neighborhoods; by designating full scholarships to the university for students from the Chicago Public School system; by placing its students in local schools as teachers' aides and tutors; by supporting the participation of faculty in programs providing accredited college-level courses to adults at or near the poverty line; by establishing and quickly expanding a University Community Service Center; by working to generate economic and employment opportunities on the South Side of Chicago; and by providing subsidies to staff and faculty who buy housing in areas beyond the traditional limits of the university's neighborhood.

Most important, the university has recently expanded its police coverage to neighborhoods beyond the university's traditional boundaries with the consent of and, in some instances, at the request of neighbors. Whereas the university campus extends north to south from 55th to 60th Streets and east to west for five blocks, its police now travel as far north as 39th Street and as far south as 63rd Street, at an annual cost of several million dollars. Community residents at public meetings are reported to have expressed satisfaction that the university at last sees them too as worthy of the same protection that upper-class members of the university community receive. And as best as I can tell, the university community, including the administration, imagines that the university will keep an extensive police force in perpetuity. The university in its public aspect has become a rough equivalent to a private security company, something like the Bel Air patrol, which posts signs on the lawns of houses it guards, promising an "armed response." Over the long term this mode of self-presentation will undermine other efforts of trust generation that rest more on collaboration than on power.

In my utopia universities would have no police. For all the good that the university's force has done to establish conditions where diverse citizens can begin to interact once again on the streets and in public spaces, we should not be content to let the project of integration depend on the display and application of force. A university seeks to advance the reach of knowledge through open intellectual inquiry and exchange, but presently this university presents itself to its neighbors armed and in uniform rather than carrying books and ideas. If the university's police force does its work well, it should help generate trust that might of itself diminish the need for policing; but if the members of our polis fail to imagine and plan for a future where the university's police will be unnecessary, we may miss the tipping point where the police cease to be a cause of trust and become rather a source of its corrosion. Now is the time to seek other methods for generating trust. Above all else, we need methods of integration based on political friendship rather than force.

How can the university make its defining features of openness and free exchange in conditions of equality the basis for its interactions with other citizens in its polis? How can these sources of strength and power generate trust? In order to expand its police coverage to 39th Street, the university has just assumed an additional annual expenditure of roughly $300,000. What if these funds were used for other acts of generosity more in keeping with the university's central mission, perhaps to support open access to the library and athletic facilities for polis residents? Educational and informational resources are distributed very unevenly within this area; in this information age, the university might aspire to invent new methods for achieving the unencumbered circulation of information and knowledge across socioeconomic and ethnic divides. The university could establish satellite sites within the community where intellectual resources would be made broadly available: for instance, courses in the humanities (through which, in this country, the majority of powerful citizens have always acquired the cultural literacy that has been the basis of their power) and clinics on entrepreneurship, legal questions, and medical issues. Or it might support the establishment of Kinko's-type office service centers throughout the polis, attaching such clinics to them. Public cultural events held at the university should be advertised in all the community newspapers of the polis as a matter of course. Or what if some of these funds were diverted to research on the problems of contemporary policing? The university police fill the same gap in Hyde Park as do private security companies in wealthy neighborhoods, but to fill a gap is to obscure a problem: too often publicly funded police are trusted neither by the wealthy, nor by the poor, and scarcely by anyone in between. The university might seek to develop policy that might eventually return the United States to a situation where city and state police are adequate to the job of establishing a sense of security for every resident— poor, rich, and middling.

But to share resources in mutually beneficial ways is only half of the business of political friendship. It is crucial to remember that even generous citizens will be distrusted if they refuse to share power. The university's new policies, especially the expansion of the university's police force, will have serious public consequences for the polis, but few of them have been discussed publicly even within the university. Our own new policies treat trust-building as central to the reversal of the boundaries exploited in the 1950s and 1960s, and implicitly aim to reconstitute strangers' habits of interaction within the polis. But such reconstitution can't occur in private by quiet administrative decisions, praiseworthy though they may be. The development of new norms for the interaction of strangers within the polis requires public discussion *among* strangers. Trust grows only through experience; habits of citizenship are fashioned only through actual interaction. Although I am reluctant to propose new committees, the effects of institutions on our patterns of interaction cannot be ignored, and sometimes the fastest route to redirecting interaction is indeed to restructure an institution. Since 1952 roughly fifteen neighborhood development corporations have sprung up in the territory of our polis. Like the original South East Chicago Commission, these neighborhood development corporations tend to take protectionist stances against other neighborhoods; collaboration across the whole area of the polis has been minimal; citizen conversations about development issues and concerns tend not to flow across neighborhood boundaries. I think it's time for a polis-wide development council, perhaps composed of the presidents of each neighborhood development corporation.[17]

Such a council could give a public airing to development plans and policy decisions that are likely to affect the polis in general. It could also propose goals for the community as a whole, carry out impact studies of projects envisioned by the university or other large institutional bodies within the polis, and cultivate a community-wide discussion on how powerful institutions within the community, and in particular the university, can reach their own goals while also respecting and responding to the goals and concerns of the community. The council might begin its work with efforts to repeal and/or amend the eminent domain laws that give private corporations excessive power over the property of their fellow citizens. These laws exemplify the sort of policy proposals that distribute power so unevenly as to make trust impossible. Although the university no longer uses these laws, their public repudiation would be a powerful symbolic gesture. During the first fifty years of this country's experiment with integration, we failed to find ways of slipping loose of habits of domination and acquiescence. This should be our main goal for the next fifty years. With a decision to set aside overly strong versions of eminent domain powers in favor of collaborative approaches to solving problems of community development, we would at last set our faces in the right direction.

Would efforts exerted toward these proposals divert the university from its central mission to educate students and advance knowledge? Would they entail an improper use of the funds of a private educational institution? Hardly. A sizeable proportion of the university's faculty purport to explain our world to us, and often also to propose methods for dealing with that world. The university's ability to analyze, explain, and respond, in intellectually coherent terms, to its own difficulties is an important test of its success at the very business at which it claims expertise. Any discoveries it might make about what, in an urban context, can convert distrust to trust, generate economic opportunity, and extend the impact of educational resources will count as valuable research around the world. Finally, any university that operates in a democratic context must admit that it educates citizens; it ought at least to know what sort of political education it provides. Most students and faculty on campus wonder exactly why relations to the community feel so poisonous. Very few know about Illinois' remarkable eminent domain laws, nor of the university's role in writing and then implementing them. How uncommonly embarrassing that at a university we accept such a high degree of ignorance about our own circumstances. We should now have the self-confidence to make the university vulnerable within the community, trusting that over the long term appropriate vulnerability will issue in vastly greater rewards, both of self-knowledge and of political friendship, than do current norms of distrust.

Even if one were to dismiss my reasons for the university to attend to its role as a political friend within its community, there remains an important economic factor. If the university were able to generate, within its polis, habits for the interaction of strangers that significantly diminished the need for police protection, it might at some future point divert the bulk of those funds to fellowships for students, books for the library, laboratory equipment, or faculty positions. It would win its own "peace" dividend.

My eye is on the moment when the University of Chicago would have no police. A commitment to political friendship opens up the possibility of pursuing a real world version of that ideal. Not only a healthier, more democratic community, but also a stronger university lie along this road.

Yours sincerely,
Danielle Allen

. . .

The ancient Greeks believed in treating strangers hospitably in case any of them should turn out to be a god. I have been advocating treating strangers well on the grounds that we are related to one another in more ways than we know, even if race and class have made it difficult for us to see those connections. During my final days of writing this manuscript, my husband, Bob, had a remarkable experience that converts the Greek proverb into modern form. We were spending our summer vacation in Los Angeles where we both grew up. One evening I had gone to visit a cousin and so did not join my husband and stepson for our usual dinner at a Mexican grill. The two of them chose their table, my stepson went to the washroom, and a bag lady stepped up to the table to ask if she could use the empty spot. Not much looking at her, my husband said yes. Police love this restaurant, and soon she was talking across the aisle to them, complaining about treatment she'd received during the day. Something about her voice struck Bob's attention. By the time Isaac got back from the bathroom, Bob was sure he knew something important about the woman. Isaac sat down and Bob said to her, "I have a surprise for you." She looked at him, confused. "For me?" "Yes, I have a surprise for you. Isaac, tell the lady your name." Isaac answered just with his first name, and Bob asked him again, "No, tell the lady your whole name." "Isaac von Hallberg." "That's *my* name!" she exclaimed. Still, she did not figure out what Bob had already realized. Finally, he had to tell her his whole name, Robert von Hallberg, and say, "And you're Marie von Hallberg, my cousin." He had recognized her voice.

"Unless we continually explore the network of complex relationships which bind us together," to quote Ellison a final time, "we [will] continue being the victims of various inadequate conceptions of ourselves, both as individuals and as citizens of a nation of diverse people." The adoption of the aspirations and techniques of political friendship by any of us, even individually, would have ramifying effects. And, happily, liberal institutions make it possible for us to interact with fellow citizens well beyond the limit of the "polis" with its 99,999 inhabitants. That number provided us with a thought experiment; liberalism allows us to extend political friendship beyond local and to national contexts. Wherever we move throughout our polity, we have opportunities to engage strangers in political friendship because strong institutional protections of rights free us to take risks on interactions that we could not otherwise afford. Nor, when we are active as political friends in our own polis, can we forget about the rest of the people with whom we share our polity. The final test of whether we have managed to cultivate political friendship in our own communities is not how we treat the 99,998 other residents immediately around us, but whether a stranger to our neighborhood, any stranger also willing to act like a political friend, including strangers from beyond the nation's borders, could land there and flourish in conjunction with us.[18] My utopia stands as a proposal to democratic citizens generally to develop their capacities for political imagination, particularly with reference to the strangers in their lives. The long-term ability of this democracy to convert distrust to trust is the reward.

Am I right about the potential of political friendship to rejuvenate democratic practice? Aristotle closes his treatise on rhetoric with words that he presents as the best way to close an argument, and which I will accordingly use: "You've heard me, you understand. Now judge."

Acknowledgments

THIS BOOK CONSISTS of revised versions of the 2003 Julius Rosenthal Lectures at Northwestern University School of Law. My thanks to Northwestern for the inspiration and occasion for this project.

For the making of this book I owe more debts than I can count; I will do my best to name those to whom they're owed: Arash Abizadeh, Marc Allen, Michael Allen, Shannon Allen, Susan Allen, William Allen, Elizabeth Asmis, Elizabeth Babcock, Ike Balbus, Selya Benhabib, Christina Burnett, Graham Burnett, Cathy Cohen, Jim Conant, Marianne Constable, Vivian Counts, Raine Daston, Jill Frank, the Franke Institute for the Humanities, Bryan Garsten, Amy Gutmann, Kevin Hawthorne, Matt Hofer, Melissa Lane, Sally and Fred Lowrance, the MacArthur Foundation, Steve Macedo, Paige Maclean, Sonya Malunda, Karuna Mantena, Patchen Markell, Maureen McLane, Charles Mills, Lucas Morel, Deborah Nelson, Northwestern University Law School, Martha Nussbaum, Josh Ober, Steve Pincus, Robert Pippin, the Max Planck Institute for the History of Science, Jim Powell, Stacie Raucci, Carol Saller, Maggie Schein, James Schulz, Laura Slatkin, Jackie Stewart, Jeffrey Stout, Alan Thomas, Richard Tuck, Lisa Van Alstyne, Isaac von Hallberg, Robert von Hallberg, Stefan von Hallberg, Ken Warren, Heather Watkins, Hank Webber, Cornel West, Melissa Williams, Iris Young, and audiences, students, and workshops at and in: Cambridge University; Washington and Lee University; Wesleyan University; University of Houston–Clear Lake; Ramsey I unit, Texas Department of Correctional Justice;

Princeton University; Harvard University; Charlotte, North Carolina; the Odyssey Project; the Universities of Wisconsin–Milwaukee and Madison; the Universities of California–Berkeley and Irvine; Northwestern University Law School; Howard University; Wesleyan College; University of Toronto; and Chicago Political Theory group.

Thanks also to the anonymous readers for the University of Chicago Press.

Notes

PROLOGUE

1. In general, I use "we" to refer to citizens of the United States. Sometimes I use it to refer to human beings generally. I have tried to flag which usage applies in each case. For a discussion of race talk and the use of the pronoun "we," see L. Balfour, "'A Most Disagreeable Mirror,'" *Political Theory* 26 (1998): 346–69.

2. Details about urban renewal come from the following texts: South East Chicago Commission, *South East Chicago Renewal Project,* no. 1 (Chicago, 1954); J. Levi, *The Neighborhood Program of the University of Chicago* (Washington, D.C., 1961); Center for Neighborhood Renewal, *People and Neighborhood Renewal* (Chicago, 1962); D. E. Mackelmann, *Elimination and Prevention of Slums and Blight in Chicago* (Chicago, 1964); M. Murphy and E. G. Yondorf, *Mid South Development Area* (Chicago, 1968); P. H. Rossi and R. A. Dentler, *The Politics of Urban Renewal* (1961; repr. Glencoe, 1963).

The recent literature on trust is extensive. Whereas most recent work has focused on trust in "government," I focus on interpersonal trust among citizens, not in institutions, government, or politicians. I adopt a definition of trust equivalent to Russell Hardin's analysis of it as a belief that someone else's interests encapsulate one's own such that that person can be expected to act with one's own interests in mind. He writes, "One of the most important and commonplace [reasons for thinking someone trustworthy] is *trust as encapsulated interest*. . . . On this account, I trust you because I think it is in your interest to take my interests in the relevant matter seriously in the following sense: You value the continuation of our relationship, and you therefore have your own interests in taking my interests into account. That is, you encapsulate my interests in your own interests. My interests might come into conflict with other interests you have and that trump mine, and you might therefore not actually act in ways that fit my interests. Nevertheless, you have at least some interest in doing so" (R. Hardin, *Trust and Trustworthiness* [New York, 2002], 1). Like Hardin, I believe that the best way to generate trust is in fact to generate trustworthiness.

Other books on trust that I have found helpful include A. Baier, *Moral Prejudices* (1994; repr. Harvard, 1996); M. Warren, ed., *Democracy and Trust* (Cambridge, 1999); S. Macedo, *Diversity and Distrust* (Cambridge, Mass., 2002); L. Guinier and G. Torres, *The Miner's Canary* (Cambridge, Mass., 2002); M. Williams, *Voice, Trust, and Memory* (Princeton, 1998); K. Cook, ed., *Trust in Society* (New York, 2001); T. Skocpol, *Diminished Democracy* (Norman, Okla., 2003); R. Putnam, *Bowling Alone* (2000; repr. New York, 2001); J. Dunn, "The Concept of 'Trust' in the Politics of John Locke," in *Philosophy in History,* ed. R. Rorty, J. B. Schneewind, and Q. Skinner (Cambridge, 1984); R. D. Putnam, with R. Leonardi and R. Y. Nanetti, *Making Democracy Work* (Princeton, 1993).

Other early major landmarks on the subject are N. Luhmann, "Trust: A Mechanism for the Reduction of Social Complexity," in *Trust and Power* (New York, 1980); F. Fukuyma, *Trust: The Social Virtues and the Creation of Prosperity* (New York, 1995); D. Gambetta, ed., *Trust: Making and Breaking Cooperative Relations* (Oxford, 1988).

Race is a frequent subtext in these discussions of trust. When scholars get down to concrete examples and want to ask questions about who counts as trustworthy and whom one can trust, racially coded examples often surface. See, for instance, A. Baier, *Moral Prejudices* (184), where workers in "the drug business" and "loyal gang members" come in for discussion. I point this out not to cast blame. Baier's work on trust is the work I most admire. Rather, I seek to draw our attention to the ways in which we often implicitly recognize that issues of trust in this country are closely tied to issues of race.

3. See J. Kaufman, *For the Common Good?* (Oxford, 2002), which revisits late nineteenth-century civic associations and lays out their connections to a culture of exclusion and domination. Putnam's earliest work tended to focus on bonding relationships among people who are like one another, but more recently he and other social scientists have turned their attention to "linking" and "bridging" relationships that bring people together across social cleavages. For the status of Charlotte, see *The Saguaro Seminar (Civic Engagement in America),* "Social Capital Community Benchmark Survey 2000," John F. Kennedy School of Government (Robert Putnam, Principal Investigator), at http://www.ropercenter.uconn.edu/scc_bench.html. A summary of the results is provided in Foundation for the Carolinas, *Voices and Choices of the Central Carolinas: 2000–2001* Social Capital Survey Results (Charlotte, 2001).

4. G. Burns, "America's Motto," *Chicago Tribune,* June 7, 2003, sec. 1.

5. John Hart Ely, *Democracy and Distrust* (Cambridge, 1980).

6. Of trust theorists, Annette Baier is the most sensitive to the issues of vulnerability involved in trust, and to the relationship between trust and confidence. A. Baier, *Moral Prejudices,* 99: "Trust, then, on this first approximation, is accepted vulnerability to another's possible but not expected ill will (or lack of goodwill) toward one." She also offers a good discussion of the relationship between cognitive and affective elements of trust (130–51) and a response to Ely-style arguments (108,

131). On this last question, see also L. C. Becker, "Trust as Noncognitive Security about Motives," *Ethics* 107 (1996): 43–61.

7. For a history of the civil rights movement, see C. Carson, D. J. Garrow, G. Gill, V. Harding, and D. C. Hine, eds., *The Eyes on the Prize* (New York, 1991); C. M. Payne, *I've Got the Light of Freedom* (1995; repr. Berkeley, 1996); S. Lawson, "Freedom Then, Freedom Now," *American Historical Review* 96 (April 1991): 456–71; A. Morris, *Origins of the Civil Rights Movement* (New York, 1984); C. Eagles, ed., *The Civil Rights Movement in America* (Oxford, Miss., 1986); W. Chafe, *Civilities and Civil Liberties* (Oxford, Miss., 1980); F. Powledge, *Free at Last?* (Boston, 1991); S. Belfrage, *Freedom Summer* (New York, 1965); D. McAdam, *Freedom Summer* (Oxford, 1988); J. Hochschild, *Thirty Years after Brown* (Washington, D.C., 1985). I am by no means the first to argue that the period of the civil rights struggle constituted a civil war. See Garry Wills, *The Second Civil War* (New York, 1968).

8. See, as an example, J. Levy, *Multiculturalism of Fear* (Oxford, 2000), 112–18. Cf. A. Buchanan, *Secession* (Boulder, 1991); L. Green, "Internal Minorities and Their Rights," in *Group Rights,* ed. J. Baker (Toronto, 1994).

9. Martin Luther King, Jr., "I Have a Dream" (speech, Washington, D.C., Aug. 28, 1963). Payne, *I've Got the Light,* 421, makes the point that studies of the civil rights movement have a tendency to "reduc[e] the movement to a 'protest' movement, treating nonviolence as if it were somehow natural while treating militance as inevitably doomed to failure." For the place of militancy in the civil rights movement, see D. Colburn, *Racial Change and Community Crisis* (New York, 1985); Rural Organizing and Cultural Center, *Minds Stayed on Freedom* (Boulder, Colo., 1991); and D. Levering Lewis, "The Origins and Causes of the Civil Rights Movement," in *The Civil Rights Movement,* ed. Eagles, 3–17.

10. Up until the 1920s African Americans were the majority group in Louisiana, South Carolina, and Mississippi. By the 1950s the balance had swung, but African Americans remained significant population blocks in these and other Southern states. A swath of roughly 200 counties stretching from Virginia through the Carolinas and across the Gulf South were still majority black counties at the onset of the civil rights movement.

	African Americans		Native Whites	
	Male	Female	Male	Female
Mississippi	479,137	507,357	591,286	589,032
South Carolina	396,112	425,965	639,891	646,011
Louisiana	424,771	457,657	876,603	891,196

Source: U.S. Census of 1950, available at www.fisher.lib.virginia.edu/census/.

11. I adopt the definition of civil war developed by H. M. Enzensberger in *Civil Wars* (New York, 1994). He argues, for instance, that "in the collective running

amok, the concept 'future' disappears. Only the present matters. Consequences do not exist" (29).

12. Martin Luther King, Jr., wrote, "It was a great relief to be in a federal court. Here the atmosphere of justice prevailed. No one can understand the feeling that comes to a Southern Negro on entering a federal court unless he sees with his own eyes and feels with his own soul the tragic sabotage of justice in the city and state courts of the South." *Stride to Freedom* (New York, 1964), 131–32, cited in C. Hamilton, "Federal Law and the Courts in the Civil Rights Movement," in *The Civil Rights Movement,* ed. Eagles, 97–117. Hamilton also writes that after those who were planning the protests in Birmingham were denied a permit, they "refused also to take their case to the state courts declaring, interestingly, in a press conference '[they] had respect for the Federal Courts, or Federal injunctions but in the past the state courts had favored local law enforcement'" (112).

13. I use the phrases "electoral minorities" and "electoral majorities" in order to include within this analysis even such cases as those of some counties in the South where a minority held all the political power, and the majority was excluded even from voting. The phrase "electoral minority" can refer to a group that, despite being the majority within the population, is a minority within the voting registers, and vice versa.

14. This argument is consistent with James Madison's arguments in *Federalist* 10 about the need to protect minorities. The thought experiment about joining a club in which one will be outvoted is akin to John Rawls's veil of ignorance experiment in *Theory of Justice.* My result is analogous to his, although my argument that majority decisions must also advance minority interests in order for democracy to be stable is not quite as robust a principle as his difference principle: "Social and economic inequalities are to be arranged so that they are . . . to the greatest benefit of the least advantaged" (*Theory of Justice* [Cambridge, Mass., 1971], sec. 46; cf. Rawls, *Political Liberalism* [New York, 1993], 291). Rawls's argument is normative, whereas mine, here, is merely pragmatic.

15. Benjamin DeMott offers an eloquent critique of attempts to draw on the idea of friendship for dealing with political problems (*The Trouble with Friendship* [New York, 1995]), in which "interracial buddy movies" are among his main targets. He treats the "friendship orthodoxy" as simplifying the problems that generate interracial distrust in the first place and relying on superficial emotional bonds to solve the problem. See also M. Rogin on *Forrest Gump* and *Pulp Fiction* in "The Two Declarations of American Independence," in *Race and Representation,* ed. R. Post and M. Rogin (New York, 1998), 88–90.

16. B. Honig, in *Democracy and the Foreigner* (Princeton, 2001), works from a similar premise: "Democracy is always about living with strangers under a law that is therefore alien (because it is the mongrel product of political action—often gone awry—taken with and among strangers)" (39). See also Sheldon Wolin's wonderful *The Presence of the Past* (Baltimore, 1989).

CHAPTER ONE

1. Two strands of political analysis come together in my approach to the idea of a "constitution." Historians of ancient politics, who study polities without written constitutions, typically analyze the changing distribution of citizenship rights and powers through law and custom in order to identify different "constitutional moments" in any regime's history. Athenian history, for instance, is generally periodized according to changes in citizenship law and in other laws and customs determining who could hold particular offices within the city. See, for instance, V. Ehrenberg, *From Solon to Socrates* 2nd ed. (New York, 1973); C. Starr, *The Birth of Athenian Democracy* (Oxford, 1990); J. Ober, *Mass and Elite* (Princeton, 1989); D. Allen, *The World of Prometheus* (Princeton, 2000).

Recently scholars have paid greater attention to how cultural habits and customs interact with institutions to route power, grafting Michel Foucault's approach to power (e.g., *Discipline and Punish*) onto a more traditional one. Examples include J. Ober, *Mass and Elite;* J. Ober, *Athenian Revolution* (Princeton, 1993); D. Allen, *The World of Prometheus;* and R. Balot, *Greed and Injustice in Classical Athens* (Princeton, 2002). Political theorist Sheldon Wolin's approach to constitutions is similar in *The Presence of the Past,* 8–31, 180–87. See also, Baier, *Moral Prejudices,* 162.

2. M. Kruman, "Suffrage," in *The Reader's Companion to American History,* ed. E. Foner and J. A. Garraty (New York, 1991), 1043–47.

CHAPTER TWO

1. Wolin, *The Presence of the Past,* 85.

2. In general, I have found the following helpful on the subject of citizenship: B. Manville, *The Origins of Citizenship in Ancient Athens* (Princeton, 1990); R. Beiner, ed., *Theorizing Citizenship* (Albany, 1995); D. Batstone and E. Mendita, eds., *The Good Citizen* (New York, 2001); J. Shklar, *American Citizenship* (Cambridge, Mass., 1991); and for a comparative perspective, B. Crick, ed., *Citizens* (Oxford, 2001).

3. Herodotus, *Histories* 9.5.

4. A. Schlesinger, *The Disuniting of America* (1991; repr. New York, 1992). On the role of the motto *e pluribus unum* in the identity of U.S. citizens, see Wolin, *The Presence of the Past.* On the idealization of "oneness," see B. Barber, *Strong Democracy* (Berkeley, 1984), 32–37.

5. Schlesinger, *Disuniting,* 13, 18.

6. The amended pledge was signed into law on June 14, 1954, having been introduced in the House as Joint Resolution 243 on April 20, 1953. The author and originator of the amendment of the pledge was Rep. Louis Rabaut (D-MI), who was known to his colleagues as a deeply religious man. Rep. Alfred Santangelo of New York made representative remarks at Rabaut's memorial service: "Louis Rabaut was a deeply religious man. His belief in God and in the dignity of man permeated his whole life and found vessels in the form of three daughters who be-

came nuns, one son who became a priest and five children who married and became parents. Little wonder then that he successfully sponsored the measure to insert the words 'under God' in our 'Pledge of Allegiance.' This bill was his greatest comfort and pride and his words 'under God' will be repeated by all Americans while our Nation lives in freedom." Rep. Carl Albert of Oklahoma wrote, "How significant is that fact in an age in which our principal concern is with the spread of atheistic communism." In *Memorial Services, Louis C. Rabaut,* 87th Cong., 2nd sess. (Washington, D.C., 1962), 34, 45.

7. Schoolchildren could not be forced to pledge, but schools could be required to offer it as a morning ritual. When Eisenhower signed the revised pledge into law, he made the following statement:

> From this day forward, the millions of our school children will daily proclaim in every city and town, every village and rural schoolhouse, the dedication of our Nation and our people to the Almighty. To anyone who truly loves America, nothing could be more inspiring than to contemplate this rededication of our youth, on each school morning, to our country's true meaning.
>
> Especially is this meaningful as we regard today's world. Over the globe, mankind has been cruelly torn by violence and brutality and, by the millions, deadened in mind and soul by a materialistic philosophy of life. Man everywhere is appalled by the prospect of atomic war. In this somber setting, this law and its effects today have profound meaning. In this way we are reaffirming the transcendence of religious faith in America's heritage and future; in this way we shall constantly strengthen those spiritual weapons which will be our country's most powerful resources, in peace or in war. [83rd Cong., 2nd sess., *Congressional Record–Senate* 100, p. 7 [June 22, 1954]: 8618]

Rabaut himself, in advocating the change before Congress, argued, "It is my hope that the recitation of the pledge, with this addition, 'under God,' by our schoolchildren will bring to them a deeper understanding of the real meaning of patriotism. Love of country is not just a blind adherence to an institution evolved out of the mind of man and established and maintained by human hands alone. This deception was the scheme establishing the wicked idolatry of the state, impregnated into the fertile young minds of the Hitler youth, and their Soviet counterparts" (*Appendix,* 83rd Cong., 1st sess., *Congressional Record* 99, pt. 10 [April 21, 1953]: A2063). And in the following year, Rabaut argued, "You may argue from dawn to dusk about differing political, economic, and social systems, but the fundamental issue which is the unbridgeable gap between America and Communist Russia is a belief in Almighty God. . . . An atheistic American . . . is a contradiction in terms" (83rd Cong., 2nd sess., *Congressional Record–House* 11, pt. 2 [Feb. 12, 1954]: 1700).

8. On the argument over where to insert the phrase "under god," see 83rd Cong., 2nd sess., *Congressional Record–Senate* 100, pt. 5 (May 11, 1954): 6348. See also the summary of the year-long debate on June 7, 1954, 83rd Cong., 2nd sess., *Congressional Record–House* 100, pt. 6: 7760–61. The insertion of "under God" between "nation" and "indivisible" suggests that the nation is now divisible by God, or by issues of religion. The pledge has, strangely enough, introduced conceptual space for precisely the sorts of problems that many of the writers of the Constitution wished to write out of politics.

9. C. M. Wiltse, ed., *The Papers of Daniel Webster,* vol. 1, *1800–1833* (Hanover, N.H., 1986), 349–93. Robert Caro writes of this peroration, "Those words would be memorized by generations of schoolchildren, they would be chiseled in marble on walls and monuments," in *The Years of Lyndon Johnson* (New York, 2002), 7.

10. The 1954 congressional debate also included recitation of a text written by Bellamy to describe writing the pledge. Bellamy had written, "Now how should the vista be widened so as to teach the national fundamentals? I laid down my pencil and tried to pass our history in review. It took in the sayings of Washington, the arguments of Hamilton, the Webster-Hayne debate, the speeches of Seward and Lincoln, the Civil War. After many attempts all that pictured struggle reduced itself to three words, 'One Nation, indivisible.' To reach that compact brevity, conveying the facts of a single nationality and of an indivisibility both of States and of common interests, was, as I recall, the most arduous phase of the task." He continues by describing the original pledge as entailing a rejection of the ideas of equality and fraternity: "But what of the present and future of this indivisible Nation here presented for allegiance? What were the old and fought-out issues which always will be issues to be fought for? Especially, what were the basic national doctrines bearing upon the acute questions already agitating the public mind? Here was a temptation to repeat the historic slogan of the French Revolution, imported by Jefferson, 'liberty, fraternity, equality.' But that was rather quickly rejected, as fraternity was too remote of realization, and as equality was a dubious word. What doctrines, then, would everybody agree upon as the basis of Americanism? 'Liberty and justice' were surely basic, were undebatable, and were all that any one Nation could handle. If they were exercised for all they involved the spirit of equality and fraternity" (83rd Cong., 2nd sess., *Congressional Record–House* 100, pt. 6 [June 7, 1954]: 7761).

11. Congressional argument included the claim that the amendment "comes at a time when throughout our land and throughout the world some people express doubt, yes, doubt and even fear, regarding the future. They see the storm clouds blowing upon the horizon and sometimes not the sun behind." They also included this claim: "Some 2000 or perhaps 3000 of my constituents wrote me in support of this joint resolution. Those who wrote me came from all walks of life. Many were children. It was by far the largest mail that I have received on any subject during the months of the 83rd Congress. It reflected a spiritual awakening in our country,

the universality and the depth of which may never have been surpassed. I was profoundly moved, Mr. Sepaer, at this evidence so clear that none could miss its significance that in time of atomic peril and of evil-portending foreign and domestic problems the American people were resting their fears in a quiet faith in God" (83rd Cong., 2nd sess., *Congressional Record–House* 100, pt. 6 [June 7, 1954]: 7757, 7761). On September 24, when President Dwight Eisenhower addressed the nation on the Little Rock crisis and warned of "anarchy peril," he concluded his speech with reference to the pledge: "Thus will be restored the image of America and of all its parts as one nation, indivisible, with liberty and justice for all" (*New York Times,* Sept. 25, 1957). His failure "to put 'Under God' in Pledge" merited an accompanying headline.

12. See n. 10, above.

13. The suggestion that modern democratic politics requires the active engagement of the imagination is not original. Benedict Anderson argued in *Imagined Communities* (London, 1983) that modernity has required citizens of large nation states to develop methods of imagining themselves into relationships with their fellow citizens. The development of national languages and newspapers that circulate throughout a whole community allows people to see and imagine themselves as part of a larger group despite the literal impossibility of ever seeing the whole nation state or citizenry at once. The impossibility of seeing the group to which one belongs requires the engagement of the imagination if politics based on such groups is to succeed.

I suggest here, in a move away from Anderson, that it is not the size of the modern nation state that requires the engagement of the imagination, but simply the attempt to base politics on "the people." For where is the people? And what is it? And how does it act? No citizen can explain her role in modern populist political regimes without fairly significant conceptual and imaginative labor by which she makes herself part of an invisible whole. See also Wolin, *The Presence of the Past;* and Barber, *Strong Democracy,* 32–37.

14. I discuss this distinction between domination and exclusion in "Invisible Citizens," in *NOMOS,* ed. M. Williams and S. Macedo (forthcoming).

15. T. Skutnabb-Kangas, ed., *Multilingualism for All* (Lisse, The Netherlands, 1995).

16. Facing History and Ourselves, exhibit at the Chicago Historical Society, with accompanying website: http://www.facinghistorycampus.org/ctp.nsf//All+Docs/ CTP+crisis+elizabeth2?Open. Dorothy Counts, the young woman who was the first African American to attend Harding High School, in Charlotte, N.C., shared the front page of the *New York Times* with Elizabeth Eckford on September 5, 1957, in the headline photo. She too was wearing a checked dress, which, in the black-and-white photography of the day, also looks like black-and-white checks. Perhaps the similarity in the dresses of the two young women accounts for the selection of those photos as a pair for the front page?

17. I am grateful to Patchen Markell for conversations on the subjects of agency and control in relation to democratic citizenship.

18. Thucydides, *History of the Peloponnesian War* 1.10.

19. This is not a new story in U.S. politics. George Washington wore a suit made of homespun cloth to his first inauguration in order to express his revolutionary country's economic independence from Britain (*The Papers of George Washington, Presidential Series,* vol. 2 [http://gwpapers.virginia.edu/presidency/inaugural/]; see also C. W. Bowen, ed., *The History of the Centennial Celebration of the Inauguration of George Washington* (New York, 1892). Robert Hayne, the Southern senator to whom Webster made the famous reply discussed above, had for his own speech to the Senate (presided over by John C. Calhoun) worn a "coarse homespun suit that he had substituted for the hated broadcloth manufactured in the North" (Caro, *The Years of Lyndon Johnson,* 5).

CHAPTER THREE

1. Although Arendt thought she was writing about the photo of Elizabeth Eckford in Little Rock, Arkansas, that appeared on the front page of the *New York Times* on September 5, 1957, the photo that she actually describes was the accompanying photo of Dorothy Counts in Charlotte, North Carolina. It is the photo of Counts, not of Eckford, that includes the "white friend of her father" to whom Arendt refers. Arendt's mistake has been frequently adopted by others on the basis of her authority. Also, it is important to point out a common misinterpretation of Arendt's essay. She is often seen as having criticized only the African American parents. In fact, she also criticized the white parents for exploiting their children (RLR 50).

The most helpful secondary materials on Arendt's essay are Elisabeth Young-Bruehl, *Hannah Arendt* (New Haven, 1982), 308–18; D. S. Allen, "Law's Necessary Forcefulness," *Oklahoma City Law Review* 26.3 (2001): 857–94; S. Benhabib, *The Reluctant Modernism of Hannah Arendt* (Thousand Oaks, 1996); J. Bohman, "The Moral Costs of Political Pluralism," in *Hannah Arendt,* ed. L. May and J. Kohn (Cambridge, Mass., 1997); L. J. Disch, "On Friendship in 'Dark Times,'" in *Feminist Interpretations of Hannah Arendt,* ed. B. Honig (University Park, Pa., 1995), 285–311; A. Norton, "Heart of Darkness," in *Feminist Interpretations of Hannah Arendt,* ed. Honig, 247–61; E. M. Budick, *Blacks and Jews in Literary Conversation* (Cambridge, 1998).

2. Ellison also commented on Arendt's article in "The World and the Jug," *New Leader,* Dec. 9, 1963, which has since been reprinted in *Collected Essays.*

3. As a novelist, Ellison was determined to achieve the "imaginative integration of the total American experience" ("On Initiation Rites and Power," *CE* 525). He invented narrative forms that connect individual psychic struggles to the larger structures of American democracy, and also reveal the meanings of that connection. The arguments I make here about Ellison's "conclusions" are based on read-

ing his two novels for the arguments constructed out of the interplay of characters and then setting these arguments against those developed in his essays. This method of reading mimics Ellison's own. He and his letter-writing companion, Albert Murray, discussed how to give the reader "an adventure" by "presenting process" not "statements." Thus, Ellison writes to Murray, "I would like more Emdee . . . or Jaygee because with them Jack could arrive at his theories through conflict . . . His ideas are not the usual ones . . . and I think much *unrevealed* revelation lies in the story of how he attained this kind of transcendence" (R. Ellison and A. Murray, *Trading Twelves* [New York, 2000], 28). Thus, I read Ellison's novels seeking to discern what the conflicts of ideas are; from there I try to assess what concerns on the part of the author led to the focus on these particular conflicts. I never take the words of any particular character as examples of Ellison's opinions, unless they are the words that have won some particular argument that his books are having with themselves. I amplify my readings of his novels with reference to his essays.

4. Both Meili Steele and Kenneth Warren have been building a body of work on Ellison's political ideas. See M. Steele, "Metatheory and the Subject of Democracy," *New Literary History* 27 (1996): 473–502; "Democratic Interpretation and the Politics of Difference," *Comparative Literature* 48 (1996): 326–42; "Arendt versus Ellison on Little Rock," *Constellations* 9 (2002): 184–206; Kenneth Warren, "Ralph Ellison and the Reconfiguration of Black Cultural Politics," *Yearbook of Research in English and American Literature* 11 (1995): 139–57; "'As White as Anybody,'" *New Literary History* 31 (2000): 709–26. There has also been a proliferation of free-standing pieces on the subject: J. M. Albrecht, "Saying Yes and Saying No," *PMLA* 114 (1999): 46–63; T. Parrish, "Ralph Ellison, Kenneth Burke, and the Form of Democracy," *Arizona Quarterly* 52 (1995): 117–48; Allen, "Law's Necessary Forcefulness"; J. Callahan, "Frequencies of Eloquence," in *New Essays on Invisible Man*, ed. R. O'Meally (Cambridge, 1988), 55–94; B. Ostendorf, "Ralph Waldo Ellison," in *New Essays,* ed. O'Meally, 95–122; S. E. Hyman, "Ralph Ellison in Our Time," in *Ralph Ellison,* ed. J. Hersey (Upper Saddle River, N.J., 1974), 39–42 (reprinted from *New Leader* 47, no. 22 [Oct. 26, 1964]: 21–22); B. Foley, "Reading Redness," *Journal of Narrative Theory* 29.3 (1999): 323–39.

On Ellison's politics (in contrast to his *theories* of politics), see J. G. Watts, *Heroism and the Black Intellectual* (Chapel Hill, 1994).

The best places to start with criticism of Ellison are A. Nadel, *Invisible Criticism* (Iowa City, 1988); K. Bentson, ed., *Speaking for You* (Washington, D.C., 1987); H. Baker, *Blues, Ideology, and Afro-American Literature* (Chicago, 1984); H. L. Gates, Jr., *The Signifying Monkey* (Oxford, 1988); L. Morel, ed., *Raft of Hope* (Lexington, Ky., 2004).

The most helpful text on Ellison that I have found is B. Eddy, *The Rites of Identity* (PhD diss., Princeton University, 1998). She addresses sacrifice, tragedy, and comedy in Ellison, as well as many of the other concepts that come up in his work.

Except for Eddy, I have not yet come across a text that investigates Ellison's idea of sacrifice, the subject of this chapter.

5. "Hidden Name and Complex Fate."

6. From T. S. Eliot's *The Wasteland* and Lord Raglan's *The Hero*, Ellison took a conviction that myth and ritual are fundamental to both human life and literature. Ellison invokes the idea of ritual throughout his essays. For instance, in "The Myth of the Flawed White Southerner," he refers to himself as "a novelist interested in that area of national life where political power is institutionalized and translated into democratic ritual and national style" (*CE* 553). To piece together Ellison's account of ritual, see particularly "Twentieth Century Fiction and the Mask of Humanity," "Art of Fiction," "Hidden Name and Complex Fate," and "Initiation Rites and Power." See also Eddy, *Rites*.

7. "Hidden Name and Complex Fate."

8. For related formulations of the idea of the democratic good, please see W. Connolly, *Politics and Ambiguity* (Madison, 1987), 15–18; and S. Wolin, *The Presence of the Past,* 4. Other theorists who draw our attention to discord, dissonance, and the mongrel nature of democratic policy are Ben Barber and Bonnie Honig. I have benefited substantially from the work of all four, as citations throughout this text indicate.

Here is another section of the interview with Robert Penn Warren:

> Warren: Here in the midst of what has been an expanding economy you have a contracting economy for the unprepared, for the Negro.
>
> Ellison: That's the paradox. And this particularly explains something new which has come into the picture; that is, a determination by the Negro no longer to be the scapegoat, no longer to pay, to be sacrificed to—the inadequacies of other Americans. We want to socialize the cost. A cost has been exacted in terms of character, in terms of courage, and determination, and in terms of self-knowledge and self-discovery. Worse, it has led to social, economic, political, and intellectual disadvantages and to a contempt even for our lives. And one motive for our rejection of the old traditional role of national scapegoat is an intensified awareness that not only are we being destroyed by the sacrifice, but that the nation has been rotting at its moral core. (WS 339)

9. This account derives entirely from Daisy Bates, *The Long Shadow of Little Rock* (New York, 1962); cf. D. L. Chappell, *Inside Agitators* (Baltimore, 1994).

10. There are some hints in the literature that integrationists preferred to start integration with girls rather than boys, because of the inflammatory power of the miscegenation issue. Of the Little Rock Nine, seven were young women.

CHAPTER FOUR

1. We can tell that Ellison meant his term "sacrifice" to be used for political and not only psychological analysis because he makes it the centerpiece of a criticism of Hannah Arendt's arguments about school desegregation and Little Rock Almost everyone with whom I have discussed these materials has objected that the term "sacrifice" does not properly belong to politics and is too dangerous to introduce to political discussion. George Kateb, for instance, worries (in personal conversation) that the effect of the term "sacrifice" in political discussion is inevitably to set the community above the individual, with dangerous consequences. My argument, however, is not that we should introduce sacrifice as an ethical term, but rather that we must recognize how much of a role it is already playing, and has always played, in democratic politics. Despite general disavowals of the topic of sacrifice, the word comes up frequently in political theory and political discussions. In fact, from a quick and casual survey, it seems that the majority of works published in political theory use the term at some point. The point I make with Ellison is that it is better to be honest about the political work being done by this idea, and to try to figure out how to deal with it, than to ignore it. My discussion is not meant to bring either military sacrifice or militarism to the fore; rather, in this chapter, I point to all the ordinary, prosaic day-to-day sacrifices that go into keeping democracy running, and that also generally go unnoticed. The United States has a fairly robust discourse of honor, recognition, and recompense for the sacrifices of soldiers, policemen, and firemen. We need some sort of analogous discourse, I am arguing, to help us deal with the sacrifices made by ordinary people.

Here and there in the political literature, one does find a recognition of the role that the idea of sacrifice has played in democratic contexts. Interestingly, the term appears with special frequency in discussions that also touch on race. W. Connolly offers an extended discussion of the "ideology of sacrifice" as an example of how citizens develop illusory ideological constructs to protect themselves from political and civilizational realities in *Appearance and Reality in Politics* (Cambridge, 1981), 65–82, 157–62. See also DeMott, *The Trouble with Friendship*, e.g., 11–23; Honig, *Democracy and the Foreigner*, e.g., 36; Wolin, *The Presence of the Past*, 49.

2. *New Oxford Annotated Bible.*

3. Shakespeare's *Hamlet* 2.2.276–96, gives further proof of the widespread currency of the story of Jepthah in the early modern period:

Ham. O Jephthah, judge of Israel, what a treasure hadst thou!
Pol. What a treasure had he, my lord?
Ham. Why
    One fair daughter and no more,
        The which he loved passing well.
Pol. [Aside.] Still on my daughter.
Ham. Am I not in, the right, old Jephthah?

Pol. If you call me Jephthah, my lord, I have a daughter that I love
passing well.
Ham. Nay, that follows not.

For Locke, Jepthah's relationship to God is a model for political action on the
part of democratic citizens. See also Locke II.21, 176. Peter Laslett writes in a note
on p. 282, "Locke evidently regarded the story of Jephthah as crucial to the scrip-
tural foundations of his case about civil society and justice. Grotius and St. Augus-
tine had used the Jephthah story for political analysis, and Locke may have had in
mind the Calvinist position expressed by Jurieu (1689, 365) that the Judges, Jepthah
among them, represented a stage between the anarchy of primeval innocence and
established sovereignty, a stage which inevitably passed because of the effects of
the Fall." Rousseau cites the Jepthah story in *Of the Social Contract* (bk. 4, chap. 8).
Honig (*Democracy and the Foreigner,* 36) offers an account via a discussion of Rousseau both of the role of sacrifice in the social contract theory and of the habits of
imagination that allow democratic citizens to ignore sacrifice.

4. He is explicit about the role of sacrifice in constitutional founding in his essays. See, for instance, "Initiation Rites and Power."

5. James Madison, "Vices of the Political System of the United States," in *Papers,*
W. T. Hutchinson, R. Rutland, et al., eds. (Chicago, 1962), 9.357, cited in E. Morgan, *Inventing the People* (New York, 1988), 52.

6. Shklar, *American Citizenship;* D. R. Roediger, *The Wages of Whiteness* (1991;
rev. ed. New York, 1999), chap. 8.

7. Honig, *Democracy and the Foreigner,* 58–62, offers a reading of the book of Ruth
that analyzes the figure of the female sacrificer in greater detail.

8. My account of the history of this idea as well as my analysis of it derives from
James K. Galbraith, "Time to Ditch the NAIRU," *Journal of Economic Perspectives* 11,
no. 1 (Winter 1997): 93–108. For related accounts of the relationship between unemployment policy and citizenship, see Connolly, *Appearance and Reality;* Wolin,
The Presence of the Past, 23–24, 32–46, 162. Interestingly, there are parallels to Ellison's language in Galbraith's analysis of how the NAIRU policy has imposed loss:
"We cannot reject the possibility that macroeconomic policy has been in thrall to
the illusion of a supposedly objective, but in fact self-induced, decline in the trend
rate of productivity growth, and that we have been running from the phantom of
accelerating inflation for more than two decades. The result: a self-inflicted wound,
a sociopsychological disability of colossal proportions" (99). On the relationship
between interest rates, the Federal Reserve, unemployment policy, and NAIRU,
see p. 101. Also, "The assignment of sole responsibility for anti-inflation policy to
the Federal Reserve, a de facto development that is technically illegal under the
Full Employment Act of 1978, is a serious underlying problem. . . . One of the serious unintended consequences of economists' preoccupation with NAIRU has
been to convey a message to political leaders that they need not feel any responsi-

bility in this area, that the inflation-unemployment tradeoff can be fine-tuned with interest rates by the Fed. It isn't so" (106). "Since Friedman's speech, orthodox macroeconomics has virtually always leaned against policies to support full employment. In spite of stagnant real wages, it has virtually never leaned the other way" (102). "When a higher NAIRU accompanies higher unemployment, it cuts against the case for a policy of expansion, since a higher proportion of the existing unemployment is seen as necessary to preserve stable inflation. When unemployment is falling, a downwardly sticky NAIRU bolsters the natural caution of many economists concerning progrowth policy intervention. In consequence, policymakers are almost *never* presented with a clear case, based on natural rate analysis and supported by a consensus of NAIRU-adhering economists, for a proemployment policy" (102). "The cost of unnecessarily high unemployment itself must therefore, to some extent, rest on the conscience of the economics profession" (103).

9. Galbraith, "Time to Ditch," 94.

10. Source for the natural rate of unemployment in 1999 and early 2000: Robert J. Samuelson, "Our Lifetime Job Prospects," *Newsweek,* June 28, 1999.

11. Galbraith, "Time to Ditch," 103.

12. Ellipses appear in the original and also indicate omissions of text.

13. DeMott, *The Trouble with Friendship,* 27–36, also criticizes the "same boat" metaphor and provides some specific examples.

14. See Shklar, *American Citizenship,* for an account of the centrality of military service and employment to the status of citizens in the United States; Wolin, *The Presence of the Past,* 32–46.

15. The arguments about trust in this paragraph rest on work done by Rogers Smith in "Trust and Worth," a paper given as the ISPS Charles E. Lindblom Lecture, 1999. There he argues, "Accounts of peoplehood . . . become stories of trust, stories told by leaders to persuade constituents that if they adhere to the political community thus defined, *they will be able to trust their compatriots, and particularly their governors, to strive to advance their own interests, values, and identities. . . .* the fundamental task facing the proponents of a particular conception of peoplehood is to persuade its would-be loyal citizenry of the distinctive worth or value (however defined) that can be realized by belonging to the community thus understood. . . . In short, people-building requires stories of trust and worth" (10; emphasis added).

16. Annette Baier recounts that the lesson about not talking to strangers, a new one for her when she moved from New Zealand to Britain and the United States, led to her work on trust in *Moral Prejudices,* 191.

17. M. Brick, "More Bad News, and the Stock Markets Are Happy to Hear It," *New York Times,* May 5, 2001, sec. C. See also M. Hulbert, "Beneath the Stock-Market Rebound, Hints of Trouble," *New York Times,* May 20, 2001, sec. 3. See also J. H. Boyd, and R. Jagannathan, and J. Hu, "The Stock Market's Reaction to Unemployment News," available at http://papers.nber.org/papers/W8092.

CHAPTER FIVE

1. The extent of agreement expected to result from arguments formulated in accord with Habermasian norms is extreme. The result of communicative action would be, in Seyla Benhabib's words, that "the consequences and side-effects which would foreseeably result from the universal subscription to a disputed norm, and as they would affect the satisfaction of the interests of each single individual, *could be accepted by all without constraints*" (*Critique, Norm, and Utopia* [New York, 1986], 304; emphasis added). Simone Chambers advocates the impartial agreements that should arise from Habermasian argument in similar terms: "To believe something is right is to believe that we have good reasons to hold this position. To believe that we have good reasons entails *the idea that given enough time,* given interlocutors of goodwill, and given a constraint-free environment, *everyone would come to the same conclusion as we have.* Thus impartial judgments are judgments that would gain *universal agreement in an ideal communication community*"("Discourse and Democratic Practices," in *The Cambridge Companion to Habermas,* ed. S. White [Cambridge, 1995], 233; emphasis added).

2. This is a paraphrase from Benhabib, *Critique,* 311.

3. She makes the argument implicitly: "The school is to the child what a job is to an adult. The only difference is that the element of free choice, which, in a free society, exists at least in principle in the choosing of jobs and the associations connected with them, is not yet at the disposal of the child but rests with his parents. To force parents to send their children to an integrated school against their will means to deprive them of rights which clearly belong to them in all free societies" (RLR 55).

4. I owe phrases in this sentence to Arash Abizadeh's excellent paper "Can Habermasian Discourse Shake the Charge of Motivational Impotence?" (presented at the annual meeting of the American Political Science Association, Aug. 29–Sept. 1, 2002). In general, this essay is one of the most useful analyses of the relevance of rhetoric to contemporary political theory presently available.

5. A. Honneth, "The Other of Justice," in *The Cambridge Companion to Habermas,* ed. White, 305. Or, as Chambers puts it, "Habermas never deals fully with the possibility that citizens might generally lack such an interest [in mutual understanding]" ("Discourse," 247).

6. There is a slippage in English translations of Habermas's arguments and in his critics' treatment of them between "understanding" and "agreement," such that the two terms sometimes become synonyms. This is really where the problems in the argument come in. It does seem reasonable to consider "understanding" a wholly illocutionary event, but not if "understanding" becomes a stand-in for "agreement." These problems arise from the ability of the German, *Einverstandniß,* to capture both ideas. For an example of this slippage, see quotations in note 1 of this chapter; and K. Baynes, *The Normative Grounds of Social Criticism* (Albany, 1992), 105–8.

204 : NOTES TO PAGES 59–66

7. As we have seen, Austin's regular examples of perlocution are "persuading" and "convincing." Habermas's are "to give fright to, to cause to be upset, to plunge into doubt, to annoy, mislead, offend, infuriate, humiliate, and so forth" (*TCA* 292). That difference says everything.

8. Baynes, *Normative Grounds,* 88–108.

9. E.g., P. Markell, "Contesting Consensus," *Constellations* 3 (1997): 388–91, especially 390; Abizadeh, "Habermasian Discourse."

10. On the issue of conventionality, and Habermas's relation to it, please see Baynes, *Normative Grounds,* 98–108.

11. For analyses of the relationship of Aristotle's writing on rhetoric to that of Plato, see A. Nehamas, "Pity and Fear in the *Rhetoric* and the *Poetics,*" in *Aristotle's Rhetoric,* ed. D. Furley and A. Nehamas (Princeton, 1994), 231–56; R. Wardy, "Mighty Is the Truth and It Shall Prevail?" in *Essays on Aristotle's* Rhetoric, ed. A. Rorty (Berkeley, 1996), 56–87.

12. As M. Walzer puts it in "Deliberation, and What Else?" in *Deliberative Politics,* ed. S. Macedo (Oxford, 1999), 58–69, "Permanent settlements are rare in political life precisely because we have no way of reaching anything like a verdict on contested issues. Passions fade; men and women disengage from particular commitments; interest groups form new alignments; the world turns."

13. I. Kant, *Critique of Pure Reason,* trans. Norman Kemp Smith (1929; repr. New York, 1965).

14. I. Kant, *Critik der Urtheilskraft* (Berlin, 1799).

15. "For these words of Good, Evill, and Contemptible, are ever used with relation to the person that useth them: There being nothing simply and absolutely so; nor any common Rule of Good and Evill, to be taken from the nature of the objects themselves; but from the Person of the man (where there is no Commonwealth;) or, (in a Commonwealth,) from the Person that representeth it" (*L* 6.7).

16. *EL* 1.5.14, 1.13.1–11, 2.8.12–15, 2.9.5, 2.9.7–8; *DC,* Epistle Dedicatory (p. 94), 10.9–13, 12.12–13, 13.9; *L* 4.4, 5.20, 10.12, 11.13, 11.16, 25.15, 29.20, 30.6–14; but compare *Leviathan* chap. 8, and Review and Conclusion 1, 4, 15.

See V. Silver, "Hobbes on Rhetoric," in *The Cambridge Companion to Thomas Hobbes,* ed. T. Sorell (Cambridge, 1996), 329–45; Q. Skinner, *Reason and Rhetoric in the Philosophy of Hobbes* (Cambridge, 1996); T. Strong, "How to Write Scripture," *Critical Inquiry* 20 (1993): 128–59; T. Ball, "Hobbes' Linguistic Turn," *Polity* 17 (1985): 739–60; W. Sacksteder, "Hobbes," *Philosophy and Rhetoric* 17 (1984): 30–46; K. V. Erickson, *Aristotle's* Rhetoric (Metuchen, N.J., 1975).

17. *Metaphora de estin onomatos allotriou epiphora* (Aristotle, *Poetics* 21).

18. Aristotle, *Poetics* 22; *R* 3.2.7.

19. Aristotle, *R* 3.2.12.

20. On the degree to which Rousseau and Kant did adopt Hobbesian arguments about the state of nature, see R. Tuck, "Hobbes' State of Nature in Rousseau and Kant" (paper given at a Harvard University political theory workshop, 1997). The

relationship of Kant to Hobbes is of course much more subtle than I am able to capture here. On Kant and rhetoric, see R. J. Dostal, "Kant and Rhetoric," *Philosophy and Rhetoric* 13 (1980): 223–44.

21. I. Young, "Justice, Inclusion, and Deliberative Democracy," in *Deliberative Politics,* ed. Macedo, 123.

CHAPTER SIX

1. My reading of Hobbes differs from mainstream interpretations on the following points: (1) the "social contract" should be analyzed not as a "contract" but as a "covenant"; this is the term Hobbes uses to describe the agreement that arises in the state of nature, and for him the term "covenant" foregrounds the importance of trust to agreement; (2) Hobbes is a theorist not merely of fear and distrust but also of trustworthiness, charity, and equity; the contents of his laws of nature present his view of the ethical content of terms such as those three (here I follow Richard Tuck in emphasizing Hobbes's interest in the positive elements of sociability); (3) Hobbes's interest in rhetoric extends not merely to his use of rhetorical techniques in *Leviathan* but also to the content of his laws of nature, which, in my view, derive significantly from his readings in the rhetorical tradition; (4) Hobbes is above all else a theorist of egalitarian political forms, and to this degree his philosophical work tends toward democratic rather than monarchic theory.

On Hobbes's philosophy in general, I have found the following texts helpful: Sorell, ed., *The Cambridge Companion to Hobbes;* D. Raphael, "Hobbes on Justice," in *Perspectives on Thomas Hobbes,* ed. G. A. J. Rogers and A. Ryan (Oxford, 1988), 153–70; A. Ryan, "Hobbes' Political Philosophy," in *The Cambridge Companion,* ed. Sorell, 208–45; A. Ryan, "Hobbes and Individualism," in *Perspectives,* ed. Rogers and Ryan, 81–106; Q. Skinner, "The Idea of Negative Liberty," in *Philosophy in History,* ed. Rorty, Schneewind, and Skinner, 193–221; F. Tricaud, "Hobbes' Conception of the State of Nature from 1640 to 1651," in *Perspectives,* ed. Rogers and Ryan, 107–24; R. Tuck, "Hobbes' Moral Philosophy," in *The Cambridge Companion,* ed. Sorell, 175–207; J. Hampton, *Hobbes and the Social Contract Tradition* (Cambridge, 1986); D. Gauthier, "Hobbes's Social Contract," in *Perspectives,* ed. Rogers and Ryan, 125–52; K. C. Brown, ed., *Hobbes Studies* (London, 1965).

For the political context in which Hobbes was writing, I have relied on C. Blitzer, *The Commonwealth of England* (New York, 1963); C. Russell, *Parliaments and English Politics, 1621–1629* (Oxford, 1979); Morgan, *Inventing the People;* S. Pincus, "Neither Machiavellian Moment nor Possessive Individualism," *American Historical Review* 103 (1998): 705–36; H. F. Pitkin, *The Concept of Representation* (Berkeley, 1967); Rorty, Schneewind, and Skinner, eds., *Philosophy in History;* J. H. Burns and M. Goldie, eds., *The Cambridge History of Political Thought, 1450–1700* (Cambridge, 1991); Q. Skinner, *The Foundations of Modern Political Thought,* vols. 1 and 2 (Cambridge, 1978); R. Tuck, *Philosophy and Government, 1572–1651* (Cambridge, 1993).

On Hobbes's relation to the rhetorical tradition, see chapter 5, n. 16, above.

On the idea of "the people": Morgan, *Inventing;* J. Elkins, "Constitutionalism and Law in a Regime of Popular Sovereignty" "(paper delivered at the 1996 annual meeting of the American Political Science Association, San Francisco, Aug. 29–Sept. 1, 1996); J. Derrida, "Declarations of Independence," trans. T. Keenan and T. Pepper, *New Political Science* 15 (1986): 7–15; J. Rancière, *Disagreement,* trans. Julie Rose (*Mésentente*), (Minneapolis, 1999); M. H. H. Hansen, *The Athenian Democracy in the Age of Demosthenes* (Oxford, 1987); R. Brubaker, *Citizenship and Nationhood in France and Germany* (Cambridge, Mass., 1992).

On the place of the imagination in political life, the central subject of this chapter, I have especially profited from Anderson, *Imagined Communities;* L. Berlant, *The Queen of America Goes to Washington* (Chicago, 1997); V. Wohl, *Love among the Ruins* (Princeton, 2002); B. C. J. Singer, *Society, Theory, and the French Revolution* (New York, 1986); L. Hunt, *Politics, Culture, and Class in the French Revolution* (Berkeley, 1984); S. Sacks, ed., *On Metaphor* (1978; repr. Chicago, 1979); P. Ricoueur, "The Metaphorical Process as Cognition, Imagination, and Feeling," in *On Metaphor,* ed. Sacks, 141–58; M. Frey, *Les transformations du vocabulaire français à l'époque de la Révolution (1789–1800)* (Paris, 1925); K. Burke, *Language as Symbolic Action* (Berkeley, 1966); Burke, *A Rhetoric of Motives* (Berkeley, 1969); Burke, *A Grammar of Motives* (1945; repr. Berkeley, 1969b); Burke, *On Symbols and Society,* ed. with introduction by J. R. Gusfield (Chicago, 1989); T. Ball, J. Farr, and R. Hanson, eds., *Political Innovation and Conceptual Change* (Cambridge, 1989); K. Baker, *Inventing the French Revolution* (Cambridge, 1990).

2. The need to find the interest of the people has, in fact, in the modern world unleashed great political inventiveness, and where the ancient world, dominated by the factionalist account, focused on three regime types, the modern world has seen a proliferation of political structures, all putatively based on the will of the people: since 1650, there have been democratic and republican city-states (the American colonies), loose-knit republican confederacies (the Articles of Confederation), large federalist unions (the Constitution of the United States), bureaucratically based empires (the Napoleonic code; Prussian centralization), escapist socialist communes (Cabet, Fourier), empires bent on "liberating" subject peoples (esp. nineteenth-century France), fascism (Italy), "National Socialism" (Nazi Germany), totalitarianism and/or communism (USSR, China), Islamic Republics (Iran), secular liberal democracy, socialist democracy, consociationalism, and corporatism.

3. *De jure regni apud Scotos* (1579), 97. My translation. A translation of his text from 1680 reads "[I]t is lawfull not only for the whole people to kill that enemy but for every one of them" (*De jure regni apud Scotos, or, A dialogue, concerning the due priviledge of government in the kingdom of Scotland, betwixt George Buchanan and Thomas Maitland by the said George Buchanan; and translated out of the original Latine into English by Philalethes* [1680], 127).

On Buchanan's break from the French Huguenots, see J. H. M. Salmon,

"Catholic Resistance Theory," in *The Cambridge History of Political Thought,* ed. Burns and Goldie, 227. Buchanan was "silent about the Huguenots' idea that people hand their power over to representatives" (Skinner, *Foundations,* vol. 2, p. 343). Cromwell claimed that Buchanan and Spanish jurist Juan de Mariana were all the guides he needed for his revolutionary aims; H. A. Lloyd, "Constitutionalism," in *The Cambridge History of Political Thought,* ed. Burns and Goldie, 272.

4. The historical argument in the following paragraphs is based on the texts in note 1, above.

5. Cited in Pitkin, *Concept.*

6. On the history of representation, see Pitkin, *Concept;* Morgan, *Inventing;* Lloyd, "Constitutionalism"; Williams, *Voice, Trust, and Memory.*

7. Pitkin, *Concept,* 244–45.

8. In English, the phrase "the people" had a relatively static existence prior to the sixteenth century (*OED*). Its earliest occurrence is a statement that an "Assemblee of the pople [MS. C peple] withouten lordes that may gouerne tham es as a flokk of schepe that has na schepehird" (C. 1400 Maundev. [Roxb.] Pref. 2).

On the language of commons versus nobility and changes in parliament, see B. Worden, "English Republicanism," in *The Cambridge History of Political Thought,* ed. Burns and Goldie, 443–78, 452. The issue of who exactly was represented in the House of Commons is a little tricky. Morgan (*Inventing,* 41) argues, "The one interest, other than geographical, that the English House of Commons could be said to represent in the seventeenth century was, as we have seen, the interest of England's gentry, men whose birth and wealth were insufficient to give them a seat in the House of Lords but sufficient to make it seem desirable to them . . . that they be present at the seat of government . . . but sat as representatives not of their class but of localities."

9. Shakespeare, 3 *Hen. VI,* iii.iii.35 (1593). The same terminology is common in the Renaissance. Thus Filippo Beroaldo (c. 1440–1504) contrasts the *status popularis, status paucorum,* and *status unius;* Vespasiano da Bisticci (1421–98) opposes rule of the *signori* to rule of the *populare;* and Gasparo Contarini (1483–1542) describes Venice (in *De republica Venetorum* of 1543) as having a mixed constitution where "a mixture of the status of the nobility and of the people is maintained (*ex optimatum et populari statu*). See Q. Skinner, *Foundations of Modern Political Thought,* vol. 2, pp. 99, 106, 111. On *populus* "envisaged as comprising not only the 'poor commons' but also the marginalised and criminalised elements of late medieval European society—the destitute, the incapacitated, the vagrants, the beggars," see B. Bradshaw, "Transalpine Humanism," in *The Cambridge History of Political Thought,* ed. Burns and Goldie, 120–21.

10. Cited in Pitkin, *Concept,* 248 (emphasis added), who cites it from Louise Fargo Brown, "Ideas of Representation from Elizabeth to Charles II," *Journal of Modern History* 11 (March 1939): 34.

11. Cited in Pitkin, *Concept,* 246 (emphasis added). Morgan (*Inventing,* 48) ar-

gues that Parliament began to claim that it collectively represented the whole realm as early as the fourteenth century.

12. There are other examples of a conjunction between early analyses of representation and the idea of "wholeness." Sir Edward Coke wrote in the *Institutes,* "[I]t is to be observed though one be chosen for one particular county, or borough, yet when he is returned, and sits in parliament, he serveth for the whole realm, for the end of his coming thither as in the writ of his election appeareth, is generall" (cited in Pitkin, *Concept,* 245). In 1641 in the *Journals of the House of Commons* (II, 330) we find that "this House" is "the Representative Body of the whole Kingdom," while "their Lordships [are] but as particular Persons" (cited in Pitkin, *Concept,* 248). The Levellers' reforms of the House of Commons were intended to make it "an equal representative of the whole" (A. S. P. Woodhouse, ed., *Puritanism and Liberty* [London, 1938], 422).

13. *A Second View of the Army Remonstrance* (1648), 11–12, 26 (emphasis added). On the Levellers, see Tuck, *Philosophy and Government,* 242–47.

14. Dudley Digg[e]s, *A Review of the Observations upon Some of his Majesties Late Answers and Expresses* (Oxford, 1643), 3.

15. R. Filmer, *Observations upon Aristotle's Politiques* (London, 1652), 40 (emphasis added).

16. Blitzer, *Commonwealth,* 129.

17. Wolin, *The Presence of the Past,* 162: "State power begins in the materialization of the activity of the people, that is, in what is produced by their labor and skill. What their consent signifies is their willingness to make over, in whole or in part, their powers and products to be used by the state. While their power is being made available to government, the loss is experienced by them as political passivity." See also p. 12.

18. For a discussion of the image, H. Bredekamp, "From Walter Benjamin to Carl Schmitt, via Thomas Hobbes," *Critical Inquiry* 25 (1999): 247–66; R. Tuck, ed., *Leviathan* (Cambridge, 1996), lii; and Barber, *Strong Democracy,* 34, who writes, "The most striking feature of the liberal inertial frame is the physicality of its language and imagery. There was a 'thingness' about Hobbesian and post-Hobbesian liberal thought that seems to have been both new and extraordinary in the history of political discourse."

CHAPTER SEVEN

1. William Connolly had adopted an ideal of "dissonant holism" (*Politics and Ambiguity,* 16).

2. Sheldon Wolin's term is "tending" (*Presence of the Past,* 89).

3. Thus, in *Elements of Law* Hobbes writes, "In all contracts where there is trust, the promise of him that is trusted, is called a COVENANT" (*EL* I.15.8–9; cf. *DC* 2.9; *L.* 14.9–33. The following citations refer to passages in *Elements of Law, De cive,*

and *Leviathan* where Hobbes uses the word "covenant" to discuss what critics typically call "contract": *EL* 1.19.7, 2.1.2, 2.1.5, 2.1.6, 2.2.2; *De cive* 2.10–11, 14–18; *L* 16–18).

4. Hobbes has argued earlier in *Elements of Law,* "By power I mean . . . power of one man resisteth and hindereth the effects of the power of another: power simply is no more, but the excess of the power of one above that of another. For equal powers opposed, destroy one another; and such their opposition is called contention. The signs by which we know our own power are those actions which proceed from same; and the signs by which other men know it, are such actions, gesture, countenance and speech as usually such powers produce" (1.8.4–5).

De cive and *Leviathan* (chap. 6) include arguments similar to the passage from the *Elements of Law* quoted above. The *Leviathan* chapter includes a long discussion of the forms of speech by which passions are expressed, which is an addition to the argument of the earlier books.

5. King, Jr., "I Have a Dream."

6. Strong ("How to Write Scripture," 158) has called Hobbes "perhaps the most egalitarian of all theorists." Raphael ("Hobbes on Justice," 153–70) also sees his politics as strongly egalitarian. Other critics, too, have discussed Hobbes's conviction that pride, arrogance, and vainglory are the worst obstacles to peace (see Ryan, "Hobbes and Individualism," 101–3; F. Tricaud, "Hobbes' Conception of the State of Nature," 123; Tuck, "Hobbes' Moral Philosophy," 184. On the status of "equality" in liberal theory, see A. Sen, "On the Status of Equality," *Political Theory* 24 (1996): 294–400.

The important point is that no one, Hobbes argues, agrees to a government that he expects to perpetuate his disadvantage (e.g., *EL* 2.1.3–5). Ryan ("Hobbes and Individualism," 92) argues that this, for Hobbes, is not a matter of "maximizing utilities" but of "satisficing." He stresses that for Hobbes "what remains firmly in the hands of the individual subject is the right to decide whether obedience is worth it" (98–99). Hobbes himself argues that trust is possible only when possibilities for equality seem real. He notes that actors "covenant in expectation of security"; if they think they may be disadvantaged by an agreement, they will simply keep their natural liberty and work independently to secure their advantage (*EL* 2.1.5; cf. *DC* 3.14). In the state of nature people trust one another enough to agree to common decisions only when agreements do not advantage one side over another, just as people trust a judge who does not promise advantage to one side or the other (*EL* 1.17.7). For Smith, the development of trust within the citizenry depends on citizens' recognition of a positive connection between politics and their well-being.

7. Useful here is Benhabib's discussion of critiques of the ahistorical, asocial, disembodied moral and epistemic subject of Kantianism. Benhabib, *Critique,* 21, writes, "More specifically [Hegel] maintains that the use of contrary-to-fact thought experiments, like 'State of nature' devices, is objectionable. . . . Such argumentations presuppose or take for granted precisely what they set out to prove."

8. *Nota bene:* this law appears in both *Elements of Law* and *De cive* but not explicitly in *Leviathan.*

9. Recent social science confirms the importance of display to the production of trust. See C. D. Parks, R. F. Henager, and S. D. Scamahorn, "Trust and Reactions to Messages of Intent in Social Dilemmas," *Journal of Conflict Resolution* 40 (1996): 134–51; S. Lindskold and M. Finch, "Styles of Announcing Conciliation," *Journal of Conflict Resolution* 25 (1981): 144–55.

Since adherence to Hobbes's laws of nature should lead the state of nature's warriors into peace, these laws must provide inhabitants of the state of nature with guidelines for how to convey the stories of trust and worth that convince people they will benefit from collaboration. I believe that Hobbes's sensitivity to the status of his laws as guidelines for rhetorical display is what assured him of the ease of following his rules: "The same Lawes, because they oblige onely to a desire, and endeavour, I mean an unfeigned and constant endeavour, are easie to be observed. For in that they require nothing but endeavour; he that endeavoureth their performance, fulfilleth them" (*L* 15.214). Scholars have recently begun to pay more attention to the importance of communication in Hobbes and to Hobbes's sensitivity to the communicative construction of our worlds: W. Sacksteder, "Hobbes," *Philosophy and Rhetoric* 17 (1984): 30–46; Ball, "Hobbes' Linguistic Turn"; Strong, "How to Write Scripture"; Silver, "Hobbes on Rhetoric"; Tuck, "Hobbes' Moral Philosophy"; Skinner, *Reason and Rhetoric.* To the best of my knowledge, however, no one has yet considered the communicative aspects of the laws of nature themselves, although Skinner (*Reason and Rhetoric*) and Tuck ("Hobbes' Moral Philosophy") have pointed out that the laws are effectively laws of sociability. Ball ("Hobbes' Linguistic Turn," 757–58) defends the idea that Hobbes had a sense of the performative aspects of language.

10. E.g., *L* 15.40. This is another point on which Hobbes is extremely consistent across the texts being discussed here. Even in his latest work, *De homine,* he writes, "That moral virtue that we can truly measure by civil laws which is different in different states is justice and equity; that moral virtue which we measure purely by the natural law is only charity. These dispositions are manners, good ones called virtues, bad ones vices" (13.9).

11. This passage is interesting for it also shows Hobbes to have expected people to behave exactly the opposite of what is normally assumed in the game theory problem called Prisoner's Dilemma. Thus Gauthier ("Hobbes's Social Contract," 127) writes, "Whatever others do, war is each person's best course of action. If others act peaceably, he is then master; if others are warlike, he defends himself." Hobbes clearly attributes to people a greater degree of intersubjective flexibility than rational choice theory allows them.

Recent rational choice and game theory experiments on trust have used "tit-for-tat" tests, whereby players treat others as they are treated. Such studies have generally found that those players who treat each other well and so are treated well in return take the most overall gains from the game. In short, current game theory literature is confirming the recognition, which goes back to the *Iliad* and to Hesiod, of the centrality of reciprocal exchange to the construction of social bonds. On these issues in the ancient texts, please see L. Slatkin, "Hesiod and Reciprocity," in *The Moral Authority of Nature,* ed. L. Daston and F. Vidal (Chicago, 2003). On tit for tat, see, for instance, M. Blais, "Epistemic Tit for Tat," *Journal of Philosophy* 84 (1987): 363–75; M. Lubell and J. T. Scholz, "Cooperation, Reciprocity, and the Collective-Action Heuristic," *American Journal of Political Science* 45 (2001): 160–78.

12. Equity, justice, and gratitude (*L* 26). In *Leviathan* (15.17) Hobbes writes, that when people do in fact "accommodate themselves to the rest," "they may be called sociable." Here consider Quentin Skinner's argument that Hobbes "is essentially a theorist of the virtues, whose civil science centres on the claim that the avoidance of the vices and the maintenance of the social virtues are indispensable to the preservation of peace" (*Reason and Rhetoric,* 11; cf. chaps. 8 and 9). I am trying to argue that Hobbes's focus on the "social" virtues constitutes a rhetorical approach to human communication.

CHAPTER EIGHT

1. In general on Ellison, see above, chap. 3, n. 4.

2. Ellison regularly makes the argument that, whereas white Americans have been able to live with illusions about how democracy works, blacks in contrast "are an American people who are geared to what *is,* and who yet are driven by a sense of what it is possible for human life to be in this society" ("What America Would Be Like without Blacks," *CE* 584). African Americans, in his argument, understand the ways the collective decisions of a democracy impose on some citizens. White Americans have been able to avoid that knowledge because one minority group was assigned to bear the bulk of these burdens. "When we look objectively at how the dry bones of the nation were hung together, it seems obvious that some one of the many groups that compose the United States had to suffer the fate of being allowed no easy escape from experiencing the harsh realities of the human condition as they were to exist under even so fortunate a democracy as ours" (583).

3. This scene has been much analyzed, partly because it was published as an excerpt of the novel before the novel appeared. See esp. M. Nussbaum, "Invisibility and Recognition," in *Philosophy and Literature* 23 (1999): 257–83; Eddy, *Rites.*

4. "Everywhere I've turned somebody has wanted to sacrifice me for my good—only *they* were the ones who benefited" (*IM* 505).

5. See above, chap. 7, n. 11.

6. The verb is used to describe winnowing and the separation of grain from chaff (*Iliad* 5.501); Cf. the Old Testament, Heb. 4:12.

7. One should note how in the prologue to the novel Ellison begins with clichéd notions of responsibility (two opposed clichés) and then moves from these to a

completely counterintuitive version of the term ("I was the irresponsible one for I should have used my knife"). This strategy of beginning with what is familiar in order to take the reader to something else is central to Ellison's writing. Thus, in "On Initiation Rites and Power," he writes, "I could not violate the reader's sense of reality, his sense of the way things were done, at least on the surface. My task would be to give him the surface and then try to take him into the internalities, take him below the level of racial structuring and down into those areas where we are simply men and women, human beings living on this blue orb, and not always living so well" (*CE* 532).

Hyman ("Ralph Ellison") and Morel (*Raft of Hope*) are among the few critics to recognize the importance of "responsibility" to Ellison. Callahan ("Frequencies of Eloquence") offers a similar reading of the Freudian slip as a comment about the mutual obligations that stabilize democracy.

8. *Why We Can't Wait* (New York, 1964).

9. Ellison discussed the symbolism of the Brotherhood Party:

Interviewer: Mr. Ellison, the Brotherhood has the characteristics of a socialistic society; I was wondering what this had to do with the Communist tradition . . .

Ellison: Here again is a fabrication, just as the machines in the paint factory are fabrications. They never existed. They're images there for certain literary reasons. I did not want to describe an existing Socialist or Communist or Marxist political group, primarily because it would have allowed the reader to escape confronting certain political patterns, patterns which still exist. . . . It was very important for this young man, this would-be leader, to understand that all political parties are basically concerned with power and with maintaining power, not with humanitarian issues in the raw and abstract state. ("On Initiation Rites and Power," CE 538)

If critics are searching for a historical basis for Ellison's story, perhaps they should try this: In 1942 A. Philip Randolph, the founder of the Brotherhood of Sleeping Car Porters, "organized rallies of 20,000 in New York, 12,000 in Chicago and 9,000 in St. Louis (In conjunction with the New York and Chicago rallies, Randolph requested that all outside lighting in Black neighborhoods be turned off, symbolizing the way Blacks were blacked out of American democracy. The blackouts were successful, perhaps a greater organizing feat than the rallies themselves)" (Payne, *I've Got the Light*, 427–28).

10. These analytical terms are not far off those Ellison himself uses to describe the political behaviors of whites who want to "get shut" of blacks and Garveyites. "Both would use the black man as a scapegoat to achieve a national catharsis, and both would by way of curing the patient, destroy him" ("What American Would Be Like without Blacks," *CE* 579).

11. "Brave Words for a Startling Occasion" (*CE* 154).

12. Ellison's transitions, puns, images, and allusions create a "ghost network of

language and craft that integrate the sundry aspects of the American [Dream/] Nightmare. . . . [T]hey reveal connections that have to be repressed so as to expedite the 'normal' flow of information" (A. Nadel, "Ralph Ellison and the American Canon," *American Literary History* 13 [2001]: 394, 397; cf. 395–400).

13. Ellison's belief in the possibility of killing off malformed practices of citizenship by overemphasizing their healthy components rests on complicated ideas about the relationship between psychology, politics, and ritual.

14. J. Benjamin, *The Bonds of Love* (New York, 1988), 25.

15. *CE* (e.g., in "The Little Man at Chehaw Station," 509); *Trading Twelves*. Clearly, this phrase would be just as much at home in an Arendtian, as in the Ellisonian, context.

CHAPTER NINE

1. J. Cooper, "Aristotle on the Forms of Friendship," in *Reason and Emotion* (Princeton, 1999), 333–34.

2. My reading of Aristotle's political theory is unusual in three regards: (1) I take the *Rhetoric* as being a crucial third piece of the political theory, along with the *Nicomachean Ethics* and the *Politics* (this is more important for chapter 10 than for this chapter, and is justified there); (2) I set next to each other Aristotle's discussions of justice in the *Nicomachean Ethics* and the *Politics,* and argue that his definition of justice in the *NE* does relate to his utopian images in both texts, and also to the comparisons he draws between good and bad regimes; I seek to discern the different analytical techniques Aristotle brings to bear on the problem of what justice is, and so I give his utopian descriptions as much weight as his actual definitions of justice; and (3) most commentators focus on Aristotle's arguments about ideal states; in fact, he was just as interested in determining the features of best-case real states; I focus on the latter more than on the former. As a result, Aristotle's pragmatic support for democracy stands in sharper relief than is typical in the scholarship on Aristotle.

On Aristotle on justice, see D. J. Allan, *The Philosophy of Aristotle* (1952; repr. Oxford, 1963); and "Individual and State in the *Ethics* and *Politics*," in *Entretiens sur l'antiquité classique XI* (Geneva, 1965); Allen, *World of Prometheus;* J. Barnes, M. Schofield, and R. Sorabji, eds., *Articles on Aristotle 2* (London, 1979); J. Cooper, "Justice and Rights in Aristotle's *Politics,*" *Review of Metaphysics* 49 (1996): 859–72; C. Georgiadis, "Equitable and Equity in Aristotle," in *Justice, Law, and Method in Plato and Aristotle,* ed. S. Panagiotou (Edmonton, 1987), 159–72; A. C. Hutchinson and D. Monahan, eds., *The Rule of Law* (Toronto, 1987); C. Johnson, *Aristotle's Theory of the State* (Basingstoke, 1990); J. Lear, *Aristotle* (Cambridge, 1988); M. Nussbaum, *The Fragility of Goodness* (Cambridge, 1986); Nussbaum, "The Discernment of Perception," in *Proceedings of the Boston Area Colloquium for Ancient Philosophy,* vol. 1, ed. J. Cleary (1985): 151–201; Nussbaum, "Aristotle on Human Nature and the Foundations of Ethics," in *World, Mind, and Ethics,* ed. J. E. J. Altham and R. Harrison (Cambridge, 1995); J. Ober, "The *Polis* as a Society," in *Athenian Revolution;* D. Ross, *Aristotle* (1923; repr. London, 1966); B. Yack, "A Reinterpretation of Aristotle's Political Teleology," *History of Political Thought* 12 (1991): 15; Yack, *The Problems of a Political Animal* (Berkeley, 1993); W. von Leyden, *Aristotle on Equality and Justice* (Basingstoke, 1985); R. Kraut, *Aristotle's Political Philosophy* (Oxford, 2003); E. Weinrib, "The Intelligibility of the Rule of Law," in *The Rule of Law,* ed. Hutchinson and Monahan, 59–84.

On Aristotle on friendship, see A. W. H. Adkins, "'Friendship' and 'Self-Sufficiency' in Homer and Aristotle," *Classical Quarterly* 13 (1963): 30–45; S. Bickford, "Beyond Friendship," *Journal of Politics* 58 (1996): 398–421; J. Cooper, "An Aristotelian Theory of the Emotions," in *Essays,* ed. Rorty, 238–57; and three central essays in *Reason and Emotion:* "Aristotle on the Forms of Friendship," 312–35; "Friendship and the Good in Aristotle," 336–55; "Political Animals and Civic Friendship," 356–77; J. Derrida, *The Politics of Friendship,* trans. G. Collins (London, 1997); N. Sherman, "Aristotle on Friendship and the Shared Life," *Philosophy and Phenomenological Research* 47 (1987): 589–613.

3. ὁμοίως γὰρ πρὸς ἀγνῶτας καὶ γνωρίμους καὶ συνήθεις καὶ ἀσυνήθεις αὐτὸ ποιήσει, πλὴν καὶ ἐν ἑκάστοις ὡς ἁρμόζει· οὐ γὰρ ὁμοίως προσήκει συνήθων καὶ ὀθνείων φροντίζειν, οὐδ' αὖ λυπεῖν.

4. Analyses of trust often reach the conclusion that trust production requires aiming at habits that lie somewhere between these two extremes. See Baier, *Moral Prejudices,* 150; R. Bentley and D. Owen, "Ethical Loyalties, Civic Virtue, and the Circumstances of Politics," *Philosophical Explorations* 4, no. 3 (Sept. 2001): 223–39.

5. Please see Allen (*World of Prometheus,* chap. 8) for an account of Aristotle's idea of the rule of law. Illegitimate states have laws but not rule according to law.

6. R. Balot, *Greed.*

7. In such contexts of rivalrous desire, some brothers and some citizens always get more, and some less, than they deserve (e.g., *NE* 8.13.4, 9.6.4).

8. Since those gathered in the assembly must make decisions on the concerns of livelihood (*ta eis ton bion anêkonta*), political friendship has to do with interests (*sumpheronta*) (*NE* 9.6.1). In the *Eudemian Ethics,* Aristotle explicitly says that political friendship is according to advantage (1242b22–23). See also Cooper, "Forms of Friendship," 333; Cooper, "Political Animals," 369–70n16; and Yack, *Problems,* 110–15, 133–40. A useful discussion of the blurring of the three registers of friendship can be found in Honig, *Democracy and the Foreigner,* 48–55.

9. Landers says of *Getting to Yes,* "A highly readable, uncomplicated guide to resolving conflicts of every imaginable dimension. It teaches you how to win without compromising friendships." Vance says, "Simple but powerful ideas that have already made a contribution at the international level." Roger Fisher and William Ury, with Bruce Patton, ed., *Getting to Yes,* 2nd ed. (New York, 1991).

10. *Epieikes* is a difficult word to translate. J. H. Freese uses "person of moral worth" (*The Art of Rhetoric,* trans. J. H. Freese [1939; repr. Cambridge, Mass.,

1975]). T. Engberg-Pedersen ("Is There an Ethical Dimension to Aristotelian Rhetoric?" in *Essays,* ed. A. Rorty, 116–41) uses "(morally) good." I translate the word as "equitable" because of its connection to *epieikeia* and because of Aristotle's definition of the virtue as involving a willingness to take less than one's legal share.

11. On equality in friendships, see Cooper, "Forms of Friendship," 319.

12. "Equality in friendship is not like equality in matters of justice. In justice—fair or proportionate to desert is the meaning of equality; in friendship—equal in quantity is the primary meaning and proportionate to desert only secondary" (*NE* 8.7.3).

13. Baier, *Moral Prejudices,* 105, cf. 180: "I have made attitudes to relative power and powerlessness the essence of trust and distrust."

14. J. Pitt-Rivers, "The Law of Hospitality," in *The Fate of Shechem, or the Politics of Sex* (Cambridge, 1977), 94–112; G. Bataille, *The Accursed Share,* trans. R. Hurley from *La part maudite,* vol. 1 (Éditions de Minuit) (1967; repr. New York, 1988); G. Bataille, *The Accursed Share,* trans. R. Hurley from *La part maudite,* vols. 2 and 3 (Éditions de Minuit) (1976; repr. New York, 1991).

15. Here I am following Cooper's account ("Forms of Friendship," 321–23) on the ways in which friendship involves interest in the other. Friendship is "wishing well" for the other's sake. In this regard, it is not simply a matter of self-interest. In the case of a friendly business relationship, one begins by exchanging, and through repetitions of exchange one comes to trust the other party enough that one can hope for the general continuance of the pattern of exchange and therefore wish the other person well *in general* and not simply for the sake of acquiring some particular thing at any one time. "A businessman looks first and foremost for mutual profit from his friendship, but that does not mean that he always calculates his services to his customer by the standard of profit. Finding the relationships on the whole profitable, he likes this customer and is willing to do him services otherwise than as a means to his own ultimate profit . . . the profitability to the well-wisher that is assumed in the well-wishing is not that of the *particular* service rendered (the particular action done in the other person's interest) but that of the overall fabric of the relationship" (Cooper, "Forms of Friendship," 327). A relationship that begins from encapsulated interest (see n. 2 of my Prologue), as in strict bargaining, develops into a more flexibly altruistic relationship.

16. But when Aristotle discusses reciprocity, which he does just after giving his definitions of justice in the *Nicomachean Ethics,* he is careful to distinguish between reciprocity and justice. Reciprocity takes a cruder measure of equality than he thinks justice should. If a policeman strikes an ordinary man, this is, in the eyes of friendship, a violation that needs to be repaid, for friendships see relations only between equal human beings. But the eyes of justice see, in the officer's striking of the citizen, a perfectly reasonable action. While the reciprocity of friendship does capture the basic elements of justice—and so can serve to recreate the basic structures of justice—it cannot allow for all the refinements that are made necessary by the hierar-

chical structure of political society. But just as justice does work that friendship does not and cannot, friendship too does political work that justice cannot. Here at last we return to the question with which we began. Why did Aristotle think that it was not enough merely for men to be just but that they also needed friendship?

17. Sherman, "Friendship and the Shared Life," 608. In this paragraph generally, I follow Sherman. The term "extended self" is hers. On the same subject, see Cooper, "Forms of Friendship" and "Friendship and the Good," esp. 338–45. The term "extended self" is equivalent to Russell Hardin's "encapsulated interest," with which I began. See Prologue, n. 2, above. For further discussions of the figure of the friend as a second self, see *NE* 9.4.5, 9.9.1, 9.9.10. As the *Magna Moralia* puts it, "my friend is a second me" (1213a12).

18. This willingness to be in debt is something the philosophers have sometimes resisted. Thus Kant: "A friend who bears my losses becomes my benefactor and puts me in his debt. I feel shy in his presence and cannot look him boldly in the face. The true relationship is cancelled and friendship ceases" (cited and discussed in A. Baier, *Moral Prejudices,* 190). This approach to reciprocity is a core element of the domination model of citizenship.

19. Those who enter the assembly together have been drawn into living together and acting together, which Aristotle considers already to be the basis for friendship (*suzên, sumpraxis, NE* 9.5.3).

20. For another critique of the sharp contrast frequently drawn between egoistic and altruistic motivation, see Baier, *Moral Prejudices,* 152–82. For discussion of core assumptions in rational choice theory, see P. Pettit, "*Virtus Normativa,*" *Symposium on Norms in Moral and Social Theory, Ethics* 100 (1990): 725–55.

CHAPTER TEN

1. Early on in the *Rhetoric,* Aristotle says, "The work (*ergon*) of rhetoric concerns matters about which we deliberate" (1.22.12). And in book 2, he says, "We know that the employment of speeches is directed towards a judgment because the need for argument and speeches, or *logon,* simply disappears once a thing is known and judged [*kekrikamen*]" (2.18.1). Aristotle treats the possibility of friendship and the possibility of trust as coextensive.

2. I discuss these issues at greater length and with more exegesis in "Aristotle and the Politics of Rhetoric" (article under preparation).

3. Ibid.

4. Aristotle himself announces that his theory of speech and its techniques are elements of the art of politics. At the end of the *Nicomachean Ethics,* he tells the reader that the discussion of the good life in the *Ethics* will continue—with a shift of focus from the individual to the polis—in his next treatise, a book on politics (*NE* 10.9.22–23). And so we get the *Politics.* That text then carries on the discussions of law that are just beginning at the end of the *Ethics.* When the *Rhetoric* be-

gins, it, in turn, points back to the *Politics* and through the *Politics* to the *Ethics*. Thus the art of rhetoric, Aristotle says, is an "off-shoot" (*paraphues*) of "that study of ethics, which is called politics" (*R* 1.2.7). Elsewhere Aristotle argues that rhetoric is one of the most esteemed faculties but should be properly understood as subordinate to the architectonic science of politics (*NE* 1.1.6).

5. Cf. a passage in the *Nicomachean Ethics*: "You cannot admit someone to friendship or really be friends before each has shown the other that he is worthy of friendship and worthy to be trusted/believed [*pisteuthei*]" (8.3.9).

6. Aristotle explains the interrelation between these different elements of believability in an important passage:

> Three things are reasons that people who speak are persuasive or believable [*pistous*]. For, in addition to demonstrative or logical proof, we trust in three things: these are a habit of success at practical reason [*phronesis*], virtue [*arete*], and good will [*eunoia*]. For speakers are false in regard to what they say or the advice they give because of all of these or because of some one of them. For if they are foolish (and therefore lack abilities at practical reason [*phronesis*], they will not have the right opinions; or if they have the right opinions, they may not utter them because of baseness (a lack of virtue); or perhaps they will in fact be both good at practical reason and equitable [*phronimoi kai epieikeis*], but without being well-minded or feeling good will [*eunoia*] toward their audience. Then it is possible for them to fail to give the best advice even though they know what it is. Beyond this nothing matters. (*R* 2.1.6)

7. On *phronêsis*, *NE* 6.10.3. See E. Garver, *Aristotle's* Rhetoric (Chicago, 1994), for the argument that the whole of one's character is relevant to the art of rhetoric.

8. Aristotle points out that audiences "give heed to those people with *phronêsis*" precisely because "their arguments are likely to be correct" (*R* 2.6.17; cf. 2.6.21).

9. E.g., S. Lyall, "Most Britons Back the War, but Mistrust How the U.S. Is Waging It," *New York Times*, April 4, 2003. But see N. Banerjee, "After the War," *New York Times*, Aug. 13, 2003, sec. A, for a counterview.

10. According to *R* 2.8, the emotions depend on relations between people, so crafting one affects the other. For other attempts to address the contrast between "warping" and the "right frame of mind," see C. L. Johnstone, "An Aristotelian Trilogy," *Philosophy and Rhetoric* 13 (1980): 7–10; A. Rorty, "Structuring the Rhetoric," in *Essays on Aristotle's* Rhetoric, ed. Rorty, 21–23; S. Bickford, "Beyond Friendship," *Journal of Politics* 58 (1996): 412–13. On the place of *eunoia* in civic friendship, see Cooper, "Forms of Friendship," 329–30.

11. *NE* 8.5. In fact, in the *Rhetoric*, Aristotle distinguishes hatred from anger primarily on the grounds that it involves no pain. S. Leighton ("Aristotle and the Emotions," in *Essays*, ed. Rorty, 218) notes this and considers the possibility that hatred is a *hexis*. Cooper admits that there is some awkwardness in treating *philia* as

a feeling. He also admits that *R* 2.4, the chapter on friendship and hatred, is anomalous, and acknowledges the distinction in the *Ethics* between *philia* and *philesis*. He notes that the chapter on friendship does not invoke the idea of pain and confesses to puzzlement about the affect involved in hatred ("An Aristotelian Theory of the Emotions," in *Essays,* ed. Rorty, 242–49). G. Striker ("Emotions in Context'," in *Essays,* ed. Rorty, 291, 301n13) also notices that the treatment of friendship and hatred is exceptional. M. Nussbaum ("Aristotle on Emotions and Rational Persuasion," in *Essays,* ed. Rorty, 311) argues that *philia* is "not an emotion, but a relationship with emotional components."

12. See the very interesting article by C. Krauss, "Canadian Families Split on Fate of U.S. Pilots," *New York Times,* February 9, 2003, sec. 1, which draws out the differing conceptual contents of four families' reactions to the deaths of their sons in a friendly-fire military accident.

13. See Honig's discussion, "Mourning, Membership, Agency, and Loss," in *Democracy and the Foreigner,* 67–72.

14. For Aristotle, such senses of loss can be a cause of civil war. On this, see Bickford, "Beyond Friendship," 404–5, where she discusses the effect of "perspectives" on politics. Rorty ("Structuring," 17–20) points out the importance of *phantasia* to Aristotle's account of the role of the emotions in rhetoric. The emotions call up certain images before the mind's eye; the rhetorician is obliged to interact with these images. That is, the rhetorician is obliged to interact with these fragments of subjectivity and not only with facts, figures, or "things in the world." Rorty writes, "I suggest that *phantasiai* are how things appear to us, *given who, what, and where we are*" (19; emphasis in the original). On *phantasia,* see also Cooper, "An Aristotelian Theory," 246–47; and "Political Animals," 373; Nussbaum, "Aristotle on Emotions," 306–7. Leighton ("Aristotle and the Emotions," 212–16) argues that it is our "expectations" that produce our subjectively differentiated emotional reactions to events. Silver ("Hobbes on Rhetoric," 340) argues that Hobbes found Aristotle's *Rhetoric* useful precisely because it addresses "the subjective dimension of the human being" which has "real consequences for the public or civic realm."

15. Aristotle reintroduces the topic of "learning" in book 3, but in a different context. He uses the language of learning to argue for a plain style of speech that can make an argument perfectly clear (*R* 3.3.1, 3.3.5). Orators must expect to teach their audiences what their arguments are (that is, convey their arguments clearly), but they must then expect the understanding that will engage those arguments to be the understanding of a judge rather than of a student.

16. Aristotle's speakers start from positions of strategic interest. Aristotle regularly uses the image of a road to describe the rhetorical experience shared by speaker and audience. The rhetorician must pick out and head to a goal or boundary point that will be persuasive (*tekmar, peras, terma, R* 1.11, 1.1.14), and the speaker is always supposed to be moving the audience toward a goal of his or her liking. Also, Aristotle describes persuasive speeches as entailing efforts "to argue against an

opponent or against some hypothesis, for it is necessary to make use of speech to destroy the opposing arguments as if they were the actual opponent" (*R* 2.18).

17. Baier, *Moral Prejudices,* 124.

18. Cf. Barber, *Strong Democracy,* 173–78.

19. Cf. R. Dagger, "Metropolis, Memory, and Citizenship," *American Political Science Review* 25 (1981): 730–31. He quotes Tocqueville: "Some brilliant achievement may win a people's favor at one stroke. But to gain the affection and respect of your immediate neighbors, a long succession of little services rendered and of obscure good deeds, a constant habit of kindness and an established reputation for disinterestedness, are required."

20. One might compare this list with Barber, *Strong Democracy,* 178–98.

EPILOGUE

1. See Roediger, *The Wages of Whiteness;* Honig, *Democracy and the Foreigner,* 19–36, 80–86; Rogin, "Two Declarations," 73–95; Connolly, *Appearance,* 65–82, 157–62.

2. *OED* online:

> c) *U.S.* A member of a minority group. Usu. in pl. **1951** *Jrnl. Negro Educ.* **20** 330 There are also other factors operating against discrimination: . . . direct campaigns of some local civic groups to encourage the hiring of minorities especially in white-collar jobs. **1965** *Amer. Jrnl. Sociol.* **71** 249 A white employer's taste for discrimination may lead him to hire Negroes, females, and other identifiable minorities *only* at a rate sufficiently below the going rate for white workers to offset the price he places upon his taste for discrimination [etc.]. **1976** *Time* 20 Dec. 11/1 He was worried about the need for new young blood in Government, for more women and minorities. **1985** *Albuquerque* (New Mexico) *Jrnl.* 11 Dec. A3/3 During the past year, UNM hired six minorities and 21 women. **1996** F. POPCORN *Clicking* ii. 62 Twice as many whites as minorities owned them [*sc.* computers].

3. There are other signs of this movement. P. Rossi and R. Dentler write, "A central goal of neighborhood conservation and renewal thus was to keep Hyde Park–Kenwood as a desirable middle-class residential neighborhood. . . . Conservation meant, first of all, bringing to a halt the white exodus. On this goal, liberals and conservatives could agree. *In effect, this meant stabilizing the numbers of Negroes at some minority proportion. The ratio—which had changed from less than one nonwhite in ten before 1950 to four nonwhites in ten by 1956—was defined as requiring firm control*" (*PUR* 50, emphasis added); M. Rogin writes, "Whereas the exclusion of blacks from American politics had permitted cleavages among whites, the entrance of African Americans onto the political stage in the 1960s introduced a race-based regime into national two-party competition. A majority among whites has voted

against a majority among peoples of color in every presidential election since 1964" ("Two Declarations," 85–86). On the diminishment of a sense of security in recent decades, see Wolin, *Presence of the Past,* 29–31.

4. University of Chicago affiliates who lived in the neighborhoods immediately around the university are a classic example. In the 1950s most "old-timers" believed that in the late 1930s, 90 percent of the university faculty had lived in a small area called the "University sector" (a sector of roughly five blocks north to south, and ten blocks east to west). In fact, in 1939, 60 percent of university faculty had lived in that area and in 1957 slightly less than 50 percent did so. The change was minimal but perceived as great. The significant change that the area around the university (extending beyond the "University sector" to include the entire Hyde Park–Kenwood neighborhood) had experienced was in overall racial composition. In 1940 less than 4 percent of area residents were African American. In 1950 that number was 6 percent and in 1956 it was 36 percent (*PUR* 16, 21, 35). University faculty seem to have represented this change to themselves as a "loss" of friends and colleagues in their immediate neighborhood of roughly the same proportions.

5. The art of rhetoric has traditionally provided its students with self-confidence. For some reflections on this, see G. A. Fine, *Gifted Tongues* (Princeton, 2001), 23–25.

6. M. Berman, "Take It to the Streets," *Dissent* (Fall 1986): 484. See also the accompanying articles, M. Walzer, "Pleasures and Costs of Urbanity," 470–75; and M. Rustin, "The Fall and Rise of Public Space," 486–94. See also Barber, *Strong Democracy,* 305–6.

7. "Increasing the penalties of enforcement institutions enhances cooperation in nonreciprocal environments, but actually diminishes cooperation among cooperators in reciprocal environments." M. Lubell and J. T. Scholz, "Cooperation, Reciprocity, and the Collective-Action Heuristic," *American Journal of Political Science* 45 (2001): 175.

8. Warren, *Democracy and Trust,* 14.

9. "On Initiation Rites and Power."

10. A. Cohen and E. Taylor, *American Pharaoh* (Boston, 2000), 183–215.

11. Ibid.

12. A powerful example of the military experience is described in D. Terry, "The Men of Olive Company," *Chicago Tribune,* May 12, 2002.

13. On the status of the Hyde Park–Kenwood program as a first, see *People and Neighborhood Renewal,* 13.

14. There were already neighborhood conservation groups that had been set up in the 1930s. What was new was the establishment of corporations with legal status that permitted them to make greater use of eminent domain and other governmental powers than had previously been possible. The second Hyde Park area development corporation, the South West Hyde Park Neighborhood Redevelopment Corporation, arrived on the scene in 1956 (*NPUC* 21). Eventually, the renewal of neighborhoods like Lincoln Park would follow the same model.

15. *PUR* 58–60, 84–88; *SEC* 48 (real-estate maneuvering, *PUR* 81–82).

16. There are, however, great practical obstacles to using these laws at present, and this does reduce the significance of their continued existence. Nonetheless, until they are repealed, they remain always available for the clever to use.

17. Aldermen do currently review all major real-estate and construction projects within their wards and provide some of the community vetting I advocate. The ward system, however, breaks the city up into neighborhoods smaller than the polis I describe, and there is still room for increased cooperation across wards.

18. Political friendship does not solidify the boundaries of the community but encourages the cultivation of habits within the community that make cosmopolitanism itself possible as a cultural orientation.

Index